P9-BYZ-844

The Classroom Struggle

The Classroom Struggle

Policy and Resistance
in South Africa
1940–1990

Jonathan Hyslop

University of Natal Press
Pietermaritzburg
1999

© 1999   University of Natal
           Private Bag X01
           Scottsville 3209
           South Africa

All rights reserved. No part of this publication
may be reproduced or transmitted, in any form
or by any means, without permission of the publishers.

ISBN 0 86980 952 0

Cover design: Blue Box

Typeset by the University of Natal Press
Printed by Kohler Carton and Print
P.O. Box 955, Pinetown 3600, South Africa

Contents

List of Organisations

AAC	All African Convention
ACA	Atlantic and Continental Assurance
AEM	African Education Movement
AHNI	Association of Heads of Native Institutions
ANC	African National Congress
ANCYL	African National Congress Youth League
ASSECA	Association for the Educational and Cultural Advancement of the African People
ATASA	African Teachers' Association of South Africa
AZASM	Azanian Students' Movement
BC	Black Consciousness
BCM	Black Consciousness Movement
BED	Bantu Education Department
BPC	Black Peoples' Convention
CAPA	Cape African Parents' Association
CATA	Cape African Teachers' Association
CATU	Cape African Teachers' Union
CED	Cape Education Department
COD	Congress of Democrats
COSAS	Congress of South African Students
CP	Conservative Party
DBE	Department of Bantu Education
DCD	Department of Community Development
DET	Department of Education and Training
EP	Education Panel
FCATA	Federal Council of African Teachers' Associations
HNP	Herstigte Nasionale Party
IFP	Inkatha Freedom Party
MK	Umkhonto we Sizwe
MP	Member of Parliament
NAD	Native Affairs Department
NEC	National Executive Committee (of the ANC)

NECC	National Education Crisis Committee
NEUM	Non-European Unity Movement
NEUSA	National Education Union of South Africa
NF	National Forum
NP	National Party
NWDTU	North Western Districts Teachers' Union
PAC	Pan-Africanist Congress
PETU	Port Elizabeth Teachers' Association
PP	Progressive Party
PTA	Parent-Teachers' Association
PTSA	Parent-Teacher-Students' Association
RSC	Regional Services Council
SABC	South African Broadcasting Corporation
SADF	South African Defence Force
SAIRR	South African Institute of Race Relations
SAP	South African Police
SASM	South African Students' Movement
SASO	South African Students' Organisation
SB	Security Branch (of the South African Police)
SOYA	Society of Young Africa
SPCC	Soweto Parents' Crisis Committee
SRC	Student Representative Council
SSRC	Soweto Students' Representative Council
TATA	Transvaal African Teachers' Association
TATU	Transvaal African Teachers' Union
TEACH	Teach Every African Child
TED	Transvaal Education Department
TLSA	Teachers' League of South Africa
TOB	Transkei Organised Bodies
TUATA	Transvaal United African Teachers' Association
UDF	United Democratic Front
UP	United Party
UBC	Urban Bantu Council
UM	Unity Movement
WECSAC	Western Cape Students' Action Committee

Preface

Jackie Cock supervised the thesis on which this book is largely based. To her I must extend my deep gratitude for support far beyond anything one might normally expect. Jackie is not just a path-breaking contributor to South African sociology, but a fine and courageous person with whom it has been a privilege to work.

The interviews on which this book draws were carried out by Thomas Nkadimeng, Barnard Matsetela, Jabu Mthembu and myself. My thanks to these research assistants. Thomas Nkadimeng is a superb researcher and I would like to pay special tribute to his skill, sensitivity and integrity. Barnard Matsetela's persistence and dedication were exemplary.

My thanks to my first editor Muff Andersson for making my work a great deal more readable than it might otherwise have been.

Isabel Hofmeyr gave me indispensable assistance with last minute proofreading.

Special thanks to Glenn Cowley and Trish Comrie at the University of Natal Press.

Thanks also to the History Workshop at the University of the Witwatersrand for providing the intellectual context for my work.

Two chapters closely follow the structure of previously published articles. I would like to acknowledge the copyright permission given by James Currey for my contribution to W. Cobbett and R. Cohen, *Popular Struggles in South Africa* (London 1988), and the board of the journal *Transformations* for my article on the ANC schools boycott in their edition no.4, 1987.

I would like to thank the History Department of the School of Oriental and African Studies (University of London), the Association of Commonwealth Universities and Professor Shula Marks for their amazing hospitality during my study leave, which enabled me to finish production of this work in the most delightful of circumstances.

A grant from the Human Sciences Research Council for some of the thesis work reflected in this book is acknowledged.

Jonathan Hyslop
September 1998

Introduction

There are two common approaches to histories of Bantu Education. The one centres on defining Bantu Education as a tool to provide South Africa's ruling classes with cheap, docile labour. The other strives to show an unbroken chain of resistance to Bantu Education.

Both approaches are flawed. The first cannot adequately account for the massive resistance to Bantu Education by students during 1976. The second cannot explain how Bantu Education succeeded for nearly 20 years.

This book attempts to synthesise the 'structuralist' and 'resistance' models.

Bantu Education, it argues, was not an unchanging policy, introduced in 1955 and remaining the same for ever after. It did change, in response to social pressures. Similarly, changes in political consciousness and organisation – affecting both teachers and students – dramatically altered the form of resistance to Bantu Education.

The battle for schooling between state bureaucracy and mass resistance was one of shifting terrains, strategy and tactics.

This book concentrates on two key regions – Gauteng and the Eastern Cape – but attempts to reflect on the national picture at every possible juncture.

My material comes from archival sources, official publications, newspapers and interviews. The Treason Trial Collection in the South African Institute of Race Relations (SAIRR) Archive at the University of the Witwatersrand, which comprises the ANC's correspondence of the late 40s and early 50s, proved particularly fascinating. There is also interesting material on the mission schools' declining years in the Cory Library at Rhodes University. The collection in the University of South Africa Archive provides invaluable information on African teachers' organisations.

A further source was interviews with some 40 teachers, carried out by my research assistants Thomas Nkadimeng, Barnard Matsetela, Jabu Mthembu and myself. Most of these teachers asked for anonymity, and I respect their wishes. I have the tapes and transcripts of the interviews in my possession.

These interviews show the impact of state policy in the classroom. They also illuminate the consciousness and activities of teachers, students, and communities in a way impossible for written sources to do.

I was primarily interested in teachers' testimony for what it could tell me about their experiences of Bantu Education. I was not trying to assess the support for particular positions among them. The teachers were a 'snowball' sample. We contacted an initial group of black secondary school teachers. They were asked to recommend others who could give worthwhile insights into their experiences. I attempted to include both older, mission-trained teachers and teachers who trained under the Bantu Education system, and to obtain interviews with teachers who had experience of both the Eastern Cape and Gauteng.

The use of distinct methods in the book – interviews, studies of documents, and studies of published material – enabled me to strengthen my findings. I tested the validity of a particular interpretation by considering whether evidence of another type confirmed or contradicted it.

Jonathan Hyslop
September 1996

CHAPTER ONE

The Educational Crisis

African Schooling in the 40s and Early 50s

Urban youth – how to control and train them. This was the National Party (NP) government's chief preoccupation in 1955, when Bantu Education was first introduced.

Bantu Education was the expression given to apartheid policy in the field of schooling. It was a clumsy attempt to resolve the urban crisis that developed in the 1940s and 50s, as a result of rapid urbanisation and industrialisation.

Government action during the 50s involved the creation of a tightly state-controlled, badly funded mass education system. The idea was to provide social control of the urban working class and forge a semi-skilled work force from among the urban youth.

The state tried to channel black political aspirations towards the racially segregated structures of rural 'homelands'. However, Bantu Education was not concerned, as Marxists believe, with the maintenance of a supply of migrant labour. Nor was it obsessed, as liberal writers argue, with a malicious, ideologically driven destruction of the mission schools – 'butchered,' in Senator Edgar Brookes' words, 'to make an ideologist's holiday'.

The 40s, the period of the Second World War and its aftermath, saw rapid urbanisation resulting from the combined forces of collapsing homeland agriculture and expanding secondary industrialisation. Housing, transport, and wages were all inadequate for the growing working class in urban areas.

Squatter movements, bus boycotts and trade unionism were the widespread response to the breakdown of these services and poor conditions. In turn, these activities fuelled the eruption of a more radical level of oppositional political activity, marked by an emerging new generation of the African National Congress (ANC) leadership.

Levels of poverty threatened the physical reproduction of the workforce. There were also new political threats.

Education, or the lack of it, obstructed social stability in the 40s.

The provincially administered system of black education, which depended heavily on mission schools with their limited state subsidy, bypassed the mass of black urban youth. Administrators and educationists attributed the uncontrollability of black urban youth, and the increased crime rate, to the shortage of schools. They feared political mobilisation would increase. Moreover, the urban workforce was not providing enough workers with the education required for semi-skilled labour in the expanding factories.

By the late 40s and early 50s, a wide spectrum of dominant class opinion had come to see the extension of mass schooling as an answer to these problems.

The social control of the black working class interested politicians, bureaucrats and capitalists alike.

The crisis of the period was also one of hegemony, with rising popular challenges to the existing social order in the political and ideological spheres. There was growing conflict within the mission schools and disillusionment and anger among African teachers.

Mission schools were in a state of near collapse. Not only was the mission school system too poor and small to cope with popular demand for education, but there were internal divisions among mission authorities, staff, students and black communities. There was a challenge to the mission schools that had historically exerted a formative influence over the rising African educated elite.

H.F. Verwoerd, as Minister of Native Affairs, tried to replace the missions with a more extensive and economically viable education system. He also tried to win popular support for Bantu Education.

The state saw itself in a precarious economic and political position. It wanted to maintain economic stability while trying to address urgent problems of urban restructuring and political control.

The Crisis in Urban Schooling

By the late 40s and early 50s, the education system was incapable of providing schooling for the growing numbers of urban youth. Afrikaner educationist and head of Diepkloof Reformatory, W.W.J. Kieser, looked at the problem in his 1952 MEd dissertation. He recorded that school inspectors estimated that of African children of school-going age living on the Rand that year, 58 138 were at school whereas 116 276 were not.

The state provision in the Cape was particularly poor. In the early 50s only 24 out of 2 296 recognised schools were state-provided.

The drop-out rate among Africans who did attend school was exceptionally high. In 1945 only 50 per cent of pupils in the Cape studied beyond the first two years of school, and only two per cent reached beyond Standard 6, according to Edgar Brookes. Secondary schooling was largely underdeveloped.

Trevor Huddleston notes in *Naught for your Comfort* that St Peter's became the first school in the Transvaal to take African pupils to matriculation level in the 30s.

The problem was compounded when mission schools increased pupil intake drastically, imposing a massive strain on their existing resources. The schools failed both the potential pupils they excluded and the minority of actual pupils they took in. The Eiselen Report was thus doing no more than giving a realistic appraisal, from its own perspective, of the existing schools in stating that they were '. . . providing education for a relatively small proportion of a backward [sic] population'.

Teachers recall the squalid level of most of the educational facilities of this period. One teacher described a Sophiatown mission school in the 30s as 'a tin shack' and said St Mary's, Orlando, was 'old looking and dilapidated' in the 50s. The same teacher recalled a school in Top Location, Sharpeville, during the war years:

> (It) was an old church building built from stone from the quarries. It was so old somebody told me it was just built before the Boer War. It had those plank windows.

Another interviewee said the school building in the 50s was 'an old library, out in Benoni location. A derelict building, no electricity, one tap, hardly any toilets'.

Nor were the teacher training facilities much better. A third teacher recalled:

> When I was a student, classroom buildings were at a very, very poor level . . . I remember, when I went for teacher's training, we had to start by making the floor ourselves . . . we just took pieces of wood meant for rafters, and we built desks.

During the 40s, reorganisation and expansion of the school system was first mooted by liberal intellectuals.

In his 1946–1947 presidential address to the South African Institute of Race Relations (SAIRR), Edgar Brookes called for compulsory education as a 'preventative against delinquency and crime'. He stated:

> In our towns thousands of children are growing up juvenile delinquents, and a state prepared to maintain a police force and reformatories is apparently not prepared to increase the expenditure necessary to keep them off the streets during their formative years.

It was clear Brookes' primary concern was with the urban crisis because of his suggestion to introduce compulsion more slowly in the rural areas.

By the end of the Smuts government's tenure of office, such ideas had penetrated the thinking of significant sections of government and administration. The Secretary for Social Welfare voiced the view that compulsory education could overcome the 'skollie' (juvenile delinquent) problem. He called for a differential syllabus that would include social and personal 'hygiene'.

The De Villiers Commission reported in 1948:

> A number of witnesses, including responsible municipal officials contended, in evidence before this Commission, that juvenile delinquency among Natives was assuming alarming proportions, especially on the Rand, and that compelling all Native children of school age to attend school would reduce the incidence of delinquency. It was argued that these children, being usefully occupied during part of the day, would acquire habits of orderliness and industry, and become amenable to discipline.

On coming to power in 1948, the NP faced the same problems of social control. The 1952 Van Schalkwijk Committee noted 'an appreciable increase in the juvenile population of the urban areas during the last decade . . . [who] fall an easy prey to the vice of the towns'. The committee bemoaned that 'absence of compulsory education in towns . . . results in greater freedom from supervision of non-European juveniles.'

The same year W.W.J. Kieser wrote how, as he saw it, 'thousands of Bantu children loaf around the locations, lacking in goals and without the necessary supervision . . . daily the number of juvenile delinquents grows.'

The state's apparatus for dealing with juvenile crime was very limited: there was only one reformatory for African male youths (Diepkloof), one for females (Eshowe), and four institutions run for less hardened offenders by the Department of Welfare. Kieser supported his argument that lack of schooling contributed to delinquency with statistics demonstrating that, of his charges at Diepkloof, 29 per cent had never been to school, whereas a further 47.5 per cent had only studied to Standard 2 or below.

Beyond the growing threat to the social order posed by juvenile crime, control of urban youth was also seen as a problem at the political level. Kieser, for example, noted that the nature and enforcement of the pass and liquor laws had brought the law into contempt among the urban black community. He also observed resentment of discrimination, and bitterness and envy towards white economic privilege. He inevitably attributed the latter to 'agitation and ideas with a strong Communist influence'.

Official thinking identified the issue of township family structures as a further source of weakness in the social regulation of working-class youth. The Van Schalkwijk Committee saw 'the neglected children of divorcees and unmarried mothers and of poor or destitute families' as being particularly vulnerable to urban 'vice'. Kieser complained: '. . . parents are not in a position to give their children the necessary guidance.' He also expressed shock at what he perceived as the unwillingness of black parents to discourage their children from engaging in theft. Kieser was concerned at the black family's failure to inculcate western gender stereotypes, reflected in the fact that one out of eight African convicted juvenile delinquents was female, compared to one out of 30 white delinquents. He was also troubled by the weakness of nuclear family patterns in the urban areas: only 305 of the 839 pupils at Diepkloof came from families in which both parents were present.

Thus it was apparent by the late 40s and early 50s that the school system, the reformatories, and the family structures were not controlling urban youth in an effective manner.

In a situation where such fears of crime and political activity were at the forefront of policy makers' concerns, the inability of the existing educational system to reach large numbers of youth became a major problem for the NP government. In laying down the blueprint for Bantu Education, the 1951 Eiselen Commission identified the relatively small proportion of youth reached by the schools as one of the major problems of the existing educational dispensation.

Thus, although the NP rulers never fully embraced compulsory education, they saw youth as a central focus of the urban crisis. They felt this issue could be addressed by the introduction of mass schooling.

The coming of Bantu Education also needs to be placed in the context of strong pressures from industry for labour with a greater degree of education, especially for employment as semi-skilled operatives. This thinking was also prevalent in United Party (UP) circles. Had the UP been re-elected to office in 1948, it would, in the short term, have followed similar educational policies to those pursued by the NP. There was a far greater degree of policy overlap between the two major white parties on this issue than one might expect.

During the 40s the growth of secondary industry, with an increasingly strong monopoly sector, generated a vast number of jobs for semi-skilled machine operatives. By 1948, two-thirds of these were being filled by black workers, of whom 50 per cent were Africans, according to Jon Lewis in *Industrialisation and Trade Union Organisation in South Africa 1924–55*. The growth of technical and supervisory staff in industry did not lead industrialists to train blacks for these positions. Industry preferred to rely on white technicians and supervisors. Far from encouraging black skills upgrading, the Smuts government's attitude was consistent with this new racial division of labour.

The third interim report of the Van Eck Commission in 1941 argued for an increased emphasis on training whites for skilled labour in industry, instead of providing them with unskilled jobs in government departments.

The Secretary for Native Affairs outlined the Smuts government's policy to the De Villiers Commission in the following terms:

> The needs of the country for native journeymen and the existing opportunities for their employment in the recognised trades are much more restricted than those for semi-skilled men. Moreover, it can be argued that the generality of the Natives should be satisfied with an intermediate position for the time being . . . the unfolding of extensive Government development schemes in Native areas will bring into being a large number of skilled posts.

Thus the UP, like the NP, did not see labour requirements as necessitating black skills training at artisan level or above. They justified this situation on the basis of largely mythical opportunities in the reserves or homelands. The policy put forward by the De Villiers Commission was representative of current business and government thinking on the issue. 'The mentality of the Native', it opined, 'makes him peculiarly suited for repetitive operations.'

There was a recognition by the UP's policy makers that a restructuring of education was required to generate the semi-skilled African labour they sought. The system they advocated clearly prefigures that realised under Bantu Education. The De Villiers Commission urged educational expansion so 'we could profitably use so many efficient Native man-hours'. Just as the Eiselen Commission was to do, they urged the linking of education and work skills – 'for their present stage of development [Africans] profit much more from practical subjects than from academic subjects.'

The difference between the NP and UP in respect of the directly labour-market oriented aspect of their education policies lay more in the energy with which the NP moved to restructure education than in their basic perception of labour requirements. When Kieser wrote that the African student 'leaves school with just enough education to make him averse to any manual work', or when the Eiselen Commission wrote, 'the general orientation of school work is too academic,' they were expressing a perception also present in UP circles and among industrialists. While it is true the NP was more sympathetic to the labour requirements of agriculture than the UP would have been, its educational policies did not, in the 50s, obstruct the reproduction of the type of labour that industry by and large required.

Once it had come to power the NP showed a clear recognition that in the short term it could not attempt to uproot urban workers. Rather, the aim was to gain effective control over the process of reproduction of the urban working class in order to utilise its labour and control its political and social life. By the early 50s, government was able to reassure industrialists that it was quite willing to support the introduction of black semi-skilled workers into industry. The proviso was that this be accompanied by a move of white workers from unskilled to semi-skilled and semi-skilled to skilled posts. The 'floating colour bar' temporarily resolved potential conflict between industry and the NP government.

The unwillingness of the NP to accept urban artisan-level training for blacks was not an important source of friction between industry and government. Neither the UP nor the industrialists showed a strong practical interest in training blacks in the trades, even though a shortage of artisans was beginning to make itself felt. Thus the NP was, during the 50s, receptive to industry's *main* immediate labour need – semi-skilled labour.

The school system's critical condition in the 40s was not, however, only one of inadequacy to accommodate the growing numbers of urban youth. Within the schools themselves, increasing signs of disintegration were evident.

The Crisis of the Mission Schools
The crisis in the mission schools first manifested itself as an economic one. The De Villiers Commission identified 'financial starvation' as one of the chief causes of the deficiencies of African education. Brookes described a situation where almost every training college and high school 'had to live from hand to mouth' and where the existing school buildings were 'from an architectural and health point of view, as well as from a purely educational point of view, very unsatisfactory'.

The principal of Healdtown complained in 1945 that although teachers were paid by the Province, all other charges – including food, medical attention for 900 people, and the upkeep of buildings – had to be met from ordinary income. This consisted almost entirely of fees. Missions traditionally did not charge pupils for books, usually bearing these costs themselves.

War-time inflation exacerbated this burden. The ability of the missions to deal with it by raising fees was undermined by the inability of parents to pay major increases. The consequences were disastrous. An inquiry into the 1946 Lovedale disturbance notes that by then the institution was £30 000 in debt.

The demand for education had put pressure on missions to take greater numbers of students than they could really teach. The Lovedale Inquiry concluded: '. . . the number of students is too large for the institution to handle effectively.' The luminous educational achievements of a few renowned mission high schools should not obscure the fact that most mission schools were poor primary schools with large drop-out rates. The Eiselen Commission was not inaccurate when it stated of schools in this era that:

> . . . the rate of elimination at an early stage is very high . . . the standards of achievement in the schools as measured by examinations and achievement tests is [sic] low.

There were major problems from the 40s onwards in maintaining the numbers of white teachers who had traditionally been present in the missions. According to Z.K. Matthews, there was a decline in the proportion of motivated white missionary teachers. The government's insistence that the missions offer white teachers the same wages as they could earn in white schools made it difficult for the missions to afford them. The turbulent mission conditions and the lack of promotion possibilities outside the state sector reinforced this trend.

The impoverishment of mission finances contributed to growing student discontent. Traditionally, students at the mission boarding schools lived on a 'starchy and monotonous' diet, as Z.K. Matthews has recorded. This continued into the 40s, exacerbating students' resentment. While more perceptive missionary figures like Brookes came to recognise the negative effect this had on student attitudes, funds were not available for the missions easily to change their menus.

By the 40s there was no significant sector of dominant class opinion, including missionaries themselves, which did not favour greater state intervention in black education.

Heads of missionary schools issued a statement at a 1947 meeting in Port Elizabeth that the institutions could not bear their financial burden without greater government assistance.

The crisis of the mission schools was also a crisis of social relations. Up until the 30s, and in many places into the 40s and early 50s, relations between mission schools and their pupils are remembered as warm and friendly. This is reflected in the generally happy memories teachers interviewed in the course of this research had of their school days. A pupil of St Cyprian's, Sophiatown, in the 20s sees the period as 'just one of my best times'. A teacher who attended the same school says: 'That's where my foundation was laid.' Close relations existed between mission teachers and their students, resulting in the high esteem in which teachers were held. Another teacher says:

> Even today I still respect my teachers, because they proved to be men of some truth, of good motivation, and they were men of good character. They were noble people . . .

One of the St Cyprian's pupils who later attended St Matthew's in the Cape comments: 'They held us in high respect also . . . in fact they loved us very much.' A student at Lemana Mission in the 40s recalls: 'The teachers discussed with us. They went to church with us. They were part of us.'

Says a member of the last generation to attend mission school in the 50s:

> The reason I respected my teachers is that they were dignified. What made them dignified? Morally . . . most of the things they did were right.

A large favourable perception of the quality of mission education underpins this assessment, as these three views reveal:

> My own time at school was very enjoyable because I'd say the education we got and the teachers we had were very conscientious . . . we could see they looked like professional people.

> I feel the missionaries were doing excellently . . . in my days the Standard 4 scholar, let me say the average one . . . they had better expression in foreign languages, in the three 'r's' . . . the counting wasn't a difficulty to them. Afrikaans wasn't a difficulty to them. English wasn't a difficulty to them. Mother tongue was just . . . sweets! . . . People who learnt with the missionaries, they applied what they learnt.

> . . . the present student just wants to be spoonfed. During our days a teacher was just there to guide you and you as a student were the one who had to go out and do the reading.

Here are several descriptions of the powerful effect the religious and moral content of missionary education had on students:

> . . . my education was always connected with church. On weekends, Saturday mornings, we used to go to what we call Anglican classes. There we learned catechism. When we finished catechism, we cleaned the church. On Sunday parents, I can say the whole community, went to church. After church we continued again with an hour of classes . . . as I consider it today, compare it with those days: obedience and Christianity close to it . . .

> . . . most of my teachers dwelt on the importance of knowledge. Not only knowing arithmetic, which was not important, but they went from arithmetic to scripture and morals.

> When I was at school, really what the teachers stressed was manners. And . . . honour your father and mother . . . I am what I am because of those values.

Like all memories, of course, these ones gloss over many of the uneasinesses of the mission world.

However, during the war years a qualitative change in the relations between mission school teachers and their pupils seems to have taken place. A rising tide of African nationalist militancy combined with the material structural problems of the missions to erode the close relationships which existed up to then.

Missionary institutions had a long record of student disturbances. The earliest recorded of these, took place at Lovedale. In 1873 a section of the students protested against alleged discrimination in favour of the Fingos. Baruch Hirson records an increase in incidents after the First World War. Student revolts took place at Kilnerton and Lovedale in 1920, and at Blythswood in 1929. In 1940 there was a strike at Clarkesbury and in 1941 a stone-throwing incident at Lovedale.

However, mission authorities and educationists generally agreed there was no precedent for the great upsurge of student revolt at the end of the Second World War. Hirson has sought to argue that incidents in the 30s were hushed up by the government. This might account for the limited numbers reported before the 40s, but it seems to assign to the government a greater degree of control over the media than it actually possessed. It is more likely that political and social conditions of the 40s generated something of a student upsurge.

Lovedale's Principal, Rev. R.H.W. Shepherd, said at the time of the 1946 Lovedale riot there had been 16 incidents in mission educational institutions in the last two years. The SAIRR counted 20 disturbances from 1945 to 1947.

From 1947 there appears to have been some decline in the number of incidents. In the early 50s conflict was revived. There is evidence of four major conflicts during 1950 (Adams, St Matthew's at Keiskammahoek, St John's at Umtata and Shawbury), two during 1952 (Mfundisweni, Faku Institution and Bensonvale), four in 1953 (Bethal, Ndaleni, Mariathal and Healdtown), and one in 1954 (Mvenyane).

The most important mission school revolt of this time was at Lovedale in 1946. It illustrates the intensity of the conflicts of this period. At 9.30 a.m. on 7 August, the institution, one of South Africa's leading missionary educational centres, exploded with student anger. A crowd of 150 to 200 male students stoned the houses of some of the staff and set fire to some small buildings and equipment. Staff who tried to intervene were stoned. When police arrived, students threw stones at them. The police fired warning shots and the students fled to the hill behind the school. At dawn they gave themselves up and 157 students were arrested. On 10 August, in defiance of orders from the mission authorities, about 80 male students marched into the town of Alice to visit their jailed fellows. The next day, Sunday 11 August, women students participated in stone-throwing and ringing the church bell. Male students boycotted church. A letter from students was handed to Shepherd demanding that those who had been arrested should not be subject to double punishment by the Lovedale authorities. The letter announced a boycott until the issue was resolved. On the Monday, none of the women students and only 30 of the men turned up for classes. Shepherd suspended classes and sent the students home. On 16 August, the pupils who had been arrested were tried in the Alice Magistrate's Court. One hundred and fifty-two were found guilty and of these 64 who were under 19 years of age were sentenced to between six and ten cuts. The remainder were fined £5 or two months' jail. The supposed cause of the whole incident was students' discontent about the rationing of sugar. However, the meaning of school violence was far more complex than this.

Before the Lovedale events were over, Healdtown, the Eastern Cape's other outstanding missionary educational institution, was shaken by similar troubles. Again, supposedly in protest over the food – in this case a reduction of the bread ration – a small group of pupils unsuccessfully tried to stage a boycott and riot on Wednesday 14 August. They set fire to a school building and cut the telephone line to Fort Beaufort. A number of the leaders of this action were expelled. The institution's authorities referred the cases of those involved in cutting the wires to the police.

Why should previously stable educational institutions have entered such a period of near-insurrection?

By the 40s, the mission system was breaking down at all levels. This breakdown affected not only institutions which were incompetent in their teaching or administration, but also the elite levels of the system. Lovedale and Healdtown between them provided half of the African students passing Cape Senior Certificate and the majority of students at Fort Hare, the country's only black university during the early 50s.

The resource-stretched missions were affected by a situation in which black youth was increasingly influenced by African nationalist aspirations. While for the mission authorities the riots were a sort of political Rorschach test which tended to summon up fantasies of all kinds of conspiracies, students were clearly becoming increasingly aware of national political issues.

The SAIRR commented in 1947 that the mission riots 'appear to be symptomatic of a general unrest among the African people throughout the country'. A missionary wrote in 1953: '. . . in the present ferment of things all over Africa all our institutions stand in the same danger of riot as we have lately seen active . . .' Another commented on the Healdtown disturbances: 'many things are contributing to a spirit of defiance and resentment in the sphere of race relations.' The Rev. A.E.F. Garrett wrote in 1953 of the 'growing disregard for discipline and authority in every area of life . . .'

There was also a certain amount of political agitation taking place in the mission schools. A missionary memorandum opined that 'many forces, all too often negative, mischievous and injurious in their approach, combine to inspire irresponsible and unworthy reactions to the church and its institutions.' Rev. B.K. Hazell of Faku Training Institution wrote in 1953 that 'subversive' literature had been distrib- uted in his district for some time. He mentioned, in particular, the Unity Movement (UM) publication, *The Torch*. In November, teachers had sold pupils copies of *The Student* which Hazell identified as 'the product of clever Communist agitation'. He said it contained a 'gar- bled' account of the recent Healdtown riots with 'the suggestion that other students in other institutions should arise in the same manner'. An awareness of international politics certainly played a role in the development of the strike wave. J. Radebe, trying to motivate his fellow students to strike at Healdtown in 1946, said:

> There is only one way of getting our way. Look at overseas. The only language the Europeans understand is to go on strike. It is the only way by which things can be put right, and we shall do that here.

Some contribution to the politicisation of the missions may have been made by returning war veterans, radicalised by their service experiences, who went for teacher training on their return. Potlake Leballo, later a major leader of the Pan Africanist Congress (PAC), went to Lovedale after leaving the army. Here he was among the leaders of the 1946 rebellion. He then managed to obtain entrance to Wilberforce Academy. Its headmaster, Rev. B.S. Rajuili, described him as 'quite interested in the disturbance of authoritative administra- tion'. He subsequently led a sit-down strike at Wilberforce, in con- junction with a group of teachers.

The testimony of former pupils of mission schools seems to confirm the shift in political attitude during the war years. One pre-war mission graduate maintains: 'In those days there was no politics – not at all.' Another, who attended school until the early part of the war, says of the student riots of this time: 'Well I think . . . that was the beginning of the spirit of nationalism among the blacks.' Speaking of an incident at his school, he says: 'The spirit of revolution was already in, it was already all over . . . revolting against whites in general, let me say.'

At St Matthew's the boarding master, a former Australian prison warder, provoked a riot in which buildings were burned because, according to an interviewee, 'his general attitude was that of a white man against blacks.' A student at Pax Training College, Pietersburg, from 1943 to 1945 did not experience any major incidents, but was nevertheless clearly influenced by the mood of the times:

> . . . as long as you don't see, if you accept everything given, it was good. I remember when I began questioning – the white want to appear to the black children as superior in mind, in everything.

Of the missionaries he reflects: '. . . their purpose was to delay what we need now.'

A student at a Catholic mission in Basutholand in the late 40s and early 50s, came to realise his differences in political outlook with a conservative Canadian teacher during his history lessons. He disapproved of the teacher's view of South Africa's past. 'Like for instance the Xhosa Wars. The Xhosas stole from the Boers, and then the Boers reclaimed the cattle.' Their clash of outlooks extended to other questions: 'About the French Revolution we had a little difference.'

There was some influence on students from politicised African teachers who would discuss political issues with them. This was alleged to have been a part of the background to the Lovedale rising in 1946. At Faku in 1953, as just mentioned, staff were selling radical literature to students. But such activities were clearly not very systematic. There is no evidence of a 'plan' by mass organisations to 'subvert' the schools of the kind in which the missionaries believed. Rather, political developments of the time were creating an atmosphere in which students were more likely to rebel.

The missionaries had formidable moral and ideological weapons to deploy against the threat of rebellion. Says one interviewee:

> . . . being a good boy was paramount. Even though we may have had complaints, we never exposed them, because of the tendency that if you speak out you are marked as a bad student, or a bad Catholic, or something like that.

These weapons could also be deployed against actual rebellion. A former scholar remembers what happened after one school strike over food:

> . . . Immediately we do that, we were called to church. We had to pray and pray and pray you know, and then in fact prayer made us submissive and . . . we could realise, well, we have offended serious.

Nevertheless, by the mid-40s it was clear the rising tide of nationalism was able to provide a legitimacy for rebellion that weakened the moral pressures of religion and authority in the mission schools.

The combination of the breakdown of the missions' infrastructure and the political changes of the time produced a breakdown in the authority of the missions over their students. The inquiry into the 1946 Lovedale riot noted that until 1939 discipline had been no problem at the school. Now, according to the inquiry, the students identified 'the European staff in the institution as part of the government machinery'. Some students 'behaved in a most unseemly way towards the teachers'. One of the teachers commented: 'The feeling among the students is that the teachers are against them.' The situation at Lovedale, others noted, was such that it was very difficult to preach in the church because of the students' tendency to make fun of the preacher.

The lack of trust also extended to strong feelings among students that white missionaries were appropriating the resources of the schools for themselves. When Radebe tried to urge his fellow Healdtown students to rebel in 1946, he denounced the fact that 'the new latrine is not finished and the Governor builds himself a new house.' What is important in this speech is the perception involved – missionaries could not be trusted to refrain from using their power in a way which bolstered their privilege as whites.

The students were sympathetic to African teachers who were subjected to discrimination within the schools. The Lovedale Inquiry noted that African staff saw the differentiated treatment to which they were subjected as having 'an unsettling effect on the minds of the students'. It also seems likely that the increasingly militant attitudes of African teachers were contributing to a breakdown of the mechanisms of social control within the schools. At Lovedale, when new rules were instituted by the head of the high school in 1946, to 'improve discipline and co-operation', these were not enforced by certain members of staff. Their attitude was described in the inquiry as one of 'passive resistance'.

Students also resented the prefect system. At a meeting between delegations from the Association of Heads of Native Institutions (AHNI) and the Cape African Parents' Association (CAPA) in 1947, the Rev. J.A. Calata argued that students resorted to strikes because they had no other way of making their grievances known. He said prefects did not convey the complaints of students to the authorities, while the students themselves were forbidden to approach principals directly. Prefects were resented for the privileges they enjoyed, such as being able to go out to movies, dances and concerts. This was compounded by the way in which the vast age range in the mission schools produced a situation where 'junior' pupils were often older than 'senior' ones who were supposed to keep them in order.

The way in which disciplinary systems fell apart under the strain of the tensions of the times is well illustrated by events which led to a 'stand-up' strike at Healdtown in 1953. Students refused their meals and refused to be seated in the dining hall, in protest against the placing of a prefect at each dining hall table. In response to this, the authorities sent about 100 students home. The prefect system had been under strain at Healdtown for some time. In 1952 there was a mass resignation of prefects. They felt their position was being undermined by the unwillingness of the housemaster, Mr Mncube, to take action on disciplinary matters. Mncube's failure to prevent fights between 'Port Elizabeth' and 'Transkei' students and the fact that students had been collecting weapons in the dormitories then came to light. Mncube resigned; but students accorded the prefects no legitimacy. In an anonymous letter to the authorities the Healdtown students complained:

> The most important point which causes us to scribble this is because our representatives are not taking our complaints to you . . . these rules are not for all our students but for the juniors and seniors who have no say in your aristocratic form of government . . . what is the use of these prefects as being our reps, they should be called your tools.

The older students felt their 'dignity' had been insulted and demanded the withdrawal of 'junior prefects in the senior area in the dining hall'. Other grudges of the students related to the quality of the food, the refusal of permission to visit the women's hostel and the carrying out of manual work (in this case getting up at 3 a.m. to bake bread).

The issue of manual work also features in other mission disturbances. There was a long-standing resentment of it on the part of mission pupils. Two teachers, who attended mission school well before the war, replied when asked what they liked least about their schools: '. . . the type of thing I did not like very much was manual labour,' and '. . . the manual work . . . we dug trenches, we dug holes.'

The new militancy of the 40s and 50s seems to have sharpened these resentments. At Lovedale in 1946 'the toolshed and gardening tools were singled out for destruction,' according to the inquiry. The social inferiority symbolised by manual labour was the issue at stake. Students' unwillingness to obey the disciplinary system of the missions was thus both a symptom and a cause of the crisis into which the missions had entered.

It was the riot over food, however, which was the most common item in the repertoire of student protest. Frequently, the issue of food became a metaphor for issues of power and authority – although there were certainly genuine inadequacies in the food in mission boarding institutions. In 1946 Dr Cooper, the Medical Superintendent of Lovedale, admitted that while the food in the institution was adequate in quantity and was fairly well balanced, 'it was monotonous and there was a shortage of vegetables.' Students at Lovedale in this period did not get tea or milk in their diet either. A former mission school student, asked to comment on what he disliked about school, says: 'Well the condition of the building was not really of the best; say the food, ja, the food definitely.'

Recalling an incident in 1945 when students at the Diocesan Training College, Pietersburg, refused to eat their food, a former pupil describes the diet:

> . . . we had yellow mealie meal and . . . the relish was kaffirbeans . . . these brownish ones. So when it was cooked, well . . . yellow mealie meal it's never just beautifully cooked. It always tastes half cooked, and then the beans had . . . weevils inside. Then we tried to eat, no good.

Such deficiencies were made worse by supply problems and government rationing measures during the war and immediate post-war period. The financial difficulties of the institutions made it hard for them to make major improvements in this area.

Food was thus a material grievance for students. But a closer examination of food riots suggests that for the students the inferior quality of their food became a symbol of, and a matter of protest against, the social domination they experienced in their daily lives. The issue of food often emerged as one which embodied the unjust relations, the authority, power and politics of a racist society: a universal focus of consistent discontent which could unite students motivated by disparate grievances.

Frequently linked to these disturbances was the students' belief that poor food represented contempt on the part of the missionaries, a lack of concern for the pupils. An anonymous student at Healdtown wrote to his headmaster in 1953:

> (i) We have been eating sour and dirty bread and raw porridge but because you do not eat these you don't worry.

> (ii) In the time of Rev. S. Mo we were given fresh fruits and fresh vegetables but see to what you give us.

The way in which food grievances highlighted other discontent is well illustrated. In the 1946 Lovedale disturbances, the students put forward the reduction of the sugar ration as the reason for their riot. However, both Shepherd and the housemaster had discussed this issue with student delegations and had pointed out there was a national sugar shortage. Moreover, students were still getting a pound of sugar a week. It thus seems highly unlikely the sugar itself was the real issue.

Similarly in the 1946 Healdtown disturbances, those students accused of being instigators by the authorities stated their motive as the reduction of the bread ration and its replacement by mealie porridge. However, when told by the teachers that the need for this had been explained to the student body, who had accepted it, they are recorded in the Principal's report as having admitted they were really motivated by a desire 'to do what Lovedale [had] done'.

A typical incident in which food became a metaphor for power took place at Mvenyane Institution, Cedarville, in 1954. On 9 March women students complained the mealie meal porridge was smelly. They were given biscuits. The school authorities investigated and found some bags of mealie meal were rotten. The bad mealies were picked out and only good ones used for the next meal. A new supply of mealies was ordered, but they were not immediately available. This was explained to the students. Staff tasted the porridge made from the selected mealies and pronounced it good, but students refused to eat it. They also rejected good yellow mealies on offer. On Saturday 13 March, staff members again tasted the porridge and found it adequate. However, the women students all walked out of the institution. Both the District Surgeon and parents who brought back their daughters tried the food and found it acceptable. Despite this, male pupils carried out their own mass walkout on 14 March. Here the food issue was clearly the focus of a power and authority struggle rather than its real content.

A minor role in the disturbances of the 50s was played by ethnic conflict. Some missions certainly housed their students on a 'tribal' basis. This must have emphasised any tendency to ethnic definitions of conflict. At Lovedale in 1946 student discontent was intensified by the fears of non-Xhosa students that they would be excluded from the institution. This erroneous impression was created by the dropping of SeTswana and SeSotho as language subjects because of insufficient numbers. In the Natal missions which had played, as Shula Marks has shown, a significant role in the development of a Zulu ethnic particularism, such incidents were especially intense.

Marks describes an incident in 1950 when the Principal of Adams College banned a Shaka Day celebration by the Zulu Society. In the outburst that followed, the Principal expelled 175 pupils. In a later incident at Ohlange Institute in 1956 there was fighting between Zulu and non-Zulu students. The comment of *The Torch* that 'at the Ohlange Institute the Zulu students are made to feel proud, different and even arrogant' is probably valid in view of Ohlange's origins in the work of the father of modern Zulu particularism, Rev. John Dube.

One aspect of mission education in the 40s and 50s apparently absent from its popular image is the way in which mission authorities were willing to use stern repression against their students in cases of disorder. The missionaries were no less willing to summon the police and to engage in mass expulsions of students than their successors. At Mariathal, Ixopo, after students had thrown stones at the Rector's office in October 1953, one of the Catholic brothers fired a warning shot. Police arrived to restore order. Four days later three car-loads of police escorted away 26 students.

On 14 May 1953, 184 students at Bethal Training Institution were arrested after a riot. Six days later another 42 were arrested after an arson incident at Ndaleni College. These are just some examples of the widespread use by mission authorities of police in response to student rebellion.

Relations between the missionaries and police during these times of conflict seem to have been cordial. The Governor of Healdtown wrote to the OC of the South African Police (SAP) at Fort Beaufort in 1953. He thanked him for the 'most ready and willing assistance' the force had given during tensions at Healdtown.

Not that this relationship was always untroubled. In the same period, the Principal of Healdtown complained that a group of black and white SAP men had infuriated his students. They had driven through the grounds of the institution making ANC salutes and yelling 'Afrika!'.

Not only students, but also black communities turned against the missions. It was true the older and more conservative section of the rural elite still felt strong links to the missions. G. Bikitsha told the Blythswood Governing Committee in 1946 there was much 'disappointment' with recent student actions. He praised the Principal of Blythswood for allowing meetings of local associations and attending them. 'Good understanding, goodwill and harmony have resulted and displaced or replaced misunderstanding.'

But already these close, paternalist relations were disintegrating under the impact of the social crises of the 40s. Black opinion was increasingly unwilling to give missions the benefit of the doubt. Brookes commented that during the Lovedale disturbances:

> . . . large sections of responsible Bantu opinion seem to have condemned the authorities and the missionary bodies without condemning the

indiscipline and licence which lies behind such action on the part of adolescents.

A teacher recalls what seemed like a deterioration in the quality of the mission schools

> . . . with the 40s brought, you know, some doubts from the communities and when it reached to the 50s it started simmering and working.

The 1946 riots were followed by numerous appeals on the part of the expelled students. Govan Mbeki, in his capacity as general secretary of the Transkei Organised Bodies (TOB), lobbied the secretary of the AHNI. He called for an inquiry into the issue, and led a TOB delegation to meet Shepherd about the dismissals. In 1950, following disturbances at St Matthew's, the Rev. J.A. Calata, as president of CAPA, convened a public meeting on the issue near the school. CAPA sent a letter to the AHNI attacking the mission for calling in the police, for discriminating against Africans in appointments and administration, and for not fully warning those involved in the riots. Following the events at Healdtown in 1953, the Rev. S. Pitts was widely criticised for his disciplinary action against students. A group of Port Elizabeth parents led by W. Tshume circulated a memorandum complaining, 'the relationship between the institution and the parents have [sic] deteriorated for the past two years.'

Popular sentiment was no longer with the missionaries.

The subsequent decade saw growing conflict within the education system. The mission system was becoming unviable in terms of its claims to guidance over teachers. The gradualist integrationism of the leading missionary ideologues was unacceptable to a rising generation pulled along by the tides of social crisis and radical nationalism. Missionaries began to be aware of the new unwillingness of black teachers to accept a subservient position. Shepherd noted in 1945:

> African teachers, particularly graduates, are claiming the same treatment and to have the same customs as Europeans who are their fellow teachers . . . African teachers feel that their salaries, as compared with European teachers doing the same work, are too low and this leads them to think there can be little or no claim on extra services.

Shepherd was responding to an observation by Rev. D.W. Semple, of Blythswood, that he found his African teachers unwilling to undertake extra-curricular activity. It was hardly surprising black teachers became increasingly resentful. Lovedale, for example, had a whites-only top table in its dining hall and its senior posts were occupied by whites. There was a strong suspicion on the part of teachers that the missions passed over suitably qualified African teachers for such posts in favour of whites. In 1952 the local branch of the Cape African Teachers' Association (CATA) criticised Healdtown on this score.

Bibliography

Oral History
Interviews with Teachers. Nos 1, 4–7, 11, 13–14, 16, 18–19.
Interview with G.M. Pitje (Manson, A.). SAIRR Oral History Archive, Accession No. 3.

Archives
Cory Library manuscripts. Series MSS 14 714, 16 452, 453, 453/9, 587/5, 598, 598/5/6.

Official publications
Report of the Commission on Technical and Vocational Training (Chairman: De Villiers, F. J.). Pretoria, Union Government, 65/1948.
Report of the Commission on Native Education (Chairman: Eiselen, W.W.M.). Pretoria, Union Government, 53/1951.
Report of the Inter-Departmental Committee on the Abuse of Dagga (Chairman: Van Schalkwijk, L.). Pretoria, Union Government, 31/1952.

Newspapers and Periodicals
Daily Dispatch. 30 October 1953.
Eastern Province Herald. 30 October 1953.
Evening Post. 30 October 1953.
SAIRR Race Relations Survey. 1946–1947. Johannesburg, SAIRR, 1948.
The Teachers' Vision. Vol. 12 No. 2, January 1947; Vol. 21 No. 4, April to June 1954.
The Torch. 10 April 1951, 3 November 1953, 24 July 1956.

Theses and Papers
Kieser, W.W.J. 'Bantoe jeugmisdaad aan die Rand en die behandeling daarvan deur die Diepkloofverbeteringskool'. MEd Dissertation, Potchefstroom University, 1952.
Marks, S. 'Patriotism, Patriachy and Purity: Natal and the Politics of Zulu Ethnic Consciousness'. African Studies Institute Paper, University of the Witwatersrand, August 1986.
Posel, D. 'Interests, Conflict and Power: The Relationship Between the State and Business in South Africa during the 1950s'. Association for Sociology in Southern Africa Conference Paper, Cape Town, 1985.

Publications
Brookes, E. *A South African Pilgrimage*. Johannesburg, Ravan Press, 1987.
Christie, P. and Collins, C. 'Bantu Education: Apartheid Ideology and Labour

Reproduction' in Kallaway, P. (ed). *Apartheid and Education: The Education of Black South Africans*. Johannesburg, Ravan Press, 1984.

Hindson, D. *Pass Controls and the Urban African Proletariat in South Africa*. Johannesburg, Ravan Press, 1987.

Hirson, B. *Year of Fire, Year of Ash. The Soweto Revolt: Roots of a Revolution*. London, Zed Press, 1979.

Lewis, J. *Industrialisation and Trade Union Organisation in South Africa, 1924–55*. Cambridge, Cambridge University Press, 1984.

Marks, S. *The Ambiguities of Dependence in South Africa: Class, Nationalism and the State in Twentieth Century Natal*. Johannesburg, Ravan Press, 1986.

Matthews, Z.K. and Wilson, M. *Freedom For My People: The Autobiography of Z.K. Matthews*. Cape Town, David Phillip, 1983.

Molteno, F. 'The Historical Foundation of the Schooling of Black South Africans' in Kallaway, P. (ed). *Apartheid and Education: The Education of Black South Africans*. Johannesburg, Ravan Press, 1984.

CHAPTER TWO

Teachers and the Crisis

Response to the 40s and 50s Educational Crisis

African teachers' organisations had existed in the various regions of the country for decades, but they had previously shown little signs of militancy.

From about 1940, however, teachers adopted increasingly aggressive stances over both working conditions and political issues.

This culminated, a decade later, in the emergence of radical leadership in both the Transvaal and Cape teachers' organisations, which waged hard-fought battles against state education policy in these regions.

We must look at teachers' activism in relation to three crucial factors.

First, the existing culture of mission-educated teachers was not simply conservative. It also emphasised service to the community. This could form an important ideological and cultural basis for teachers' rejection of the state's attempt to control and direct black educational aspirations.

Second, the new radicalism found its roots in structural, socio-economic problems facing teachers. Poor pay and working conditions dating from the Great Depression were influencing factors. So too was the lessening of professional autonomy and status caused by the educational policies of the NP government.

Third, African nationalism played a vital role in shifting teachers' political perceptions.

Teachers and Ideology

Teachers occupy an ambiguous social position that makes them particularly vulnerable to the social pressures of other groups. This was especially the case in South Africa's racial order of the 40s and 50s, when teaching was the main career opportunity open to blacks with some education.

According to Muriel Horrell, there were 13 953 African teachers in

1946, compared with 3 203 nurses, 2 697 clergymen, and 289 interpreters and translators. There were fewer than 100 doctors, lawyers, journalists, lecturers and law clerks, and only 69 social workers.

How teachers reacted to ideological and political pressures is extremely complex. The very ambiguity of their position allowed for differing responses. Some teachers, fearing loss of their relatively prestigious employment, took deeply conservative positions. Others, feeling the pinch of economic hardship, responded to popular radicalism with alacrity.

The existence of a culture of 'professionalism' among teachers had important effects. Professionalism could spell a conservative political response. It could emphasise the distinctions between teachers and other employees. It could also emphasise the specialist competency of the teacher and an active commitment to education. In this regard, it could be a radicalising factor. Degrading treatment and contempt for teachers' skills by the authorities could (and did) produce a sense of outraged professionalism among teachers. The form of 'professionalist' ideology that existed in the missions was a particularly ambiguous one. It contained an emphasis on education as a social service that could underpin a sense of grievance at educational injustice.

Certain aspects of teachers' ideology and culture stimulated a conservative response to their situation. For teachers, the access to teacher training often made the difference between a professional career and a life of manual labour. A teacher who attended a mission school orphanage from 1925 to 1931 recalls his contemporaries generally became farm labourers. By going on to attend Pax College from 1932 to 1937, he joined a stratum who could obtain skills and professional qualifications. Within Pax itself, different streams of instruction provided entrance to careers of varying levels of prestige. At the college while some took teaching, 'others took tailoring and carpentry'.

Teachers' outlooks often represented a strong identification with aspirations to upward social mobility. Teachers formed a prestigious top layer of African communities. 'During my time,' says a St Peter's graduate, 'teachers were regarded by the community as highly respected people, and behaved themselves properly.' The social prestige of university graduate teachers was vast and could awaken longings for social advancement by their pupils. A teacher at one state high school in Southern Transvaal (now Gauteng) recalls how on Parents' Day the Headmaster would

> Parade his staff . . . in front of us in their gowns. If I tell you we had a staff of 32, 26 of them graduates, you understand if they stood there, 26 of them in their gowns with their various colours, you looked at a wonderful scene. This motivated you to reach that stage.

Another teacher had the same experience: '... when I first saw them in their gowns, as graduates, I said "I must get that gown."'

The strain of attempting to attain educational success was such that many collapsed under it. Of his contemporaries at St Peter's, the most prestigious of mission schools, a teacher says, poetically:

> ... some have become lawyers,
> some have become doctors,
> some have become teachers,
> some have become jailbirds,
> some have become drunks.

The political implications were complex. For some teachers the fear of losing what they had won through immense personal struggle inclined them to caution. This made them receptive to conservative ideologies that emphasised the separation of education from politics and from community life. Missions provided teachers with a set of ideological values, originating in the culture of 19th-century (mainly British) muscular Christianity. This provided an important support to the tendency of some teachers to see themselves as a caste apart. This ideology was to provide a basis of group cohesion well after the end of the missionary era. The high Victorian character of this culture is quite startling. To give two examples: in 1959 teacher organiser W.D. Ntloko wrote: 'The temptation to quote Tennyson when I introduce myself to the teachers is quite irresistible,' whilst in 1968, G.L. Kekana told his audience at a Cape teachers' conference the ideal teacher was 'a Christian gentleman'.

Such an outlook pointed teachers toward an apolitical view of their role. It emphasised the need to maintain the continuity of educational services and to stay aloof from social conflict.

Yet there was another side to the ideology and culture of mission education. It also provided the basis for a strongly developed social conscience on the part of teachers, which could help to make them responsive to the needs of their communities. For one teacher, his training at St Matthew's in 1937 to 1939 emphasised:

> First, as a teacher, you had to set an example. You should lead an exemplary life. Next, I should be in constant touch with the community I am serving, and be conversant with what is taking place in the lives of the people I'm working with. I agreed with [these ideas]. They helped me very much.

Teachers trained between the early 30s and the mid-50s often talk about the intrinsic value of education and community service:

> ... The most important thing in teaching is to assist the student. Well the cheque comes because to be able [to] live you need money, but then the money must not be the most important aim.

This service is often seen as providing personal fulfilment, as these views from other teachers reveal:

> I enjoy being useful to the children and guiding them and exchanging views with them on whatever issues – social, political, and so on.

> I took up teaching as a calling. I wanted to serve African people. I think I've been able to accomplish it throughout my teaching career.

The ideal of service through education was propagated by dedicated African mission teachers. Of the teacher who arranged for him to do teacher training, a respondent says: 'His dedication to the education of the people – yes, that is what brought us into the game.'

The uncle of another black teacher 'influenced me towards helping the black community in teaching'.

Simplistic critiques of the colonial character of mission education miss the ambiguities of 'service to the community'. The concept could provide resources for radicalism as well as conservatism.

The sense that teachers were committed to delivering an important service seems to reflect their positive experiences of their own teachers. Among both African teachers and white missionaries a remarkable degree of elan and enthusiasm seems to have prevailed. This was transmitted to the pupils. A number of mission-trained teachers educated in this era spoke in interviews of how they had experienced their instructors as inspirational or exemplary:

> The way he taught us made us like teaching.

> At high school I found that the teaching of a child, the method the teachers had brought to us was one of the most inspiring ideas in life. I was very keen on educating other people.

> . . . even when I was still at the primary school, I dreamt myself being a teacher. I dreamt myself being a teacher and just working like a certain mistress, Janet, who was one of my teachers, and conducting my lessons like she did and even being playful with children like she used to.

A student of Lemana Mission in the 40s tells how he named his first-born son after two of the mission's brothers. Another says he wanted to teach because he did not want to disappoint the missionaries who had arranged his schooling. This strong sense of vocation on the part of teachers existed in state as well as mission institutions. At Alexandra schools in the 40s the teachers, according to one of their pupils:

> strived very hard to do their work. They motivated us a great deal, and they were almost role models for what we aspired to.

The culture of mission education did advance certain conformist and imperial values, which had the effect of inducing some teachers toward conservatism. That culture also emphasised the responsibility of teachers to the community they served, and the need for the teacher to make an exemplary contribution to community life.

In the 40s, facing deteriorating conditions in the schools, and in the 50s, facing a state intent on a policy which attacked African educational achievements and aspirations, many teachers felt compelled to oppose this process. The ambiguous ideology of professionalism had helped create certain elements of teachers' culture that could provide cultural and ideological sources of rebellion. Among the teachers quoted above who speak so warmly of mission-era education, quite a number were involved in early teacher militancy. Some also participated in the ANC's educational campaigns of the mid-50s.

The resources of conviction generating teachers' revolt in this period came from unexpected sources.

Pay and Conditions as Radicalising Issues

The second feature of teacher radicalisation in the 40s and 50s was a revolt against low pay. Austerity policy pursued by the state from early in the 30s held down teachers' wages. Wartime inflation worsened their plight. By the early 40s teachers were moving to wage militancy. This reflected, simultaneously, a fear of deteriorating status and a reduced social distance from the working class. Structurally, teachers' economic conditions posed a threat to their professional and 'middle class' social standing. The relatively high prestige teachers enjoyed inside black communities bore no relation to the low wages they received.

The Great Depression had serious adverse effects on the economic position of African teachers. The first national salary scales for African teachers were gazetted in March 1929, to be retroactive to April 1928. Because of the onset of the depression, the state introduced drastic cutbacks in expenditure. Consequently, the scales were not implemented. The Transvaal African Teachers' Association (TATA) brought a successful legal test case against the Transvaal Director of Education over this issue. As a result, about 500 teachers were able to claim back-pay from the provincial administration. The pattern had been set for a decade of retrenchment, stagnant or declining real wages, and pay cuts. In early 1931, teachers' pay was cut by 15 per cent. Between 1932 to 1934, urban teachers received a 7 per cent cut. Rural teachers earning more than £50 a year got an 8 per cent cut.

In terms of a new policy, all newly appointed teachers in the Transvaal were treated as unqualified teachers for salary purposes.

From 1937 to 1938, those who had suffered cuts from 1932 to 1934 received a refund. Teachers who had been penalised by other austerity measures obtained no compensation.

The early 40s brought only very limited improvements in the pay position. Following an interview between a teachers' delegation and the Secretary of Native Affairs in late 1941, teachers' salaries were raised in 1942. Thereafter annual pay rises were instituted. However, there was still considerable discontent over pay. This was exacerbated by the effects of inflation. The price of clothing more than doubled between 1938 and 1948. Food prices also rose sharply in the same period.

In response, TATA launched a salary campaign in 1941. The leadership of the campaign included S. Lesolang (chairperson), David Bopape (later an important member of the Communist Party), and A.P. Mda (who was to become the theoretician of the Africanist current within the ANC). Bopape, who was secretary of the campaign, travelled all over the province, organising a mass protest meeting at the Bantu Men's Social Centre, Johannesburg, in late 1941. Through the campaign's activities, pay improvements were secured.

This was followed by the 'Blanket Campaign'. Teachers took to wearing Basotho-style blankets to work, protesting that they were unable to buy themselves suits or dresses. However, E.M.J. Phago describes the teachers' expressed need for more militant action and to obtain broader support.

There was a call for a mass demonstration, to be held in central Johannesburg on Saturday 6 May 1944. R.L. Peteni, in *Towards Tomorrow: The Story of the African Teachers' Association of South Africa*, describes how, at 9 a.m., a 'mile long procession of teachers, parents and school children' left the Bantu Sports Ground.

The excitement of this demonstration still lives in the memories of participants. A teacher recalls:

> I think the whole Reef came together in the Bantu Sports and they demonstrated through Eloff Street with placards.

Another teacher speaks in similar terms:

> All the teachers who could afford it came into Johannesburg and we moved street by street carrying posters . . . Eloff Street, Bree Street, in fact the whole of Johannesburg.

Banners and posters demanded free universal education, more schools and featured the slogan 'A Hungry Teacher Cannot Teach a Hungry Child'. Police made an attempt to stop the demonstration. The teachers then called for women to go to the front of the procession. Because of the reluctance of the police to attack them and the determination of the demonstrators, the police had to give way. A rally after the demonstration was addressed by Dr A. Xuma, ANC President-General. He pledged his organisation's support for the teachers.

The demonstration might have been a prelude to even more militant action. However, the actions of some of TATA's leaders and the government's shrewd handling of the situation prevented this from occurring. The organisers of the pay campaign had planned a one-day strike to follow the demonstration. But during the post-demonstration rally, TATA's president instructed teachers to return to work on the next working day.

The government responded by sending the Minister of Native Affairs, Major Piet van der Byl, to address the TATA conference at Witbank in July. The government subsequently raised the level of teachers' annual increase and appointed a commission of inquiry into African teachers' salaries, which recommended a uniform salary structure for the whole country and all-round increases. Although the inquiry's recommendations were not implemented until 1948, the government's actions seem to have been sufficient, in combination with the passivity of the TATA leadership, to bring the campaign to a halt.

The TATA conference bemoaned the inadequacy of the new pay scales, but it organised no protest against them. A former member still feels the improvement in pay after the demonstration was 'a meagre one, not worth mentioning at all'. Yet TATA's activism over pay faded away.

Part of the reason may have been corruption in TATA's leadership. According to a former member, the considerable resources mustered in the aftermath of the demonstration were embezzled by at least one official:

> Let me tell you thousands, hundreds or thousands of funds were offered by the able, sympathetic people along the Reef and Pretoria alone. We were unfortunate money wasn't properly looked at, because shortly after that we only got information that — had resigned . . . leaving our purse, our treasure, with no pay.

However, the demonstration was an extremely significant event. It was the first time South African teachers organised in 'trade-union' fashion, seeking to gain their objectives by mass action.

This period saw a growth of teacher discontent over wages in the Cape and Transvaal, even though in the former province it did not manifest itself as dramatically. A June 1944 issue of *Inkundla ya Bantu* describes a 'mammoth' meeting of CATA at Willowvale threatening militant action over pay demands. CATA's journal, *The Teach-*

ers' Vision, kept up a strident demand for better pay, for example commenting acidly on the Royal Family's visit in 1947:

> We hope that [the new pay scales] will coincide with the arrival of His Majesty and his family in South Africa so that the latter may see the good things our democratic government is doing for us.

The Impact of Nationalism

The third major factor contributing to teacher radicalisation in the 40s and 50s was the work of African nationalist activists. Material problems alone cannot explain why teachers' political attitudes shifted into the particular form they did – that of an increasing receptiveness to African nationalist political ideology – during this period.

The initial wage agitation was conducted in terms of a fairly 'non-political' ideology. Yet this seems to have fed into the growing political self-assertion of teachers in subsequent years.

At a political and cultural level, the emergence of a new generation of young progressive teachers, linked to the African National Congress Youth League (ANCYL) and the Non-European Unity Movement (NEUM), made an important impact. The tendency towards politicisation was reinforced by black urban community organisation around educational issues in the 50s. It certainly began to place teachers under popular pressure to act on political issues in the education field.

The 40s saw the entry of a growing number of young teachers into active participation in the nationalist movement, especially its Africanist wing. Much of the impetus for this came from teachers who had studied at Fort Hare University. Many of its graduates from the 40s subsequently became major leaders of the ANC or the PAC. These included Nelson Mandela (who graduated in 1940), Oliver Tambo (1941), Robert Sobukwe (1949), Tennyson Makiwane (1947), Duma Nokwe (1949) and G.M. Pitje (1944).

Tambo was secretary of Fort Hare Student Representative Council (SRC) in 1941. Following a dispute between the students and the university authorities, he was expelled for refusing to sign a pledge of good conduct. He was thus unable to complete his studies for his postgraduate teachers' diploma. Pitje recalls that student strikes took place in 1941 and 1942.

A branch of the ANCYL was founded at the university in 1948. It supported a nurses' strike at Lovedale. This, together with other clashes with authority, led to its banning by the University Senate. Sobukwe headed the SRC in 1949. He played a leading role in urging a more radical political programme on the Cape region of the ANC.

Many Fort Hare graduates entered the teaching profession, carrying their political convictions with them.

At the founding meeting of the ANCYL at Johannesburg's Bantu Men's Social Centre on Easter Sunday of April 1944, teachers played a key role.

Despite their commitments in the broader political sphere, the ANCYL was active in TATA. Oliver Tambo was prominent at the association's 1947 conference at Lemana. He raised the issues of compulsory education, TATA's relations with political bodies and trade unions, and the ill-treatment of farm labourers in the Bethal district.

A related development with significance for teacher resistance was the emergence of the school boycott as a form of community and student resistance to the state, with the Brakpan stay-at-home of 1944. This movement erupted over the sacking of David Bopape, a leading political activist teaching at the Amalgamated Mission School in the town. He was sacked by the NP Town Council at the instigation of a certain Dr Language, head of Brakpan's Native Affairs Department (NAD), (and in his spare time, the Ossewa Brandwag's 'native expert'). The motive was apparently Language's displeasure at Bopape's involvement in community politics.

This resulted in a boycott of classes by 2 000 pupils, and a one-day stay-at-home by the entire 7 000-strong workforce of the location. This event was an important pathbreaker of combined action by students and community on political issues relating to education.

The radicalisation of teachers in the Cape followed a different route from that of the Transvaal. The politics that became dominant in CATA derived primarily not from the mainstream of African nationalism represented by the ANC but from the All-African Convention (AAC). This was an affiliate of the NEUM, a smaller, Cape-based black nationalist organisation. The NEUM is often characterised in a way typified by Eddie Roux's comment in *Time Longer than Rope*:

> African intellectuals, particularly teachers, found that their profession made it impossible for them to participate in mass movements involving physical danger or imprisonment. At the same time they were more politically conscious than the masses and realised the enormity of the colour bar. They therefore sought psychological compensation in extremist programmes, which in fact were never implemented.

A similar view is expressed by H.J. and R.E. Simons in *Class and Colour in South Africa, 1850–1950*, who see the NEUM as largely confined to 'Coloured' and African intellectuals. In their view, the NEUM emphasised the tactic of the boycott as a way of avoiding direct conflict with state authority. They claimed the NEUM concentrated on passive propaganda activity, much of it directed toward sectarian attacks on other organisations.

How accurate is this view? The NEUM did rely heavily on teachers for its active support. Unlike the ANC, it was unable to create long-lasting structures of mass support. The NEUM's emphasis on the boycott as the be-all and end-all of political strategy did often lead to mere passivity. It generally failed to put forward any tactical or strategic proposals beyond the unification of black organisations within its 'federal structure' and the carrying out of boycotts of state political institutions. It was virulently sectarian toward other organisations.

However, the NEUM was not as marginal to conflicts during the 40s and 50s as its critics may lead one to expect. The leadership of the ANC and PAC also drew heavily on the black 'middle class'. The NEUM's members faced considerable repression from the state and combatted quite vehemently those teachers who advocated protection of their professional position as a priority. The boycott tactic did not always lead to passivity. In the Eastern Cape during the 50s, the NEUM achieved some brief successes in stimulating activity by rural people in boycotting government attempts to impose new systems of agriculture, local government and education. While the NEUM was often quite as sectarian, arrogant and abstentionist as its critics suggest, the movement was far from being a totally marginal force in popular struggles in the Cape during the 50s.

This was particularly so in the field of education. With the foundation of the NEUM in 1943, its affiliate, the AAC, began to spread the movement's influence among Cape African teachers. The CATA journal *The Teachers' Vision* carried articles by writers who advocated the NEUM views. One of these writers, under the pseudonym 'Vuy-Vuyi', propounded a Marxist-influenced account of South African society: 'We are oppressed not because we are black but because we must be exploited.' Vuy-Vuyi advocated the AAC's political line, without mentioning the name of the organisation. He argued CATA should take a more overtly political stance. AAC militants took the view that African teachers could not organise in a purely 'professional' manner, because the racial inequalities of South African society would always prevent their making progress in that way. The AAC felt the only solution to teachers' problems was for CATA to abandon its existing strategy of lobbying the Cape Education Department (CED) and to link with a political mass movement. Vuy-Vuyi wrote on this theme:

> How can professional dignity abide in the tin shanties we use as class-rooms? How can we feel dignified in hunger and rags and in the presence of the starved and sickly children whom we have to teach? And when we realise all these disabilities are an outcome of our being

discriminated against by reason of our colour, we cannot help but feel that smug respectability is our greatest enemy . . . holding annual conferences and forwarding resolutions to the Department is a feeble and hopeless method to fight the odds against us.

At the 1944 conference of CATA, affiliation to the AAC was unsuccessfully proposed (an attempt to affiliate the association to the ANC also failed). However, the AAC was working on fertile ground. The manifold discontent of the Cape African teachers gained it growing support. This discontent was manifest in *The Teachers' Vision*, which carried numerous articles critical of the national political dispensation. There were frequent complaints about such matters as racist language and attacks on the official prohibition on teachers' participation in politics. CATA was committed to the principle of 'education of the whole community wholly financed by the state'. It advocated a single education department for all race groups, a demand which in itself raised questions of national politics.

While the NEUM was generally insignificant in the Transvaal, it did manage, during the late 40s and early 50s, to exert an ideological influence over limited numbers of important individuals in teachers' politics there. Indeed, Es'kia Mphahlele claims that at one stage the AAC's influence on Rand teachers was greater than that of the Africanist current of the ANC.

Thus in the 40s, the preconditions for a radical teachers' movement emerged. Teachers had suffered economically. They had been pushed into mobilising in an active and militant manner for the first time. The politicisation of Fort Hare, the rise of the ANCYL and the NEUM, brought an infusion of political activism into the profession. Brakpan events provided a new model of political action involving community, school students and teachers. New radical teachers' leadership was able to harness teachers' concern over the degeneration of education and their own social position. This created a considerable wave of teacher resistance to state education policy in the 50s.

The Rise of New Teachers' Leadership: 1948 to 1955

What forms did teacher radicalisation take during the NP's accession to government in 1948?

Teacher resistance became a central feature of the disintegration of schooling, which the NP would have to address if it were to restore the hegemony of the dominant classes. Reasserting control and attempting to create a new hegemonic order which could incorporate teachers, were central features of Bantu Education.

Wage militancy, teacher political activism, community action and growing moral revulsion over state policy were trends which prepared the way for dramatic changes in teachers' organisations. The end of the 40s and the beginning of the 50s saw the two leading African teachers' organisations in the country swing strongly to the left. It was the beginning of a period of political combativeness on the part of teachers.

Undoubtedly the election of the NP government and the enunciation of its black education policy in the Eiselen Commission Report (1951) were important precipitants of these trends. The NP's victory undermined African hopes of a retreat from segregationism. This weakened gradualist ideologies of social change among teachers. The Eiselen Report, with its apartheid orientation and proposal for centralised government control of education, was seen by teachers as an obstacle to African aspirations. Teachers viewed it as a threat to their professional autonomy.

By the late 40s and early 50s there was a perceptible change in the mood of teachers. New radical leadership took over TATA and CATA. Both bodies waged vigorous campaigns against the introduction of Bantu Education policy. They were able to raise considerable support among teachers for this stance during the early 50s.

In the Transvaal this leadership came from a loose grouping based in Johannesburg's Orlando township. The social dynamics of the township help to explain why teacher radicalism was centred there. Orlando was established by the Johannesburg Municipality in 1932. It was to be a 'Model Native Township'. Orlando was initially more attractive to higher-income sections of the African population, who were probably drawn by the relatively good quality of the housing available there. Consequently, it came to have a much larger intermediate social stratum than any other township. But despite its size, the 'middle class' of Orlando was not particularly privileged. It shared the township with growing numbers of the urban poor. Transport costs and living expenses were high. According to a Johannesburg Municipality study in 1948, 96 per cent of Orlando's population lived in unsatisfactory and unhygienic housing conditions because of overcrowding. Overall, the middle class of Orlando had little to show for its academic or commercial achievements.

The resulting frustration was an important force behind the politicisation of Orlando in the late 40s. Orlando East ANCYL and ANC branches were the second largest in the Transvaal. They were not regarded as among the most radical branches, but ANC influence was strong. It affected pupils and teachers. When Pitje came to teach at Orlando High School in 1945, he found the school students were highly politicised. Many were members of the ANC. They attended meetings conducted by the major figures in the ANCYL. The Orlando teachers were part of a 'middle class' which was numerically strong, particularly frustrated, and thus open to political activity.

The new leadership of TATA arose in the course of conflicts within the association in the later 40s. After the 1944 demonstration, there was a backlash from rural teachers. They saw their colleagues on the Rand as being too militant. This sentiment produced an ineffective and conservative, rural-based TATA leadership from 1945. E.M. Malepe, President from 1945 to 1947, failed in his attempts to set up a permanent office in Johannesburg and to establish TATA's magazine, *The Good Shepherd* as a monthly publication. J.M. Lekgetha, President from 1947, was unable to comprehend the political issues posed for teachers by the coming of the NP to power in 1948. At the TATA conference of that year, in Lydenburg, he said he hoped the new government would do more for African education, 'as the Prime Minister had held out hopes of fair play and justice towards Africans'. Finally, at the 1949 conference, the more radical urban teachers revolted. After an all-night sitting filled with acrimony and allegations of intimidation, voting took place at 5 a.m. Lekgetha was thrown out of office. He was replaced by R. Tshaka, the candidate of the urban faction. This led to a split at the 1950 conference of the association. When the discussion ended, the rural delegates remained behind and resolved to break away from TATA. Their new organisation, the Transvaal African Teachers' Union (TATU) had a base in the rural north and west of the province. However, TATA retained the allegiance of the urban Southern Transvaal, especially the Rand, Witbank and Pretoria. TATA thus became largely an organisation of politically aware urban teachers – in Mphahlele's words, 'a hard core who believed in the African and took no instructions from the Transvaal Education Department' (TED).

This constituency elected a group of young radical teachers from Orlando High School to the leadership of TATA in 1951. Zeph Mothopeng became president, Mphahlele became secretary, and Isaac Matlhare editor of the association's journal.

The TATA executive appears to have been the first group of leaders of an African organisation in the country to address the sweeping implications of the Eiselen Report. TATA mounted a campaign against the commission's recommendations. It was to be a number of years before the attention of the mainstream of the African nationalist movement became focused on the significance of the proposed new educational system. Mphahlele comments bluntly: 'The African National Congress was caught with its pants down as far as the introduction of Bantu Education was concerned.'

He writes: 'It took the ANC a long time to digest the message of our campaign in 1951 and 1952.' The TATA executive launched a speaking tour of the Transvaal, during which they elaborated a sharp critique of Bantu Education. Their views in many ways anticipated what was to become the standard African nationalist analysis of Bantu Education as a mechanism of racial domination. According to Mphahlele:

> We travelled to various parts of the Transvaal to address teachers' and parents' meetings . . . we warned people against the dangers of the proposed system not only for the child but for Africans as a people with a historical destiny. This education for slavery had to be resisted because its philosophical underpinnings were wrong.

At least some teachers of his generation share Mphahlele's high estimation of the role of contemporary teachers' organisations in opposing Bantu Education. One says of TATA and CATA:

> They were the group who knew the dangers. They were aware the government was removing these things from the missionaries and not giving them equal education.

The TATA executive convened two conferences on the Eiselen Report in March 1952, one in Johannesburg and one in Pretoria. Both rejected the report. They manifested their animosity toward white liberals by voting to refuse an invitation to discuss the issue with the SAIRR. The meeting also decided to boycott the upcoming festival commemorating the 300th anniversary of Van Riebeeck's landing at the Cape. The organisation tried to strengthen its links with the community by building or revitalising parent-teachers' associations. This was only successful in a few cases. Mphahlele comments: 'Most of the teachers did not understand the full implications of what we were saying.'

Their activities quickly brought the three TATA leaders into conflict with the Principal of Orlando High School, Godfrey Nakene. He enthusiastically supported the plans for Bantu Education. Nakene was allegedly involved in financial corruption over school fees and text-book purchases. His staff was divided into his supporters and his antagonists. Nakene reported the TATA leaders to the TED for being involved in the production of a community newspaper, *The Voice*. The TED wrote to them, referring to the paper as a 'subversive publication' and asking them to confirm or deny their connection with it. Presumably for strategic reasons, they denied being involved and asked the TED for the source of its information. *The Voice* had carried material critical of the Eiselen Report. This presumably attracted official displeasure.

Following a visit by a police Special Branch (SB) officer to Orlando High School, Mphahlele and Khabi Mngoma were charged with publishing a newspaper without printing their names and address. They were acquitted on a technicality. In a memo to the TED, the TATA leaders detailed Nakene's mismanagement of the school. But Nakene arranged for the TED to institute a commission of inquiry into the school's staff relations.

Nakene had little difficulty in convincing the commission of his point of view. It devoted most of its efforts to unsuccessful attempts to find evidence the three had tried to spread their political views in the classroom. In July 1952, Mothopeng, Mphahlele and Matlhare were sacked, with one month's pay instead of notice. TATA responded with a statement noting they had never been charged with any breach of regulations. TATA asserted the real reasons for the dismissal lay in TATA's opposition to the Eiselen Commission, the TED's policies and the Van Riebeeck Festival.

It soon became apparent the Orlando community would not accept the sackings. When Nakene announced the dismissals to the school, students booed him. On 10 August, a Parents' Protest Committee convened a mass meeting at Donaldson Orlando Community Centre. About 500 people attended. A resolution was sent to the TED Director warning that a school boycott would be called and alternative classes organised for students unless the three were reinstated. The meeting also passed a resolution of no confidence in the school board. It called for the resignation of Nakene within seven days. The community response confirmed TATA's success in mobilising popular support for the campaign against Bantu Education.

When the TED failed to respond to the community's demands, a definite decision was taken to launch the school student boycott on Monday 25 August and to set up alternative classes. The boycott received the support of more than two-thirds of Orlando High School's students. About 100 attended the alternative classes at the Donaldson Centre.

On the second day of the boycott, the authorities struck back. Mothopeng, Mphahlele and Matlhare were arrested and charged with incitement to public violence. The boycott began to lose momentum. Students started to return to school. However, on Thursday 4 September, a successful student rally boosted support. A big parents' rally was held on the Sunday which also helped revive the campaign.

Their plan was to sue the TED for wrongful dismissal of the three.

When the three appeared in court on 8 and 9 September, the Crown's case rapidly fell apart. Students called as Crown witnesses denied the three had incited them to violence. They said they had given statements to that effect only because the SB had threatened them with three years in Diepkloof Reformatory if they did not co-operate.

On the second day of the trial, the prosecutor dropped the charges. Nakene, who was called as a Crown witness, was publicly humiliated. He was accused of making a profit on the sale of school books by denying students the 10 per cent discount to which they were entitled. The instructing counsel for Mothopeng was his ANC colleague, Nelson Mandela. It was an important psychological and moral victory.

After this success, the student boycott gained momentum. A TATA emergency conference at Brakpan on 13 September supported the demand by the three for reinstatement. The conference expressed confidence in their leadership and voted funds for their defence. Addressing the conference, Matlhare argued the sackings were an attack on those African intellectuals who had 'turned their backs on the old reactionary road of deputation and humble requests to authorities'.

The boycott came apart when, in October, a shooting incident outside Orlando High School gave the police an opportunity to arrest a substantial number of students. Eighteen appeared in court in early November on charges of public violence. The tide of opinion in TATA turned with the boycott's failure. Mothopeng, Mphahlele, Matlhare and their colleague V.K. Ntshona, who was Assistant Secretary, were all voted out of office at the TATA conference in July 1953.

An important factor in this defeat seems to have been the authorities' refusal to negotiate with TATA as long as the radical group was in the leadership. This resulted in a 'standstill' in relations between teachers and the authorities. In the words of one veteran teacher:

> The Department would not have any discussions with the teachers' organisation as long as it was led by those men, because of their political views. Their case was turned down, and the teachers voted these people out . . .

Thus many teachers, while sympathising with the Orlando group's cause, were susceptible to the argument that the organisation was not representing them effectively to the authorities.

The new leadership seems to have been constituted through an alliance between relatively conservative teachers such as S.P. Kwakwa, the new President, and a section of the more radical teachers. The latter was led by Pitje of the ANC, who became a magazine editor. The alliance appears to have been based on a common emphasis on the importance of reuniting with TATU. This position had been rejected by the previous leading group.

Kwakwa's success was partly based on his being seen as a man who could restore negotiating relations between TATA and the TED. One teacher comments:

The only progress made in the negotiations came when Mothopeng was succeeded by Kwakwa. Kwakwa was acceptable to the Department, to negotiate, to have discussions with.

The ANC's attitude to TATA and its leaders had been a complex one. ANC militants intervened in the structures of TATA. ANC members in the Orlando TATA branch tried to persuade their colleagues to support the 1950 ANC/Communist Party strike against the Suppression of Communism Act. Pitje also disseminated the ANCYL's Africanist ideology at TATA meetings. The Orlando ANC gave active backing to the three during their reinstatement struggle. The Parents' Protest Committee was headed by the ANC Branch Chairperson, I.M. Maseko, and ANCYL members served on it. But, at a national level, the ANC displayed limited interest in TATA's campaign against Bantu Education. Mphahlele approached ANC leaders about the political implications of the new education system during 1952. His approach failed to elicit much response.

Perhaps because the ANC was not, at this stage, giving priority to educational issues, the NEUM's affiliates appear to have had some following among Rand teachers. The NEUM paper, *The Torch*, gave regular coverage to the Orlando teachers' struggle. Its Cape affiliates CATA and the 'Coloured' Teachers' League of South Africa (TLSA) held meetings to support the campaign. The NEUM's orientation to education issues allowed it to gain some influence over teachers. But suspicion of the Orlando group's links with the NEUM generated hostility from some ANC leaders like Pitje.

However, the Orlando teachers' leadership was far from being politically homogeneous in their outlook. Mphahlele seems to have been influenced by both the ANCYL and the NEUM. During the mid-50s, he moved rapidly toward the ANC. He was the main speaker on culture and education at its 'Congress of the People' in 1955. Mothopeng, a long-standing member of the Africanist current in the ANC, became a prominent leader of the PAC. What united such politically diverse individuals in the 1951 to 1953 period was their critique of Bantu Education. They fought for their ideas, at a time when the mainstream of the African Nationalist Movement had not yet fully addressed itself to the political significance of educational issues.

To fully understand the politics of TATA, we need to note the central role of Orlando teachers in the rise of Africanist opposition in the ANC and, eventually, in the emergence of the PAC. The May Day strike of 1950, in which the ANC co-operated with the Communist Party, divided the ANC into a non-racial faction, which supported the alliance, and an Africanist one, which opposed it. Africanist dissent on the Rand crystallised around the leadership of three Orlando teachers –

Mothopeng, Peter Raboroko and Potlake Leballo. Under Leballo's direction, the Orlando East ANCYL became increasingly critical of the ANC's links with non-African organisations and the influence of 'foreign ideologies'. It was also critical of the ANC's view that the boycott of state institutions was a tactic rather than a principle. Africanists in the leadership of the school boycott included not only Mothopeng, but also the ANC Branch Chairperson, Maseko, who led the Parents' Protest Committee. In 1953, Maseko became involved in an Africanist ANC faction known as the 'Bafabegiya'. He was consequently expelled from the ANC the next year.

Teachers were extremely prominent in the Africanist opposition. Nine out of the 15 most prominent Africanists were present or former teachers. Many teachers within the ANC tended toward the Africanist faction. This Africanist trend was reflected in the handling of education issues within the Orlando ANC. In 1955 there was a move to set up a breakaway branch of the organisation in protest against the national leadership's postponement of the implementation of the school boycott of that year. The role played by Orlando teachers in the development of Africanism can partly be accounted for by the factors discussed earlier in this chapter. As part of an unusually large and confident township 'middle class', these teachers found their aspirations frustrated by the conditions of material life in Orlando. They responded by focusing their hostility on whites as a group. On top of this came the diminution of teachers' status and autonomy, as they were subjected to the controls of Bantu Education. G. Gerhart suggests a further reason for the feelings of frustration that fostered Africanism: the lack of professional mobility. Of the 15 most prominent Africanist leaders, nine attempted, without success, to break into the fields of medicine or law. The emergence of Africanism in Orlando may thus be attributed, in large part, to the economic, political and career frustrations of a 'middle class' consisting largely of teachers.

In the Cape, the rise of a new leadership in the teachers' association came slightly earlier than in the Transvaal. The pro-AAC wing of CATA, which came to be known as the 'progressives', did not have it all their own way. Some teachers voiced annoyance at what they saw as the progressives' neglect of basic material issues. CATA president H. Masiza opposed a more political orientation. He argued that until a strong class of wealthy Africans emerged, 'so long will our leaders, politicians and organisations clamour vainly for our rights'.

But the general trend of events was in the AAC's favour. The 1948 CATA conference was able to secure affiliation to the AAC. Here, CATA adopted a statement of policy which declared: 'Our struggle is inseparable from the general struggle of the African people.' It committed CATA to unite with other bodies in order to 'co-ordinate their struggles in the fight against their common oppression – the fundamental oppression of the black man'. While 'other bodies' was interpreted in a sectarian sense, meaning only other NEUM affiliates, this shift toward full political commitment represented an important change in the political attitudes of CATA's base. A prominent CATA member, R.S. Canca, vividly described this process in *The Teachers' Vision* in 1949:

> For a long time the African teacher imagined himself to be somewhere between the oppressed and the oppressor. Hence we refused to identify ourselves with the struggling masses for we considered ourselves to be above them. We mainly believed the oppressor would suddenly change his heart and admit us into his society. But events show us that all laws that affect the miner, the garden boy, the kitchen girl affect us too. We cannot so much as attain a single one of our objectives unless and until black South Africa has attained its freedom.

CATA's affiliation to the AAC involved the incorporation of the NEUM's political strategy into every aspect of CATA's activity. Even CATA's demands relating specifically to education were seen as confronting wider questions of political power. Thus *The Teachers' Vision* declared:

> To seek equality between the white and black teacher is to seek full social, economic and political equality between black and white South Africans. Our slogan 'Equal Pay for Equal Work' therefore implies that our struggle is the general political struggle for the emancipation of the African.

The accession to power of a new leadership in CATA had a galvanising effect on its organisational growth. Membership rose from a mere 612 in July 1949 to about 3 000 in July 1952. These figures represented, respectively, about 10 and 50 per cent of the total number of African teachers in the Cape. This spectacular growth indicates a receptivity on the part of a substantial section of teachers to CATA's new approach.

During this period CATA undertook a number of initiatives. The association was active in campaigning on the issue of salaries. During 1950, it used the hearings of the Eiselen Commission as a platform to voice its views. A memo to the Commission demanded state financing of education 'at the same rate per child irrespective of race or colour'. It urged the use of English as the medium of instruction. It also opposed regulations introduced by the authorities to reduce the school population as a solution to school overcrowding, drawing attention instead to the numbers of unemployed teachers. The efforts to build links with African teachers' associations in other provinces did not meet with great success. This was largely because of the grip of conservative strains of 'professional' ideology on those bodies. It was also because the relevant organisations in other provinces objected to CATA's AAC affiliation. *The Teachers' Vision* reported that at a meeting of the Federal Council of African Teachers' Associations (FCATA) at Bloemfontein on 17 December 1949, the Cape delegation were told that although teachers in other provinces were:

> just as political minded [sic], if not more so, than their brothers in the Cape, they had learned the importance of divorcing duty from political convictions, and they would not subject their professional associations to the chaperonage of any other bodies, which it was feared may only result in professional inefficiency.

While the TATA of the early 50s had a certain amount in common with CATA, it never forged closer links. This was despite a meeting to discuss unity between the CATA leaders and Ntshona and Mphahlele in Kimberley in April 1953. More progress was made in constructing links with the TLSA, the NEUM's affiliate organising 'Coloured' teachers in the Cape. CATA and TLSA leaders met in Port Elizabeth in March 1951. They formed the Cape Teachers' Federal Council as a co-ordinating body. In June 1952 CATA and TLSA held a joint conference in Cape Town. At this gathering CATA's president, L.S. Sihali, proclaimed: 'We have realised it is high time these artificial barriers were knocked down.'

However, the NEUM never succeeded in creating a teachers' union embracing all black teachers in the Cape.

A significant feature of CATA's activity in this period was that it began to forge links with the rural population in certain areas of the Eastern Cape (especially the Transkei). This was to have important consequences in the mid- and late 1950s. NEUM leaders saw CATA members as a cadre of activists through whom the organisation's influence could be spread into the rural areas. K. Hassim, a notable NEUM figure, comments in retrospect: 'it was the teachers who were often our link with the countryside.'

After the Second World War the AAC boycotted the government's soil rehabilitation scheme and the various unpopular forms of black representation. Peasant organisations and vigilance committees sprang up, with which the NEUM claimed to have links. It is difficult to determine the extent of the NEUM's influence in the rural Eastern Cape and Transkei in this period. CATA members were certainly active in rural agitation.

On 15 March 1952, a meeting of 'Iso Lomzi' (Vigilance Committee) of Willowvale was held at Ciko School. Three CATA activists, N. Honono, Makasi and Jadazweni, attacked the Bantu Authorities Act in their speeches. On 30 March the same year, there was a conference of the Transkei Organised Bodies at Baziya. The main speaker was W. M. Tsotsi, a CATA member and AAC General Secretary. He spoke about inequalities in access to land between blacks and whites. N. Honono also played a prominent part at the conference. He attacked Bantu Education and the Bantu Authorities – which, he said, made people responsible for their own oppression.

In 1954 it was reported that the education authorities had called a celebration of the establishment of the first Bantu Authority in the Cape, at Willowvale. Teachers were each asked to bring a bottle of brandy while parents were requested to bring sheep, goats and a bullock. The celebration was successfully boycotted by CATA and AAC supporters. Only two sheep materialised as donations, and no teachers participated. 'The local magistrate became very hostile toward the teachers,' reported *The Torch*.

The Report of the Eiselen Commission was published in 1951. Its recommendations were made law in 1953, but this was only put into full effect in 1955. There was thus a lengthy period between the government's giving notice of its intention to transform the system of African education and the execution of that design.

During this period CATA's publications emphasised its view that the government sought to use education as a way of generating cheap labour. *The Teachers' Vision* commented in 1954: 'The aim [of Bantu Education and Bantu Authorities] is to increase the power of the "herrenvolk" by producing ignorant, docile CHEAP LABOUR, CHEAP TEACHERS, CHEAP GOVERNMENT [sic] of an oppressed people divided into suicidal factions and feuds among themselves – "Bantu Culture".'

CATA's critique of Eiselen's system underlined the ethnically divisive role it would play. Tsotsi told a CATA meeting at Mfula on 2 October 1951 the government aimed 'at starving Africans of education, sending them back to tribalism'.

The 1952 CATA annual conference called on its members to organise the people. CATA advocated a boycott of school boards and committees. Its view was that by setting up these bodies in every community, the state was attempting to make the African people operate the 'machinery of their own oppression'. In order to prevent this happening, CATA argued, no one should serve on the boards or committees or in any other way support the administration of the new schooling system. The immediate difficulty with this strategy was that it did not provide any scope for action in the period before 1955, before the new community-based administrative apparatus was set up.

CATA was, however, active in the field of propaganda. On 3 November 1953 the Western Province branch of CATA held a public meeting of more than 500 people in Langa to denounce the Bantu Education Act. On 14 December 1953, CATA organised a nationwide teachers' conference at Queenstown to consider how to fight the Act. It was attended by 200 delegates from all over the country. During 1954 CATA issued and distributed two pamphlets attacking Bantu Education, 'Yemk' Imfundo' and 'Verwoerd Speaks Out'. In April of the same year, 220 Transkeian teachers and some parents attended a conference on Bantu Education, convened by CATA at Davies Mission School. They passed a resolution condemning Bantu Education and affirming solidarity with CATA.

CATA's active political role attracted hostile state attention. The CED, which had for many years recognised CATA as a representative organisation of African teachers, withdrew its recognition in 1951. Chief Inspector F. de Villiers told a CATA delegation this was done because CATA had affiliated to a political organisation which aimed to 'upset the present policy of the government'. Dr W. de Vos Malan, the Superintendent-General of Education in the Cape, publicly threatened teachers and school managers who engaged in politics. Dr Eiselen himself threatened CATA in a radio talk in December 1953. He warned teachers not to attend the Queenstown conference.

From 1953 onwards, SB members began to attend all CATA meetings. In November 1952, CATA President L. Sihali and local CATA Branch Chairperson M.T. Moerane, were sacked from the Bantu High School, Queenstown, apparently for political reasons. Two members of CATA, M. Mali and J.N. Hlekani of Cradock, were instructed by the police not to teach for six months. On 19 July 1954, the police carried out a series of raids on the homes of CATA activists. Books, papers, minutes of meetings, accounts and address lists were confiscated.

The Rise of Teacher Conservatism
The conditions of the early 50s did not lead to uniform teacher radicalisation. Some wanted to preserve their professional status and material benefits (such as they were). This factor resulted in the birth of teacher groupings which conceived their professional role as one of avoiding any participation in wider social conflicts. They felt this would both ensure the maintenance of educational standards and secure their own social position.

Many teachers felt strongly they had something to lose by engaging in militancy. Teaching provided most of the opportunities of employment open to Africans with some education in this period. The loss of a teaching post thus threatened the teacher with a precipitous fall into the proletariat. In addition, sections of teachers felt their social posi-

tion was undermined by activities which reduced rather than emphasised the differences between themselves and the African people as a
whole. Given the struggle which attainment of a teaching post represented for the individual and his or her family, it is not surprising many
were unwilling to put the opportunities it represented in jeopardy.

There were elements of the ideologies present in the mission education tradition that underpinned political quietism. During the early 50s
groups and organisations reacted against the new radicalism. The
struggles between the right and left wings of the teachers' movements
certainly added to the fragmentation of the education system in this
period.

Notably though, the more conservative organisations were generally weak in the 50s. The temper of the times, with a rising African
nationalist movement holding the promise of drastic social change,
made the ideological attractions of cautious co-operation with the
authorities very limited. It was to be only in the 60s, when hope gave
way to despair, that the pragmatic approach of the 'professionalist'
teachers' organisations established in the 50s would flourish.

The defeat of the TATA radicals and the determination of the new
leaders to unite with the apolitical TATU were to have severe consequences for the development of teachers' politics in the Transvaal.
Although the legacy of the period from 1951 to 1953 lingered for a
while, in that some campaigning activity was mounted against Bantu
Education, the bland unity appeals allowed an apolitical grouping to
dominate TATA. The reunification with the more conservative TATU
in 1957 cemented the hegemony of the right wing. It allowed Transvaal teachers to become dominated by a conservative organisational
machine which retained its grip for years.

Substantial anti-Bantu Education activity did continue throughout
late 1953 and early 1954. In October 1953, TATA held a special
conference in Pretoria to consider the Bantu Education Act. The Act
was rejected and methods of fighting it were discussed. TATA continued its efforts to organise strong parent-teacher associations (PTAs).
In November 1953, the founding meeting of the Moroka-Jabavu PTA,
attended by 200 people, began planning a boycott of schools in protest
against the Bantu Education Act. In February, the PTA convened a
meeting of 500 parents and teachers at Morris Isaacson Hall which
supported the boycott. The meeting was clearly influenced by the
NEUM. There was a report on the Queenstown anti-Bantu Education
Conference. The meeting passed a resolution which, in true NEUM
rhetoric, pledged participants 'to teach the people not to work the
machinery of oppression themselves'.

By mid-1954 there had been TATA activity toward forming PTAs in

Sekhukuneland, the Johannesburg townships, Lady Selbourne (Pretoria) and the East Rand.

However, the deeply divided 1954 TATA conference at which KwaKwa and Pitje fought bitterly with NEUM supporters, did not help the future development of TATA. These hostilities were manifested when the Klipspruit branch, of which Ntshona was chairperson, was censured for sending a delegate to the Queenstown conference. The TATA conference passed a resolution expressing disapproval of sending delegations and resolutions to the TED. This was the last gasp of TATA militancy. TATA demonstrated its turn away from political action when, in 1955, it refused to participate in the ANC's school boycott on the grounds that children should not be 'used' in the struggle against Bantu Education and 'that even a Bantu Education was better than no education at all'.

The bland appeals to unity raised by TATU found a ready response in the KwaKwa group. TATU was plagued by organisational and financial weaknesses. It was thus increasingly interested in a merger. Following negotiations conducted by KwaKwa, TATU and TATA finally amalgamated at a 1957 conference in White River to become the Transvaal United African Teachers' Association (TUATA).

The second half of the decade, during which Bantu Education was effectively implemented, saw an absence of oppositional response from organised teachers in the Transvaal.

A much clearer split between right and left developed among Cape teachers. Two pressures were crucial in this development. On the one hand, more conservative teachers became alarmed at the political stance of their organisation. At the same time, they were intimidated by the prospect of conflict with the state. On the other hand, the authorities saw CATA as an obstacle to the introduction of Bantu Education. The resulting tensions in CATA led to a break-away and the formation of the Cape African Teachers Union (CATU). This split was primarily over whether, as CATU believed, a teachers' organisation should represent purely 'professional' interests, or, as CATA argued, it should concern itself with broader political questions. It divided those who felt the post-war radicalisation of teachers had undermined their social position from those who saw their interests as lying in political action.

CATA's right wing comprised two groupings. One was the North Western Districts Teachers' Union (NWDTU), the constituent organisation of CATA in the Kimberley area. The other group was led by I.D. Mkize, the Principal of Langa High School in Cape Town. NWDTU amalgamated with CATA in 1947. The graft never took. After 1938, at CATA conferences, NWDTU delegates opposed the association's political orientation and made unsuccessful attempts to disaffiliate CATA from the AAC.

The Kimberley branch defied CATA discipline by giving its own evidence to the Eiselen Commission without consulting the executive. Their militantly apolitical outlook was voiced by a speaker at a 1950 NWDTU meeting. He attacked both the ANC and the AAC. The speaker was quoted in *The Teachers' Vision*:

> Are we going to achieve . . . change by preaching any one political philosophy? My answer to this is an emphatic NO. Rather we will achieve this end, by helping the child to such wholeness of development that he cannot only adapt himself to, but co-operate in devising new social forms.

Thus, the NWDTU counterposed education to politics as a means of achieving social uplift. On 4 August 1951, the NWDTU broke away from CATA, on the grounds of the latter's AAC affiliation.

I.D. Mkize's history was very different. As CATA President from 1947 to 1950, he supported CATA's pro-NEUM policies. For reasons which are unclear, his political views thereafter shifted rapidly to the right. During 1952, his actions hastened a major conflict in CATA. The majority of CATA became incensed over Mkize's participation in the Van Riebeeck Festival, which CATA had committed itself to boycotting. Mkize's attendance at a SAIRR conference was, according to *The Torch*, viewed as a 'collaborationist' action. Clearly, these incidents were merely pegs from which hung far weightier differences. Mkize had abandoned CATA's refusal to participate in state-run or liberal institutions in favour of a gradualist strategy of seeking partial reforms and concessions.

Conflict escalated. CATA charged that Mkize had tried to sabotage its 1952 conference by complaining to the Cape Town Native Commissioner about CATA's use of certain funds. At the conference an attempt to disaffiliate CATA from the AAC was heavily defeated. On 18 August, Mkize split the annual general meeting of CATA's Western Province section (the Western Province Bantu Teachers' League), taking 62 members with him. From mid-1952 to mid-1953, he was active in attempts to found a secondary school principals' association or a new teachers' association. These efforts successfully culminated in the founding conference of CATU. This gathering, held in Grahamstown's Municipal Hall from 23 to 25 June 1953, brought together the NWDTU and Mkize's supporters. In his presidential address to the congress, Mkize gave a thorough summary of the views of the split supporters. After 1947, he claimed, 'there was growing on the part of the teacher an unhealthy interest in politics.' He said this had led to the disintegration of CATA and harm to African education, the undermining of the loyalty of staff to principals, bad results, the closing of some schools and the lowering of the prestige of others.

C.N. Lekalake's vice-presidential address explained that CATU sought CED recognition. He said an exchange of views between the two parties was 'essential and beneficial to the profession'. That the authorities also sought such a relationship was made clear by the guest speaker, Dr E.G. Schnell of the CED. He stressed the need for a 'responsible body of African teachers to advise the Department on Native Education'. Recognition of CATU was granted by the CED before the union's next conference.

In the period after its formation, CATU was successful in building links with other provincial African teachers' associations prepared to co-operate with the education authorities. It became the Cape component of FCATA. However, as an organisation committed to the special interests of teachers and opposed to political campaigning on community issues, it had little ability to attract broad support in a period of political upheaval. When, in August 1953, Mkize convened a public meeting in Langa at which Chief Inspector De Villiers was to speak, fewer than 10 people showed up. A number of these were NEUM supporters who proceeded to denounce the CATU president. While CATU was able to establish the kind of professional lobbying relationship with government envisaged by Mkize, this did not mean CATU members were necessarily content with all aspects of their lot. They were all aware of the adverse effects of aspects of Bantu Education on their position as teachers and even to some extent of its political role.

There was harsh criticism of Bantu Education at the 1954 CATU conference. The discussions 'disclosed convictions that the Africans were going to be given an inferior type of education'. Delegates voiced fears of lower exam standards. There was also criticism of the double shift system and of the fact that teachers had no say in the adoption of syllabi. Thus, while the concrete issues which alarmed CATU members were ones which adversely affected their professional autonomy and status, there was also a strong suspicion of the basic aims of Bantu Education. This underlines that it was not so much differences on educational issues that were behind the CATU/CATA split. Rather, it was differences over whether or not teachers' organisations should take an overtly political stance, and whether the relationship of teachers to the authorities should be one of confrontation or co-operation.

The split posed some difficulties for CATA. In April 1953, the Pondoland region disaffiliated at its conference. Visits to the district by executive members and an emergency conference were needed to bring it back into line. In November, attempts to disaffiliate Xalanga and St John's branches were defeated.

But in general CATA weathered the split fairly well. Its leadership positively welcomed its 'purifying' effects. L. Sihali told the 1954 conference: 'CATU was a new organisation today because it was free from traitors, collaborators and disrupters.'

While this response reflects the lack of realism of CATU's leaders, it was indeed the case that the conservative teachers were not in a position to attract a strong following during the 50s.

Bibliography

Oral History
Interviews with Teachers. Nos 1, 4–7, 10–11, 13, 16, 18–19.
Interview with David Bopape (Cachalia, D.). SAIRR Oral History Archive, Accession No. 4.
Interview with G.M. Pitje (Manson, A.). SAIRR Oral History Archive, Accession No. 3.

Archives
University of South Africa Archives. Pretoria. Series AAS 212.

Newspapers and Periodicals
Africa South. Vol. 1 No. 1 October to December 1956 (Sihali, L.S. 'Bantu Education and the African Teacher').
Inkundla ya Bantu. Vol. 7 No. 82, 17 July 1944 (cited in *Molteno* (see below)).
The Teachers' Vision. Vol. 10 No. 3, March 1944; Vol. 10 No. 4, June 1944; Vol. 11 No. 1, September 1944; Vol. 11 No. 2, December 1944; Vol. 11 No. 3, September 1945; Vol. 12 No. 1, September 1946; Vol. 12 No. 3, March 1947; Vol. 15 No. 4, June 1949; Vol. 16 No. 1, September 1949; Vol. 16 No. 3, March 1950; Vol. 16 No. 4, June 3 1950; Vol. 17 No. 1, September 1950; Vol. 13 No. 2, December 1950; Vol. 17 No. 3, March 1951; Vol. 15 No. 4, June 1951; Vol. 21 No. 3, January to March 1954; Vol. 22 Nos 1–2, October to December 1954.
The Torch. 19 June 1951, 2 October 1951, 16 October 1951, 4 December 1951, 10 February 1952, 25 March 1952, 8 April 1952, 1 July 1952, 8 July 1952, 21 July 1952, 5 August 1952, 12 August 1952, 19 August 1952, 26 August 1952, 9 September 1952, 16 September 1952, 23 September 1952, 14 October 1952, 21 October 1952, 4 November 1952, 11 November 1952, 25 November 1952, 13 January 1953, 27 January 1953, 17 March 1953, 24 March 1953, 7 April 1953, 30 June 1953, 21 July 1953, 18 August 1953, 20 October 1953, 10 November 1953, 4 December 1953, 22 December 1953, 2 March 1954, 3 August 1954, 12 October 1954, 28 December 1954, 11 January 1961.

Work in Progress. No. 31, May 1984. Hassim, K. 'Interview: Hassim on APDUSA'.

Theses and Papers
Eales, K.A. 'Jordan Ngubane, Inkundla ya Bantu and the African National Congress Youth League, 1944–51'. BA (Hons) Dissertation, University of Natal, (Pietermaritzburg), 1984.
Giffard, C. 'The Hour of Youth has Struck: The African National Congress Youth League and the Struggle for a Mass Base, 1943–52'. BA (Hons) Dissertation, University of Cape Town, 1984.
Kieser, W.W.J. 'Bantoe jeugmisdaad aan die Rand en die behandeling daarvan deur die Diepkloofverbeteringskool'. MEd Dissertation, Potchefstroom University, 1952.
McIntosh, A. 'Africanism Within the African National Congress and its Basis in Orlando in the '50s'. BA (Hons) Dissertation, University of the Witwatersrand, 1983.

Publications
Bundy, C. 'Resistance in the Reserves: The AAC and the Transkei'. *Africa Perspective*. No. 22, 1983.
Gerhart, C. *Black Consciousness in South Africa: The Evolution of an Ideology*. Berkley and Los Angeles, University of California Press, 1978.
Horrell, M. *South Africa's Non-White Workers*. Johannesburg, Ravan Press, 1956. Cited in Gerhart, C. *Black Cnsciousness in South Africa: The Evolution of an Ideology*. Berkley and Los Angeles, University of California Press, 1978.
Houghton, D. *The South African Economy*. Cape Town, Oxford University Press, 1973.
Huddleston, T. *Naught for your Comfort*. London, Collins, 1981.
Karis, T. and Carter, G. *From Protest to Challenge: A Documentary History of African Politics in South Africa 1882–1964*, Vols 3 and 4. Stanford, Hoover Institution Press, 1977.
Lewis, G. *Between the Wire and the Wall: A History of South African 'Coloured' Politics*. Cape Town and Johannesburg, David Philip, 1987.
Lodge, T. *Black Politics in South Africa Since 1945*, Johannesburg, Ravan Press, 1983.
Lodge, T. 'The Parents' School Boycott: Eastern Cape and East Rand Townships, 1955' in Kallaway, P. (ed). *Apartheid and Education: The Education of Black South Africans*. Johannesburg, Ravan Press, 1984.
Majeke, N. *The Role of the Missionaries in Conquest*. Johannesburg, Society of Young Africa, 1952.
Manganyi, N.C. *Exiles and Homecomings: A Biography of Es'kia Mphahlele*. Johannesburg, Ravan Press, 1983.
Matthews, Z.K. and Wilson, M. *Freedom For My People: The Autobiography of Z.K. Matthews*. Cape Town, David Phillip, 1983.
Molteno, F. 'The Historical Foundation of the Schooling of Black South Africans' in Kallaway, P. (ed). *Apartheid and Education: The Education of Black South Africans*. Johannesburg, Ravan Press, 1984.
Peteni, R.L. *Towards Tomorrow; The Story of the African Teachers' Associa-*

tion of South Africa. Morges (Switzerland), World Confederation of the Teaching Profession, 1978.

Phago, E.M.J. *A Short History of the Teachers' Association in the Transvaal.* TUATA, December 1966.

Roux, E. *Time Longer Than Rope.* Madison, University of Wisconsin Press, 1978.

Sapire, H. 'The Stay-Away of the Brakpan Location, 1944' in Bozzoli, B. (ed). *Class, Community and Confict: South African Perspectives.* Johannesburg, Ravan Press, 1987.

Simons, H.J. and R.E. *Class and Colour in South Africa, 1850–1950.* Harmondsworth, Penguin, 1969.

CHAPTER THREE

Bantu Education

The Late 50s and Early 60s

State education policy in the period from 1955 to 1962 shows the features of a policy forged under the pressure of the urban crisis.

First, the state created a much larger education system than had ever existed before. This allowed it to draw the bulk of urban working-class youth into the schools. Education was set on a firmer footing than before, as an agency of socialisation.

Second, the state developed financial mechanisms. These allowed it to base its new education system on exceptionally low levels of expenditure. Thus, it overcame the economic obstacles to educational expansion.

Third, the re-organisation of education provided a new articulation between the labour needs of industry and the school. In this, the requirements of industry for semi-skilled labour were far more adequately met than had previously been the case.

Fourth, the NP government used education in its attempts to create a new hegemonic social order. It tried to lure black parents into the school system through the establishment of school boards and committees. It tried to generate divisive ethnic identification with African cultural and linguistic groups, by emphasising the use of African languages in the schools. The aim of such practices was to create a political consciousness that would accord with the ethnically divided bantustan system.

Yet the state was not forced to act in a way that was functional to capital. Verwoerdian bureaucrats on the one hand, and predominantly Anglophone industrialists on the other, had distinct ideologies and interests. However, the specific circumstances of the 50s induced the former to act in a way that did not conflict with the needs of the latter. The depth of the urban crisis, the scope of political mass mobilisation, and the delicate state of the economy forced the state to address the urban issues most urgently. It refrained from major attempts to uproot the urban workforce. The consequent urban restructuring was in line with capital's needs. In the end, this relationship was to break down.

The NP's Response to Urban Crisis

Crisis, originating in the collapse of reserve agriculture, secondary industrialisation and rapid urbanisation, threatened the social order in fundamental ways. On the one hand, slum housing, crime, inadequate schooling facilities and poverty threatened the very reproduction of the working class as a workforce with the appropriate level of skills, work discipline, and physical capacity required by urban employers. On the other hand, the community movements, trade unions, and African nationalist political campaigns that arose in response to these conditions posed direct political challenges to the dominant classes.

The urgency of the situation dictated that the policies of the period before about 1962 were driven by considerations of social control and labour reproduction. The long-term NP ideological vision of the establishment of autonomous black political entities and of a purely migrant black workforce in white areas played a lesser role. The 50s did see the setting up of the legal and administrative equipment necessary to the achievement of Verwoerd's 'Grand Apartheid' dreams. However, the state could not fully use this apparatus until it had resolved the existing urban crisis. The NP realised it could not wish away the existing black working class.

To provide minimal conditions of social reproduction within the urban areas, the NP permitted major expansion in urban housing and education. It also followed a largely pragmatic policy in relation to urban employers' utilisation of black labour. It deviated considerably from its formal commitment to migrant labour and the relegation of blacks to unskilled work in the urban areas. Simultaneously, it tried to destroy popular and working-class political resistance, crushing the ANC, the PAC and trade unions in the early 60s. There was little indication of outright subordination of the labour needs of urban industry to the NP's long-term ideological goals.

Bantu Education policy did, in the short term, achieve success in stabilising the education system. However, it eventually created new problems for the state that would generate a greater crisis by the 70s. The low level of expenditure on black education ensured material inequality would continue to be a major grievance. The attempt to establish a new hegemony assisted in creating some social forces willing to work with the government. It also generated new sources of resentment by damaging the education system. It was, in the end, incapable of winning the allegiance of the mass of the people. Government's insistence on emphasising primary education, with the policy of job reservation, was to generate chronic shortages of skilled labour. The creation of a mass education system was eventually to turn school students into a powerful social force with a common identity. The victory of Bantu Education was decisive, but temporary.

Schools and Social Reproduction

Bantu Education did address a task that wide sections of the dominant classes wanted resolved. As shown earlier, there was widespread agreement between NP, UP and liberal political forces that a state-directed restructuring of education was a priority.

The ideological approach that entered into the formation of NP education policy differed from the education policies advocated by the UP and liberal circles. The NP's Sauer Report of 1947 advocated a strongly restrictive attitude towards black urbanisation. The migrant labour system was to be reinforced and the black middle class was to grow in the reserves, which were to be the centres of black development. This reflected, in part, the weight of agricultural interests within the NP. Their access to supplies of plentiful cheap labour was threatened by the drift to the towns. The UP's Fagan Commission of 1948, on the other hand, advocated a gradual and controlled move toward a permanently urbanised labour force, and toward fostering an urban black middle class. Fagan's findings reflect the need of industrial capital for a permanent, 'stabilised' urban workforce. In practice, the NP's policies during the 50s did not conflict with the needs of industry to anything like the degree that these ideological differences might suggest. The NP did show clear recognition that it could not sweep away the urban working class. The NP leadership accepted the black urban proletariat would stay in place for the future.

In key areas, government policy harmonised with the need of capital to secure the reproduction of a permanent urban proletariat. The state was obliged to impose its solution to the problems of the urban areas before it could move on to grandiose social engineering.

Mass housing schemes were developed during the 50s in Soweto, Kwazakhele (Port Elizabeth), Duncan Village Extension (East London) and Nyanga (Cape Town), to name only the most important. The brunt of this was borne by the communities, and by employers, through taxation. This massive growth in housing was accompanied by a growing differentiation in the types of housing provided in the townships. Migrants were placed in hostels and residents in houses. Increasingly, different types of houses were provided for different economic strata. Thus, housing policy clearly played a central role in the reorganising of the reproductive process of urban workers.

The establishment of the Bantu Education system was a turning point. The mission school system had manifestly been unable to provide an education system that could exert social control over black youth. The introduction of Bantu Education meant the establishment of a mass education system embracing the bulk of working class youth.

The first year of the implementation of the measures provided for in the Bantu Education Act (No. 47 of 1953) was 1955. In the following decade, the numbers of African students in school doubled, from about one million to about two million.

The 50s saw this educational restructuring focused on the urban areas. For example, school student numbers in the urban Southern Transvaal grew faster in the period 1957 to 1962 than those in mainly rural Northern Transvaal (see Figure 1). Thus the late 50s marked a dramatic adaptation in the education system to the task of containing and controlling urban youth.

AFRICAN PUPIL NUMBERS

Year	(Rural) Northern Transvaal	(Urban) Southern Transvaal
1957	243 688	231 143
1962	299 144	310 784

Figure 1: Growth of African school student population in the urban Southern Transvaal outstrips growth in the rural Northern Transvaal (DBE Annual Report, 1962)

Education policy unfolded in a way not centrally at odds with the needs of employers for a stable, permanently urban and semi-skilled workforce. Though the NP's educational blueprint projected a rural-based future for black education, this thrust was not rigidly implemented. The new form of education met the criticisms put forward earlier, by both the NP and the UP, of the ineffectiveness of the missionary-dominated schools. By bringing the bulk of urban African youth into a few years of basic schooling, Bantu Education provided a mechanism of social control, which could be used to fight crime and political militancy. Also, it generated a semi-skilled workforce. To a large extent, the Eiselen Report met liberal educational demands.

Opposition politicians like the liberal Margaret Ballinger and D.L. Smit and liberal administrators like J. Dugard welcomed the Eiselen Report. They supported Eiselen's call for central government control of African education, while disputing whether this should be under the control of the NAD. Nor did they object to the commission's advocacy of vernacular languages in primary school, as this was already regular practice up to Standard 4. The white opposition, whether liberal or mainstream UP, agreed with the NP on a 'basic elementary education' for all children as rapidly as possible. Only when it became clear how linked to apartheid policy and how under-financed Bantu Education would be, did white politicians on the left of government became critical of state education policy.

The racist and inegalitarian character of the new system should not obscure important parallels between Bantu Education and mass schooling in industrialising societies elsewhere. If one examines the growth of mass schooling in late 19th-century Europe and North America, for example, one sees noteworthy similarities to the South African situation. There too schooling was seen by dominant social groups as a response to the need for social control over working class youth. It was also a means of producing appropriately trained labour, and for political socialisation of youth.

Bantu Education was unique in its racial ideology. It was far from unique in its role of providing an educational structure appropriate to industrialisation.

The Financing of Bantu Education

The NP government of the 50s was constrained from providing adequate finance for black education by several factors.

Its own racist base and ideology generated strong political pressures against expenditure on black education. Employers were unwilling to pay, through taxes, for social services for their employees. The South African economy was less robust than in either the preceding or the subsequent decades. The new policy enabled the state to reconcile its need for a new mass education system with its unwillingness to pay for it. It did this largely by transferring the economic burden onto the shoulders of black communities, thereby enabling the state to institute cheap educational reorganisation.

The NP built Bantu Education on a shallow foundation, characterised by rigid cash limits. In 1945, J.H. Hofmeyr, as the UP's Minister of Native Affairs, had decoupled expenditure on black education from the income from black taxation. The two were previously linked. Black education became a charge on the general revenue.

The Bantu Education Act of 1953 ruled that all expansion of expenditure on African education had to come from expansion in the level of African taxation revenues. In 1955 the statutory contribution of the state was pegged at R13 million, a level at which it was to remain until 1972. Four-fifths of taxes received from Africans were to be channelled toward education. Dugard suggests, interestingly, that this was Verwoerd's concession to the most extreme wing of the NP. They were opposed to any substantial spending on black education.

The policy put an enormous financial strain on the resources of the education system. Per capita expenditure on African education fell from the equivalent of R17,08 in 1953 to R12,46 in 1960. The consequence was a grossly inadequate level of material provision in the education system. A teacher comments:

> It got worse in that the population of school-going children increased and funds were tied. So the material progress did not match the human population that was coming in.

The concrete breeze-block buildings thrown up in the townships of this period provided cheap school accommodation at the expense of any modicum of comfort. In the words of a teacher:

> . . . when it became too hot the children tended to fall asleep and no amount of motivation would make them alert, and in the winter [it] would be too cold so they were more concerned in trying to keep themselves warm.

Another teacher comments that whereas mission school classrooms *looked* like classrooms, once one entered a Bantu Education school 'it took time to acclimatise to a place that looks like a stable.'

Because of government educational financing policies, pupil teacher ratios worsened from 42,3 to 1 in 1946 to 54,7 to 1 in 1960. Sometimes, says a former pupil, 'teachers . . . had to teach classes of up to 65 or 70 per session.'

As a further cost-saving device, the government introduced the concept of double session teaching. Primary school teachers took two separate classes a day in shifts. This had severe and deleterious consequences for the quality of the education provided. The same student remarks:

> The teachers would be too tired to teach in the afternoon. They would find it boring teaching the same subject. The pupils who would come in the afternoon wouldn't be as alert as pupils who came in the morning.

> The morning group up to 11.30, they were all right. Now when those coming in the afternoon . . . it was impractical. They didn't learn much. The children came. They played a bit, became tired.

By 1958, 70 per cent of primary schools were teaching double sessions, and there are reports of instances where teachers had to take three sessions a day.

The approach of the state to the financing of black education harmonised with the desire of capital to avoid subsidising social services through taxation. Maximal effort was exerted to make the wages of African workers, rather than taxation of employers, provide the basis for the reproduction process in the townships. The state sought, for example, to avoid any expenditure on the care of pre-school urban children. When Ekutuleni Mission, the only Nursery School Teachers' Training College for African women was closed in 1958, a NAD spokesperson commented: 'We would be glad if Bantu parents would take more responsibility for this type of thing.'

The state also sought to extricate itself from any responsibility for the maintenance of students. It aimed to replace boarding schools with day schools and to reduce expenditure on school feeding from R893 000 in 1955 to R50 000 in 1964.

The consequences of government refusal to spend adequately on education, combined with its attempt to use education to further the bantustan system, led to a growing demoralisation among teachers. As one put it:

> I think the mission schools provided a better type of education since they prepared the child for a higher . . . calling. They also prepared the child for a meaningful role in life. Bantu Education on the other hand apparently deprives the child of his self, of his personality and of his realisation.

Such feelings resulted in the decision of many experienced teachers to resign from the new education system. As one teacher remembers:

> . . . The older teachers knew the differences and implications between Bantu Education and the old system, the Transvaal Education Department. So they resigned.

These resignations affected the quality of the educational services. With the simultaneous development of larger scale, low-grade teacher training programmes, there was a decline in the average level of teacher qualification.

Though in the 50s such educational horrors occasioned little comment from business, by the end of the next decade official parsimony in education spending would become a serious issue. Industry became aware of the gross deficiencies of such an educational order in providing skilled labour and social stability. In the 50s such considerations did not disturb the smooth meshing of industrial needs and state educational policy.

Educational Re-organisation and Industry

There is usually, in educational policy formation, a battle between different dominant class interests, bureaucratic interests and mass pressures from below, which all go into deciding the outcome. However, as suggested earlier, in the 50s the state was not yet attempting to uproot the industrial working class (as it would try to do in the 60s). It was willing to accommodate industry's immediate need for urban semi-skilled labour. In monopoly industry, automation increasingly eliminates the split between unskilled hands and artisans which marks small, competitive industry. As the skills of the artisan are increasingly replaced by machinery, the high-grade technician who can repair and set up factory machines is in demand. On the other hand, to draw on the argument of H. Braverman, (*Labour and Monopoly Capital: The Degradation of Work in the Twentieth Century*), the machine operator emerges as a new kind of labourer: the semi-skilled worker who requires skills of literacy and numeracy and an internalised work discipline.

The generation of such semi-skilled labour was an important part of the new education system's early aims. State officials believed four years of schooling was sufficient to provide basic literacy, some knowledge of English and Afrikaans, and a basis for further education. Thus these first four years were deemed capable of providing a level of education appropriate to semi-skilled work.

A flexibility was shown by the state in reconciling its formal commitment to job reservation with industry's need for semi-skilled labour. The utilisation of black labour in these semi-skilled positions, rather than in artisan positions, was really at issue. Potential conflict between government and industry was largely averted via the device of the 'floating colour bar'. White workers were upgraded and blacks moved into the positions they vacated.

Clearly there were differences of long-term interest between industrialists and government, especially around whether blacks would ultimately provide urban artisans. It was becoming increasingly clear that white labour could not provide a larger number of artisans. Demand for black skilled and clerical labour hardly existed during the 50s, compared with that for semi-skilled labour. Conflict was further postponed by the slow growth resulting from the slump of the late 50s. For the time being government policy on labour did not present major obstacles to urban industrial employers.

Bantu Education was not an exception to the complementarity that existed between the NP's policies of the 50s, and the skill needs of industry. The NP's educational policy in the mid-50s concentrated on building up the first four years of primary education as its main initial objective. Dugard, a regional director of Bantu Education at this time, says of his role: 'Our first aim was to promote literacy by making it possible for as many children as possible to complete the first four years of school.' The basis of this four-year emphasis was explained by the Minister of Bantu Education, W.A. Maree, in 1964. He asserted in a parliamentary debate that a Standard 2 (or four-year) education gave a child an ability to read and write in his own language. He claimed it provided a child with a reasonable knowledge of the two official languages, and a basis for further education.

In the urban areas this emphasis was encouraged by state policy. This made it possible for white municipalities to finance the building of African lower primary schools. Higher primary and secondary schools could only be established where community-based school boards paid half the cost. This priority was even built into the physical structure of the townships. Plans for township expansion in this era included space for new lower primary schools, but old buildings had to be used for higher primary and secondary schools.

Racist ideology triumphed over capitalist 'rationality' in the field of technical training. The number of training places for blacks sharply declined. This was not a major issue for employers. They showed little interest in the training of black artisans. The state also showed a willingness to assist industrialists in obtaining suitable employees. It systematically channelled people with appropriate abilities into different levels of the school system and toward different levels of the labour market. During the 50s, the National Bureau of Education and Social Research embarked on a project to develop intelligence tests for use in African schools.

Education and the NP Bid for Hegemony

Verwoerd and his cohorts did aim to create mechanisms for the incorporation of blacks within their new political order. The homelands would provide the arena within which black political advancement and educational development would take place. The NP government therefore sought to establish a means to secure the allegiance of sectors of the black population to a conception of their future in the homelands. In order to do this, structures would have to be set up to create the illusion of self-determination.

Verwoerd quite explicitly outlined his aims in education in these terms in his 1953 speeches to Parliament on Bantu Education. He called for a form of black participation in black educational administration

> ... which will make him ['the Bantu'] feel he is co-responsible for his education but that he is also assisted by the guardian ['the European'] in so far as he is incapable of assuming co-responsibility for it ...

The school boards and committees were the means chosen for this purpose. They would play the essential ideological role of winning parents' allegiance to Bantu Education. They would also provide a means of squeezing black communities financially, in order to subsidise the kind of cheap mass education at which the NP was aiming. Verwoerd argued black parents should be made co-responsible for their children's education and that

> . . . that co-responsibility is two-fold – it is co-responsibility for control, but associated with that is co-responsibility in respect of finances.

In this sense contemporary Marxist analyses such as E.N. Mathonsi's *Black Matriculation Results: A Mechanism of Social Control*, which see the system as purely about the creation of black labour power at low levels of skill, fall short of the mark. Verwoerd was a sufficiently shrewd political actor to understand he could not rely exclusively on force to dominate a subject population, with any chance of success. Nor was he sufficiently foolish to believe it would be possible to maintain black subordination while holding the barriers to career advancement at 'certain forms of labour'. Verwoerd made several notorious, but widely misinterpreted orations on black education from 1953 to 1954. It is clear from his words he intended to impose strict limits on black educational and career advancement in white areas. However, he held out on, the other hand, a new hegemonic vision to co-optable sections of blacks. Verwoerd proposed homeland structures as a key part of the material underpinning of black acquiescence. Discussions of Bantu Education often treat Verwoerd's strictures on black career advancement as if they were new features of political discourse. Of course they were not. 'Civilized labour' had a long and broadly based history in white politics. What *was* new was Verwoerd's aim of opening new structures of black incorporation through the homelands.

Accordingly, the Bantu Education Act gave the responsible Minister sweeping powers. He could provide for black participation in educational administration by establishing 'such regional, local, and domestic councils, boards, or other bodies as he may deem expedient'. He could place any government school under bodies such as the 'Bantu Authorities'.

Regulations laid down that the school committees, which were immediately responsible for a particular school, would be partly elected by the parents. In both rural and urban areas, four to six of the committee members could be elected by parents; clearly this was aimed at drawing local communities into the new system. In order to strengthen the strata participating in homeland structures, the local authority was given the right to nominate six committee members. However, these nominations were subject to approval by Pretoria, and the Secretary of Native Affairs could appoint a further two members of the committees. In the urban areas, the remainder of school committee members, comprising a majority, were direct appointees of the NAD or the Local Native Commissioner.

The committees were to be the key link to the community, controlling school funds, erecting new buildings, and advising the school boards. What real power was embodied in the system subsisted, however, in the school boards. These were wholly appointed bodies, with one school board controlling a group of school committees. In the urban areas all the members were appointed by the NAD. In the rural areas the members were nominated by the NAD and by the 'Bantu Authority'. Horrell argues that as the homeland system developed, the proportion of homeland authority appointees was allowed to increase. The boards had considerable powers over local schools and teachers.

From 1955 all African teachers' salaries were paid as subsidies to the school boards. This meant the boards effectively controlled hiring and firing (although the NAD could force the board to sack a teacher by withdrawing his or her subsidy).

From this brief description some of the inherent weaknesses of the system ought to be apparent. The hegemonic aims of the school committee structure were undermined by the NAD's reluctance to concede real control to parents, by insisting on a majority of appointees. The NAD wanted parental participation without giving up real control. The boards did something to strengthen the power of homeland authorities. Their appointee-dominated structure, their control of the school committees, and the fact that they were not responsible to the parents of local students also undermined their legitimacy. This structure tended to encourage the emergence of tyrannical school boards, subservient to the NAD and resented by local parents and teachers.

Despite these inherent weaknesses and fierce organised opposition from popular movements, the establishment of the boards went forward with a degree of success for government. This was especially so in the less politically volatile rural areas. By 1956, 4 000 committees and 300 boards had been established. This did not constitute a particularly effective social base for Bantu Education. It did demonstrate there were substantial social groupings that Verwoerd could rally around the new system.

Another dimension of Verwoerd's attempt to develop a new hegemony was the greater emphasis given to African languages in schooling. Under the mission education order, English (or sometimes Afrikaans) was used as a medium of instruction within the primary phase of education. Sometimes this began from the earliest years of schooling. However, Verwoerd's attempts to emphasise ethnic diversity among so-called 'tribal' groups led to a reversal of this policy. Now

African languages would be the sole means of instruction in primary school. English or Afrikaans would only be used as the medium of instruction in secondary education. Teachers who experienced both systems perceive the result as having been a sharp drop in the standard of English among secondary school pupils, and even university students. For teachers this policy was a destructive one. It sought to increase linguistic differentiation among blacks. It also made it so much more difficult for pupils to succeed at the secondary schools. Here are the views of three teachers:

> Before Bantu Education was introduced it was so easy to teach students, man. You find that . . . those children can write English, speak English, official languages, easily, easily, easily . . . It's different now, teaching in a high school is difficult.

> Now you talk of a mine where gold and the rest are dug. The trouble is now this child has been taught for about eight years in mother tongue. Now merely spelling of a mine, you find that it's writing m-a-n-e.

> When they go to universities they can't even express themselves fluently, because they are used to an African language . . .

Teachers resented this policy. Many felt African languages often lacked the vocabulary for some of the concepts they were required to teach. Says a teacher:

> . . . we had such a difficulty in for instance the teaching of Arithmetic in the vernacular. Take a thing like Geography in the vernacular. When you come to something like the 'Roaring Forties,' what do you say in Zulu or Xhosa?

This problem could even affect the task of explaining concepts to secondary school students who had a weak background in English. As another teacher put it:

> You can't teach a student in matric some of the very difficult words used to explain a simple name that can be given in English. You haven't got it. It makes it so difficult for the teacher and worse for the child to grasp those new terminologies.

As the teachers' comments suggest, Verwoerd's strategies were inherently flawed as tools for building hegemony. The authoritarian manner in which his policies were imposed meant that any gains the regime might make would be undermined by new and deep resentments.

Bibliography

Oral History
Interviews with Teachers. Nos 1, 4, 6–8, 11, 13–14, 18–19.
Interview with G.M. Pitje (Manson, A.). SAIRR Oral History Archive, Accession No. 3.

Archives
Cory Library manuscripts. Series MS 16 598/5.
University of the Witwatersrand Archives. Johannesburg. Series AD 410, 1953.

Official publications
Statutes of the Union of South Africa. Act No. 47 of 1953. Pretoria, Union Government, 1953.
Native Affairs Department. Bantu Education Bulletin 1957. Pretoria, Union Government, 1957.
Department of Bantu Education. Annual Report for the Calendar Year 1962. Pretoria, Government Printer, 1963.
Department of Education and Training. Annual Report 1986. Pretoria, Government Printer, 1987.
Hansard. Vols 82–83. Col. 3581, 1953.

Newspapers and Periodicals
Fighting Talk. July 1956.
Rand Daily Mail. 3 June 1964, 22 October 1964.
SAIRR Race Relations Survey: 1955–1956. Johannesburg, SAIRR, 1956.
The Star. 23 May 1966.
The Torch. 25 January 1955, 12 April 1955, 7 January 1958, 4 February 1958.

Theses and Papers
Hindson, D. 'The Pass System and Differentiated Labour Power'. Law Society Seminar Paper, University of the Witwatersrand, 1985.
Posel, D. 'Interests, Conflict and Power: The Relationship Between the State and Business in South Africa during the 1950s'. Association for Sociology in Southern Africa Conference Paper, Cape Town, 1985.
The 1961 Education Panel. 'Education and the South African Economy'. (Second report). Johannesburg, Witwatersrand University Press, 1966.

Publications
Brandel-Syrier, M. *Reeftown Elite: A Study of Social Mobility in a Modern African Community on the Reef*. London, RKP, 1971.
Braverman, H. *Labour and Monopoly Capital: The Degradation of Work in the Twentieth Century*. New York, Monthly Review Press, 1974.
Christie, P. and Collins, C. 'Bantu Education: Apartheid Ideology and Labour Reproduction' in Kallaway, P. (ed). *Apartheid and Education: The Education of Black South Africans*. Johannesburg, Ravan Press, 1984.
Dale, R. and Esland, G. *Mass Schooling*. Milton Keynes, The Open University Press, 1977.

CHAPTER FOUR

The ANC's Campaign Against Bantu Education

The ANC School Boycott: 1955 to 1956

By the early 60s, the Bantu Education system had been securely established throughout the country.

Yet during the period in which it was being set up, sufficiently widespread resistance to the policy had arisen for this outcome to have appeared far from a foregone conclusion. The dire material and political consequences of the new policy, as outlined in the previous chapter, made such resistance almost inevitable.

Why was the state so successful in implementing its policy? Why was Dr Verwoerd, as Minister of Native Affairs until 1958, and later Prime Minister from 1958 to 1966 able to bring into being an education system that accorded so well with his 'Grand Apartheid' designs?

These questions cannot be answered simply with reference to the strengthened position of the state in the 60s, following its successful repression of oppositional political movements and the development of the economic boom. Most of the resistance to Bantu Education had been subdued well before the end of the 50s.

The most vigorous campaign of popular resistance to Bantu Education was the ANC's school boycott from 1955 to 1956. This involved not only keeping large numbers of students out of primary school, but also the establishment of 'Cultural Clubs'. These were, effectively, alternative schools, set up through a body called the African Education Movement (AEM). Despite its considerable achievements, the campaign eventually collapsed for reasons which throw much light on the dynamics of educational conflict in South Africa.

First, a striking feature of the campaign, considered in the light of later events, was its inability to evoke a mass political movement of youth. The social conditions of the 50s generated a 'gangster' urban youth sub-culture which did not generate transformative possibilities.

Second, although the cultural clubs constituted a bold attempt to break the state stranglehold on education, the initiative lacked the resources to sustain itself. The AEM was unable to provide the material resources for alternative schooling for more than a tiny proportion of black youth. The attempt to sustain alternative schooling over a long period of time became even more unrealistic. Moreover, sectors of the ANC themselves developed unrealistic expectations of the possibility of sustaining educational alternatives on a large scale outside the state system. This hampered the AEM in developing a workable policy.

Third, the capacity of the state to provide a mass education system drew the mass of urban youth and their parents into the new system. This fatally undermined the attempt of the ANC to build opposition to government policy through a strategy based outside the state system. Because Bantu Education schools could provide some form of child care and educational certification, they were sufficiently attractive for the large majority of black parents. Bantu Education's triumph was that it increased the availability of educational provision. Township parents overcame their scruples about its ideological content and impoverished material character.

Conventional accounts of Bantu Education fail to deal with its astounding success in drawing black youth into a new educational order. This is not to say it attained much popular support at a political level.

The building of vast townships in the 50s was not only a defeat of battles by dwellers in inner city slums to hold on to their localities. It was *also* an attempt to contain the pressures of mass squatter movements and attendant discontent. Equally, Bantu Education was *not only* about the crushing of ideological diversity in the schools. It was also part of an attempt to contain the potentially explosive needs of urban youth and the educational aspirations of parents.

The establishment of Bantu Education cannot be explained purely by repression or purely by ideology. The success of the state in stabilising the system in the 60s had two components. First, the state successfully used force against popular movements. Second, it was engaged in a struggle (only fragmentarily successful) to impose a new educational ideology.

The new school system provided a decisive material element in consolidating popular acquiescence. The school boycotts and other campaigns against Bantu Education failed to gain their professed objectives. However, they increased the pressure on the state to attempt to contain educational aspirations through further school provision. All of this is not to minimise the racist, discriminatory and materially impoverished character of Bantu Education. It is merely to state that it represented the outcome of a struggle over educational restructuring. In that struggle, the popular classes were not passive bystanders.

So the apparent victory of the state contained the seeds of the destruction of the new educational order.

The Course of the Boycott

The ANC was initially slow to respond to the passage of the Bantu Education Act in 1953 and to the government's plans for its implementation during 1955. However, an ANC conference in Durban in December 1954 decided on an indefinite boycott of primary schools beginning on 1 April 1955.

In March, because of the lack of membership response, the ANC's National Executive Committee (NEC) decided to postpone the boycott of schools. Instead it would concentrate on a boycott of school boards and school committees. In the Transvaal there was considerable pressure from members and local leaders for the school boycott to go ahead. Another conference in Port Elizabeth, from 9 to 10 April, supported the principle of an indefinite boycott. The date for the national implementation of the boycott was left to the NEC. However, local boycotts could begin earlier with the NEC's permission.

On 12 April a boycott started on the East Rand. It spread to townships nearer central Johannesburg. From 23 April, boycotts took place in the Eastern Cape. Thousands of school pupils participated, but the boycotts did not spread significantly beyond these two regions. On 23 May, a conference in Johannesburg established the AEM. It set about creating and servicing the cultural clubs mentioned above – alternative educational facilities for school students. The clubs were vigorous well into 1956. However, outside of a few areas of particular militancy, most black scholars stayed inside the school system.

Gradually, support for the boycott eroded. By late 1956 the ANC had decided to abandon the strategy.

Youth Culture and Politics in the 50s

Since the mid-70s youth has played a central part in political struggles in South Africa. Youth involvement in struggle can have few historical precedents. It comes as something of a shock to realise that the 50s urban youth were relatively unpoliticised. This was partly the result of organisational problems on the side of the ANC. It was also due to the culture generated by the structural position of urban youth in that era.

From the early 50s, the ANC made efforts to recruit substantial numbers of young people. However, it faced important organisational difficulties. Its youth wing, the ANCYL, had emerged in the 40s. This intellectual ginger group of young leaders tried to change the policy of the ANC in a more militant direction. As an organisation, the ANCYL was ill adapted to attracting young people to its ranks. As an ANC document of the early 50s put it, the ANCYL

> consists mainly of intellectuals who feel they must watch over the policy of the ANC and no attempt is made to organise sections of young African workers, scholars or peasants.

As an ANCYL publication admitted, the ANCYL 'has but scratched the surface in its efforts to create a genuine mass youth movement in this country'.

The geographical base of the ANCYL was limited to those areas where the ANC had very strong support. At its 1954 conference there were only delegates from the Cape and Transvaal. There was no representation from Natal or the Orange Free State. Details of an ANCYL provincial conference in 1955 show its Transvaal organisational structures were confined to the Rand. There were no branches in the Pretoria or Vereeniging areas or the rural areas.

The ANC leadership began, from the early 50s, to direct the ANCYL toward changing itself into a more substantial organisation. In 1953 Robert Resha, the ANCYL's Transvaal leader, made a call through *The African Lodestar* for the ANCYL to establish ANC and ANCYL branches throughout the Transvaal. ANC Secretary General Walter Sisulu subsequently called on the youth to make 1954 a year of 'Mass Youth Action against Fascism'. Duma Nokwe, the ANCYL's Assistant National Secretary, advanced a policy of creating a 'Mass Youth League'. He proposed doing this by holding 'mass youth conferences'.

The ANCYL's 1954 conference resolved to strengthen its activity and organisation. This direction toward the building of a mass youth organisation was continued into the period of the boycott.

The ANCYL made some quite vigorous attempts to implement these policies in the period 1954 to 1955. They embarked on a drive to convene mass meetings of youth, at some of which new ANCYL branches were formed. By 1955, the Transvaal ANCYL claimed at least six new branches on the Rand and one in Klerksdorp. The ANCYL showed more involvement in practical political campaigns than before. It played a prominent role in resisting removals in Sophiatown/Western Native Townships and in Germiston. It was logical the ANCYL should play an important part in the education boycott campaign. An ANCYL working group plan listed their tasks. Students' committees were to be formed at all levels to organise students. Special organisations for students were to be revived or set up. Mass meetings were planned. Bulletins on Bantu Education were to be distributed. ANCYL members were to make contact with parents and teachers. The ANCYL was to be involved in the establishment of the broadly based anti-Bantu Education committees, which would co-ordinate the boycott in each area. To some extent these plans were implemented. On the Rand, there was considerable activity by the Western Areas, Germiston, Natalspruit, Benoni, Brakpan and Alexandra ANCYL branches.

However, these attempts to organise youth politically on a mass scale were, generally, extremely unsuccessful. The NEC commented at an ANC conference at the end of 1955 that the ANCYL had failed to become a mass movement of the youth. The NEC said the ANCYL relationship with the ANC was far from satisfactory. The Transvaal ANCYL's report for 1955 explains that despite the establishment of some new branches, some of the established branches had deteriorated and collapsed. Although most branches had recruited members, most had also lost members.

By 1956, the ANCYL seems to have been at an extremely low ebb. ANCYL leader T. Makiwane commented that the ANCYL's work in the Transvaal was 'at a virtual standstill'.

To some extent these difficulties arose because the ANCYL aimed at an older and more intellectual constituency. A 1954 ANCYL publi-cation urges readers, 'Have you enrolled your son/daughter in the Youth League?' This suggests something of an inability to address young people directly. Similarly, a 1956 edition of the same journal identifies 19- to 36-year-olds as the target group for ANCYL recruit-ment. This lack of interest in recruiting teenagers was clearly incom-patible with the aim of a 'mass youth organisation'. Yet the school boycott was supposed to have been directed at primary schools.

The ANCYL was also handicapped by a number of more technical organisational considerations. Its members were frequently used as ANC foot-soldiers in campaigns and thus neglected building up the ANCYL. There was a lack of infrastructure. The Transvaal ANCYL didn't have one full-time official. A frequent leadership complaint was that the ANCYL did not organise cultural activities.

The ANCYL's work was disrupted by the long factional battle between the ANC leadership and the Africanist grouping. In the Transvaal, the Orlando ANCYL branch under Potlake Leballo was the Africanist's stronghold. This grouping was particularly opposed to the ANC's 'Congress of the People' initiative. It was highly critical of the education boycott. Controversy with the Africanists seems to have absorbed an enormous amount of the ANCYL leadership's energy.

It would be unfair and inaccurate to identify internal difficulties as the main cause of the ANCYL's inability to evoke a mass response from urban black youth. The level of mass politicisation of youth was negligible in the 50s. The ANCYL's constituency was far less easy to mobilise than that of student militants in the post-1976 era. As an ANCYL journal put it in 1955, 'many of our young people still believe they are not interested in politics'.

In its 1956 report, the ANCYL's Sophiatown branch executive warned against the danger of targeting the 'mighty few politically serious youth'. The Sophiatown ANCYL clearly found the majority of young people had interests quite distinct from theirs. 'We can strengthen [the branch] by catering for the ordinary sporting and social youth. By having interests in their activities [sic]. They in turn will have interest and confidence in the ANCYL movement.'

What explains the contrast between the urban black youth in recent decades and the 50s youth?

The inadequacy of state provision for the reproduction of the working class in the 50s meant urban youth was drawn into a 'gangster' sub-culture. There was the absence of an effective school system. There was a lack of employment prospects. The permanently urbanised proletariat was a recent development. All these factors forced youth to seek individual, and often criminal, rather than collective and political, solutions. Writer Don Mattera was a member of a Sophiatown gang. He captures very clearly the way in which the 'gangster' or urban youth made organisation difficult for the ANC:

> But at this time there were more tsotsis and gangsters than people at work. So there was this social problem. So the politician could not organise successfully because he was being hampered by the social disorder.

The advent of Bantu Education largely changed this youth culture in the 60s and 70s. Township youth of the 50s was patchily reached by the school system. Bantu Education, on the other hand, drew in a larger proportion of youth than the mission system. It provided some experience of an under-resourced, inferior and repressive education system. The rapid expansion of the education system provided youth with a common set of political problems. It provided a common identity and a structure within which they could react to those problems.

A somewhat anarchic spirit prevailed among the bulk of urban youth. However, parental authority was more evident among regular 50s school-goers than in more recent times. This inhibited the emergence of self-organised school student movements. The tendency of young people to impose their political will unilaterally on their elders became a major political problem in the 80s. By contrast, the 1955 boycott was an adult-controlled action. There is no evidence of clashes of opinion between students and parents. It is probable that between the 50s and the 70s there was a shift in authority relations within the family. This must be central to an understanding of post-1976 student movements.

'People's Education': Strengths and Limitations
The first limitation of the boycott's possibilities was the lack of self-organisation and political awareness among the youth.

The second was the material inability of the AEM to provide an institutional alternative in the education field. The ANC clearly did envisage itself as providing a different vision of education.

'People's Education for People's Power', a major slogan and strategy of popular political movements in South Africa in the 1980s was often perceived as an entirely new development. But in a strictly historical sense 'People's Education' is not a new concept. During the 1955 to 1956 boycotts, the ANC advanced the slogan of People's Education in exactly the same sense in which it was used in the 1980s. An ANC leadership document of 1955 defines People's Education as: 'Democratic-Liberatory education . . . it will be democratic in control, organisation and purpose . . . it will be liberatory in object because its main object will be to equip the people and the youth to fulfil their historic task of liberating themselves.' The impact of the concept was, however, limited during the 50s. There was some attempt, during the decade, to popularise the slogan. Peter Ntithe, an ANCYL activist, greeted a 1955 Sophiatown conference on Bantu Education with the words: 'Long live the People's Education.' However, the slogan was not widely taken up.

What did People's Education achieve during the 50s? It did briefly sustain a remarkable level of organised alternative schooling activity. In national terms, though, it was limited in its impact and hampered by a lack of resources. The cultural clubs were prevented by the Bantu Education Act from presenting themselves as schools or teaching formal courses. Considering the lack of available resources and funding, the AEM did a remarkable job. It sustained networks of clubs on the Rand and in the Eastern Cape through the period of the boycott. Members of the ANC and Congress of Democrats (COD) provided co-ordination and support for these projects. The club at Korsten in the Eastern Cape provided 'games, physical exercises, health talks and singing'. It also had a feeding scheme for the children. The New Brighton Club catered for about 1 000 children and boasted a well-trained choir. The Veeplaats Club had 900 children, the one in Brakpan, 800. At Kleinskool the club was so effective that after a year, 75 per cent of children in the area were attending its programme of 'games, Bible studies, singing . . .'

The back-up provided by the AEM was very competent, considering its lack of financial resources. Club leaders were provided with a timetable and guidelines. Training groups for leaders were held once a fortnight. Larger scale training courses were also run occasionally, especially during 1956. At these training courses talks were given by prominent figures like Resha, J. Radebe, Norman Levy, Helen Joseph and (on one occasion) Eddie Roux. The AEM supplied clubs with good quality educational material, on roneod sheets, covering games, stories, history, geography, maths and English. Most of the material did not have a specifically political orientation. Recommended reading included Alan Paton's *Cry, the Beloved Country*, an interesting choice considering the disfavour into which the book later fell in ANC circles. Culturally, the material drew on diverse traditions. African folk tales and western nursery rhymes featured. The material was directed to the passing on of real skills. However, some of it did address social and political issues. A well-written history lesson sought to make quite complex points: For example that the 17th-century Dutch colonists thought in terms of a Christian/heathen rather than a white/black distinction, and that South Africa had been settled by blacks before the arrival of the whites.

Club leaders were advised to explain the Bantu Education Act and the campaign against it to their students. They were asked to teach them the Freedom Charter. One draft programme recommended, as well as a 'talk by Anglican priest or any denomination', discussions on the lives of popular leaders. These included Johannes Nkosi, Bill Andrews, Dr Dadoo, Moses Kotane, Albert Luthuli, J.B. Marks and Mao Tse Tung. The participating children seem to have identified clearly with the aims of the boycott. Huddleston records that when Sophiatown children passed the Bantu Education school they would give Congress salutes and yell 'Verwoerd, Verwoerd'. Those attending the clubs sang the song: 'There are only two ways for Africa . . . one way leads to Congress and one way to Verwoerd.'

The AEM's activities were thus an exemplary use of extremely limited resources. Within months of the call for a boycott, there was a network of clubs and training facilities for leaders and a supply of educational materials.

Nevertheless, the achievement of the AEM should not be exaggerated. It reached a very small proportion of the school population. By mid-1955, the numbers at cultural clubs on the Rand were as follows:

Alexandra Township	200
Benoni	327
Brakpan	800
Germiston	320
Jabavu	89
Moroka	49
Natalspruit	289
	2 074

Attendance in the Eastern Cape, at the beginning of the boycott (or early 1956, according to the availability of figures) stood at:

Malmaison Location (1956)	141
Missionvale (1956)	50
New Brighton	1 000
Fairview	(not given)
Despatch	287
Uitenhage	455
Veeplaats	900
Korsten	600
Kleinskool	102
Walmer	60
Kirkwood	296
TOTAL	3 891

The total number attending the clubs was about 6 000, out of the more than one million African children in school in the mid-50s. In national terms the clubs reached only just under one school child in every 166. This clearly did not constitute an alternative system of education.

Nor could the AEM overcome the problem of the lack of political structures for youth. In June 1955 there was an attempt to launch a youth organisation known as the *Baputsela*. It was modelled on the scouts and guides movement, but had a progressive political content. However, it seems to have rapidly faded away. Despite considerable enthusiasm from the youth for participation in the cultural clubs, the AEM could not help to structure mass youth politics.

Activists of the 1955 to 1956 boycott suffered an absolute and crushing defeat. During the second half of the 50s, enrolment in Bantu Education schools rose from less than one million to more than one-and-a-half million. The schooling system was effectively restructured as Verwoerd had envisaged.

Why was it impossible to sustain a People's Education initiative alongside Bantu Education? Obviously, state repression played an important role in undermining the boycotts. But there were also under-lying ambiguities and difficulties in trying to provide a counter-hegemonic education system which were not squarely faced.

Repression by the state certainly confronted the boycott movement. In April 1955, Verwoerd expelled 7 000 boycotting children from their schools. In July, he decreed they were to be readmitted the following year. This was on condition their parents gave undertakings about their behaviour, and the school committees investigated their cases. In the same period, 116 teachers were removed from their posts. There were constant raids on cultural clubs by the police. This placed severe limitations on the type of activities the clubs could offer. Even an item like a blackboard could be used by police as evidence of an illegal school. The state strove to disrupt AEM activities. In January 1956, 30 Eastern Cape club leaders were stopped from travelling to Johannes-burg for a training course at Alexandra. The AEM decided to hold a course in Port Elizabeth at Easter. However, a ban on meetings forced them to move it to Uitenhage. On the second day of the course, the SB and the location superintendent arrived. They took away organisers Helen Joseph and Norman Levy. Municipal police tried to take the names of those at the meeting, but the delegates refused to co-operate. The SAP then arrived in force and ordered the meeting to disperse, which it did after singing in defiance. The next day the course contin-ued, in secret, in the countryside. The police discouraged hall owners from allowing the clubs to use their facilities. Where students mounted pickets at schools, these were broken up by the police.

However, police action and Verwoerd's threats did not drive the bulk of those participating in the clubs back to school. The clubs sustained themselves well into 1956. The repression was limited com-pared to the situation in the 70s and 80s. There are no reports of the use of fire-arms against school students, nor of arrests or substantial numbers of them. In the 70s and 80s, boycotts sustained themselves far longer than in the earlier period. The harassment cannot explain the campaign's lack of success.

Problems of organisation and tactics may have had an impact on the anti-Bantu Education Campaign's fate. The ANC certainly had diffi-culties in the area of organisation.

At its 1954 conference, the NEC complained about bad admini-stration at the provincial committee level. Branches, some running to 1 000 members, were unwieldy.

At the 1955 conference, the NEC said it was handicapped by the local leadership's inability to send membership fees and levies to the national organisation. There were also some tactical problems in the way in which the school boycott was organised. The NEC pointed out the danger of treating education as a sectoral issue. It noted Bantu Education was directed against 'the entire liberatory struggle'. It said the campaign 'should not be handled in isolation from other campaigns'.

The wrangle within the ANC as to when and where the boycott should start also caused difficulties for the campaign. According to the ANC's Cape organiser, T.E. Ka Tshunungwa, it created 'a confused situation' and 'dampened spirits throughout the country'. These setbacks were linked to problems of local-level organisation. When the NEC met in March 1955 to decide on whether to go ahead with the boycott, no local reports were available. Ka Tshunungwa felt the leadership did not adequately communicate conference decisions to members. But again, these tactical and organisational issues do not provide the key to the boycott's limited impact. The ANC was able to launch campaigns which drew enormous popular support during the 50s. Whatever problems they experienced do not seem to have prevented their drawing a widespread following. There is no reason to assume organisational difficulties dealt a fatal blow to the anti-Bantu Education campaign.

The fundamental weakness of the campaign was its lack of clarity. Was it, or was it not, seeking a permanent alternative system to Bantu Education?

In ANC policy discussions and activities three distinct views of the role of the cultural clubs emerge. These three views were often used in some combination. The AEM's activities were variously portrayed as:

- a protest against the Bantu Education Act, which would be of limited duration;
- a temporary provision of cultural activities and child care, but not an all-round education for school students, during the course of a boycott of indefinite length;
- an attempt to establish an alternative, popular education which would continue until the collapse of the NP government.

This lack of clarity led inevitably to disillusionment.

A popular movement can create its own educational structures on a mass scale in periods of mass mobilisation. But in a modern industrialising country with millions of school students, no movement can sustain such a popular educational system outside of state structures for long. A popular movement which does not control the state simply cannot find the material resources to support tens of thousands of teachers. It lacks the rudimentary educational equipment, the complex bureaucratic planning required for the maintenance of any permanent mass education system. Popular education movements are therefore likely to be undermined by their material weaknesses. But they are also liable to be debilitated by their own status as 'alternative' institutions. If an existing social order remains intact, the student is going to be faced with the need to enter the labour market. It rapidly becomes clear to both parent and child that the student from a state school will have certification which will be accepted by employers. A student who has been through an 'alternative' education system lacks certification and will be negatively affected in terms of employment opportunities if the employer knows of his or her background. The result of these factors was likely to be a steady drift of students away from People's Education and towards state schools.

A People's Education movement which tries to maintain itself as a separate entity from the state system is liable to wither away. More viable for such a movement would be a strategy of providing some limited alternative activities for students inside the state system. This could be combined with an attempt to change aspects of state education policy and to transform school practices through community and student activity at a local level.

The idea that a new educational system could be built outside that of the state was totally unrealistic. It led, inevitably, to the failure of the campaign and disillusion on the part of parents and students.

When the notion of a campaign on the Bantu Education Act was first floated by the ANC at its December 1953 conference in Queenstown, no tactics were specified. The aim was identified as the repeal of the Act. An ANCYL working committee set up to plan the campaign saw it as a short-term protest. In its view it should attempt to be a 'countrywide demonstration'. It should try to counter the effects of Bantu Education 'primarily by raising the political consciousness and understanding of the Youth and Students'. The action should take the form of 'withdrawal of children from schools for a defined period'.

However, once the boycott movement developed some momentum, it began to open itself up to other ideas. Some elements of the ANC saw the cultural clubs as a permanent alternative to Bantu Education.

'Once the people have rejected Bantu Education,' an ANC publication stated in November 1955, 'they will find an alternative to Bantu Education and to the entire slave education of this country.' Similarly a COD document of the same year describes the AEM programme as 'a direct alternative to the school education'. This grew into a somewhat triumphalist view of what the clubs and the boycott could achieve. At the 1955 conference of the Transvaal ANCYL, the campaign was prematurely described by the Provincial Executive as a 'victory'. The executive went on to assert: 'The uncompromising implementation of the decision to withdraw the children must lead to destruction [of Bantu Education].' The AEM evolved the idea of a system of home education. The AEM would provide material that students could study under parental supervision. Such a scheme had even greater material problems inherent in its realisation (provision of study kits, illiteracy among parents and so on). It was also interpreted in a way which fed into the idea of an AEM 'alternative', setting out to provide 'a start in formal education'.

The rampant ambiguity about the future of the boycott is demonstrated by a 1955 article in *Fighting Talk*. 'How much of an alternative do [cultural clubs] provide? . . . frankly we must answer . . . not very much.' The author goes on to assert, contradictorily: 'There will be Cultural Clubs as long as there is Bantu Education.'

Substantial elements of the ANC leadership were clear from the beginning about the limitations of what they could provide in the educational sphere. Their problem was that the creation of the clubs generated unrealistic expectations. Robert Resha had told the conference that launched the boycott of the 'practical impossibility of providing alternate primary education'. He saw the clubs as strictly limited to cultural and recreational activities. In assessing the campaign at the end of 1955, the ANC's NEC recognised the difficulties created by the ambiguity on the issue:

> We must beware of creating the false impression that by isolated local boycotts the Bantu Education Act can be defeated . . . we must not deceive ourselves or the people into believing that in the immediate future we can, with our resources, substitute a national education system. We have no state budget behind us.

By late 1956, the NEC had followed through the logic of this view by calling off the indefinite boycott.

The ANC came increasingly to realise the material difficulties standing in the way of any alternative educational system. At the conference in late 1955, the NEC criticised the 'undue emphasis' laid on alternative facilities. This, it concluded, had strengthened the argument that Bantu Education was better than no education. (This was presumably because of the disillusionment caused by the limitations of the service AEM could provide.) As Congress leader Z.K. Matthews commented in retrospect, 'the boycott failed principally because of the difficulty of organising an alternative programme for the children.'

By late 1956, the cultural clubs were in a state of collapse, chiefly because of a simple lack of funding. The 1956 conference of the Transvaal ANC identified lack of money to pay club leaders as the main problem. But even before this collapse, the clubs simply could not provide adequate resources for the numbers of children attending. In September 1956, the Brakpan Cultural Club reported that with 'about eight' leaders it was endeavouring to cater for 758 children, all meeting in the open air. Even given the limited extent of the boycott, the AEM lacked the material resources to undertake the task it was attempting.

Bantu Education as 'Material Factor' in Acquiescence

The most important reason for the defeat of the boycott was the capacity of the state to provide mass schooling. 'We must cry for our children,' said an ANC speaker in Moroka in June 1955, even as he urged parents to participate in the boycott. Parents' concern for the future employability of their children ultimately undermined support for the boycott.

As the NEC recognised in its assessment of the campaign at the end of 1955, all it could offer a parent through the campaign was an act of 'political conviction'. Parents were generally unwilling to make this sacrifice, as even strong proponents of the boycott like Huddleston acknowledged. Even among parents who could be persuaded to participate in the boycott there was a steady decline in support. The Veeplaats Cultural Club, for example, started with 900 children in 1955. This had fallen to about 500 at the beginning of 1956.

The restructuring of education enabled the schools to draw in vast numbers of new pupils. Acquiescence, not allegiance, brought children into Bantu Education structures. However, the absence of widespread resistance in education from late 1956 to mid-1976 surely cannot be satisfactorily accounted for purely in terms of coercion or brain-washing.

The urban working class parent desperately needed schools. As Z.K. Matthews put it, in explaining the failure of the school boycott, schools kept pupils 'safe from accidents and juvenile delinquency' while their parents were at work. Alternative schools did not have the capacity to replace regular schools in this role. Politically conscious people and most teachers rejected Bantu Education. Others, however, especially those with no previous access to the school system, welcomed it. A teacher who was working at the time comments:

> Now most of the parents were illiterate, they felt that now anyone can get educated . . . Those who realised the set up reacted with more support to the missionary schools . . .

The same teacher found that parents often did not grasp the reasons teachers were resigning in protest against Bantu Education. He believed the expansion of the numbers of students made a favourable

Davenport, T.R.H. *South Africa: A Modern History*. Johannesburg, MacMillan, 1981.

Dugard, J. *Fragments of My Fleece*. Pietermaritzburg, Kendall and Strachan, 1985.

Hlope, S.S. 'The Crisis of Urban Living Under Apartheid Conditions: A Socio-Economic Analysis of Soweto' in Murray, M.J. (ed). *South African Capitalism and Black Political Opposition*. Cambridge, Mass., Schenkman, 1982.

Kane-Berman, J. *South Africa: The Method in the Madness*. London, Pluto, 1979.

Lewis, J. *Industrialisation and Trade Union Organisation in South Africa, 1924–55*. Cambridge, Cambridge University Press, 1984.

Mathonsi, E.N. *Black Matriculation Results: A Mechanism of Social Control*. Johannesburg, Skotaville, 1988.

impression upon communities. He says it was only those aware of
education issues who grasped the meaning of the new school system:

> . . . it appeared the changes meant you could pursue any type of educa-
> tion you desired . . . It is only those who knew education, and what it
> must consist of, who knew it was a destruction coming in.

Another teacher comments in similar terms: 'It was mainly activists
who reacted. Black communities just didn't know about [the]
differences . . . [between mission and Bantu education].'

The expanded material provision of schooling underpinned the
attitude of those sections of black communities prepared to live with
the new system. A veteran teacher, says of his community's response
to the educational expansion:

> . . . I think they liked it – because the state built attractive schools. That's
> what I think – better than the mission schools. They had in mind that
> these are good for us.

In a similar vein, another teacher takes the view that:

> [The community] were pleased because the department built more state
> schools and as a result more children could be accommodated.

In one interview a teacher said his community viewed the expansion
of the education system during the early years of Bantu Education

> . . . with approval because indeed . . . this is one positive side of Bantu
> Education, that more people used to come, were able to get into school.

One interviewee's comments suggest there was existing black feeling in favour of greater state intervention in education on which the
NAD could capitalise:

> . . . the blacks felt the time had come now when the government should
> also take over the education of the blacks. That was the major change
> which the Africans advocated at the time.

The ideological elements of Bantu Education also exerted a certain
appeal. The remark of a woman teacher suggests how the Verwoerdian
attempt to mobilise ethnicity in the new education policy met with a
degree of success:

> [The community] thought it was a good thing, that the use of Bantu
> language would make it easier to cope.

She also found initial student reaction against Bantu Education was
not widespread: 'I think they didn't know it then, that this Bantu
Education was killing them.'

One teacher interviewed felt that with the exodus of politically conscious teachers from 1955, the teaching profession itself became increasingly reconciled to the new system:

> Most of the teachers are children of Bantu Education. So I don't know what you think about your mother. Generally, the younger teacher seemingly has no odds against the department.

The power of the schools to attract parents' support is borne out by the events surrounding the 1955 to 1956 boycotts. The numbers of students in schools nationally *increased* during the schools boycott by about 85 000. Even in the ranks of the ANC itself, members were suspended in about 25 Cape branches for sending their children to school.

By late 1956, the major campaign of resistance to Bantu Education had come to an end. In part, this resulted from repression, in part, from tactical and strategic uncertainty over the aims of the campaign. In part, it was the result of the attractions of an expanded school system.

But at the same time, there were hidden dangers for the regime in expanding the school system. The creation of a mass education system would, in the long run, forge a new culture of youth in the 70s with a receptiveness to politicisation absent in the youth of the 50s.

Bibliography

Oral History
Interviews with Teachers. Nos 4–6, 8, 11, 13–14, 16, 18.

Archives
University of the Witwatersrand Archives. Johannesburg. Series AD 1137, AD 1812.

Newspapers and Periodicals
Counter Attack. 18 April 1955.
Fighting Talk. November 1955.
New Age. 6 December 1956.
SAIRR Race Relations Survey. 1952–1953. Johannesburg, SAIRR, 1953.
The Torch. 19 July 1955, 21 June 1955.

Theses and Papers
Giffard, C. 'The Hour of Youth has Struck: The African National Congress Youth League and the Struggle for a Mass Base, 1943–52'. BA (Hons) Dissertation, University of Cape Town, 1984.
Mkatshwa, Fr S. Keynote address in the Report of the National Consultative Conference on the Crisis in Education: Soweto Parents' Crisis Commit-

tee. Held at the University of the Witwatersrand, 22–29 December 1985. Johannesburg, SPCC, 1986.

Publications

Hastings, A. *A History of African Christianity*. Cambridge, Cambridge University Press, 1979.

Horrell, M. *A Decade of Bantu Education*. Johannesburg, SAIRR, 1964.

Huddleston, T. *Naught for your Comfort*. London, Collins, 1981.

Lodge, T. *Black Politics in South Africa Since 1945*, Johannesburg, Ravan Press, 1983.

Lodge, T. 'The Parents' School Boycott: Eastern Cape and East Rand Townships, 1955' in Kallaway, P. (ed). *Apartheid and Education: The Education of Black South Africans*. Johannesburg, Ravan Press, 1984.

Lodge, T. 'The Parents' School Boycott, 1955' in Bozzoli, B. (ed). *Town and Countryside in the Transvaal*. Johannesburg, Ravan Press, 1983.

Matthews, Z.K. and Wilson, M. *Freedom For My People: The Autobiography of Z.K. Matthews*. Cape Town, David Philip, 1983.

CHAPTER FIVE

The Failure of Resistance

Teacher and Student Opposition to School Boards

The ANC school boycott was not the only form of resistance to Bantu Education. There were boycotts of school boards and committees and teacher resistance in the Cape. The continuing, deepening protest in the mission schools was another manifestation of popular resistance to the restructuring of education.

The educational bureaucracy could defeat or contain these forms of opposition between the mid-50s and the early 60s. The state established the school board system despite attempts to disrupt this process. Teacher activists in the Cape were victimised and organisation was difficult. No coherent social movement of school student resistance emerged. Sectarian division among Cape teachers further undermined their organisation.

These defeats appeared to pave the way for educational dominance by the Verwoerdian regime. There was growing participation in the school boards and committees. However, the best the state could achieve was acquiescence. While there was an acceptance of existing social arrangements, there was little allegiance to or identification with them.

The school boards and committees operated with a lack of real authority that prevented them from building a permanent and secure social basis. Teachers were reduced to political passivity. However, they were alienated by the arbitrary behaviour of the school boards and the racism of education department officials.

While the tradition of student rebellion faded in the rural boarding schools in the 60s, it was to re-emerge to much greater effect in urban schools in the 70s.

Resistance to School Boards and School Committees

The school boards provided more conservative members of local communities a degree of control over teachers. The attractions of this factor were sufficient to draw many participants into the boards and committees. However, in the longer term, the arbitrary actions and corruption of the boards and committees further alienated teachers from the new education system. This became an obstacle to ensuring their willing participation in it.

Political movements of the time saw school boards as an intrinsic part of Bantu Education's imposition of a totally separate and inferior education system. An ANC press release issued after the NEC meeting in Durban on 6 March 1955 called for a boycott of the boards and committees. The NEUM also opposed the board system. Its newspaper, *The Torch*, saw such a boycott as the main strategy against Bantu Education. Although nationally insignificant compared with the ANC, the NEUM could affect the struggle over this issue in the Cape: it controlled CATA.

During the two years following the introduction of the board and committee structure, there were many instances of resistance to its establishment. J. Dugard, then Regional Director of Bantu Education in the Cape, writes in *Fragments of my Fleece*:

> ... where the ANC was active only very brave men would agree to be government nominees on the boards and it was quite impossible to organise meetings to choose representatives of parents.

In the Eastern Cape and Transkei there was fierce opposition to the boards and committees. A Grahamstown meeting to elect a committee was broken up by ANC members from East London. In the Tsomo and Mount Ayliff districts about 25 out of 40 school committees were subject to successful boycotts. The Magistrate at Peddie admitted that he had experienced much difficulty with school committee elections because of local opposition. He had been reduced to nominating members.

In the Elliot district in 1955, the boycott was so successful the authorities were unable to find a single local dignitary to sit on the school committees. The School Inspector, Education Department Regional Organiser and Predikant (all white) had to form themselves into a school board.

At Tsolo the local people voted to refuse to hire out their school buildings to the NAD. They also voted to boycott the school boards and committees. There was a public meeting called by the Native Commissioner and the Circuit Inspector at Whittlesea, Queenstown district, in early 1956. Here a spokesperson is reported in *The Torch* as having told the officials:

> We are a progressive community and don't want Bantu Education. We want the same education that's given the whites, and possibly something

better if the brains of the whites are so degenerated that they can't progress.

The Torch also reported on a major meeting at Bumbana in the Umtata district on 10 February 1956. It broke up without discussing Bantu Education after the authenticity of the chiefs present had been challenged and officials of the NAD had been brusquely treated.

The campaign against school boards and committees also achieved some success in the Western Cape.

Cape Town proved a particularly difficult nut for officials to crack. Initial attempts to get parents at Langa Township to elect committees failed. On 31 August 1955, election meetings were held at five schools. However, only one of these meetings agreed to organise elections. The vote was taken as a suspect secret ballot conducted by the Sub-Inspector. At the Methodist School, an audience of 100 shouted down the Native Commissioner, S.J. Parsons. They informed him they would have nothing to do with any committee he set up. Not one person supported the election of a committee.

Langa High School parents verbally attacked Rev. Mbizela who supported the idea of the committees. Parents urged that 'those who accepted the Act be treated the way witches were treated in the olden days'.

By September 1955, only six out of 19 'Bantu' schools in the Peninsula had elected committees. Renewed NAD initiatives to organise elections in early 1956 were no more successful. At Langa High School the Rev. Lediga, Chairperson of a meeting to set up a school committee, had to run home to escape from an angry crowd. At Langa Methodist School those refused admission to an election meeting forced their way in – 'the women led the men in'. After the parents had refused to allow the chairperson to close the meeting, he left via the window.

The school board members failed to show up for the meeting they had convened at St Cyprian's. According to *The Torch*: 'The people reaffirmed their stand against any form of assisting in the mental enslavement of their children.' The secretary of the school board in Athlone, Ngo, arrived under police escort for an election meeting. Finding that the meeting refused to make nominations for the school committee, he was reduced to making the nominations himself, with the SAP as seconders.

There was resistance in some places in the Western Cape outside Cape Town as well. Parents at Langabuya High School in Paarl voted in May 1955 not to elect a school committee. This was after a speaker suggested, '. . . it would be better if Dr Eiselen came to explain things himself.'

The school boards and committees were stamped, in the popular imagination, as organs of an oppressive system. However, there were also those who sought to enter the system. In the homelands, local elites were prime candidates for such incorporation. Furthermore, there were those opposed to the existing order, but who did not see the boards and committees as worth opposing. All of this is reflected in the fact that despite strong opposition, the state did manage to put the system in place.

By 1956 there were 300 school boards and 4 000 committees nationally, according to the SAIRR survey for that year.

Dugard reports education officials found in the rural areas that it was possible to get 'men and women of some standing in the community' to serve on the boards.

In urban areas, building support for the boards and committees was more difficult. Wilson and Mafeje's work suggests that the boards often consisted of clergy and ex-teachers who lacked popular support. Some prominent figures, such as Dr W. Nkomo and Paul Mosaka, advocated joining school boards to fight Bantu Education from within.

Not all ANC members adhered to their organisation's line of a total boycott of the committees. At an ANC public meeting at Dube in June 1955, a speaker advocating a school boycott argued that those who emphasised the boycott of the boards 'forget that in School Boards there are elements [who are present] only because they are getting their bread'.

In New Brighton in Port Elizabeth, some ANC members participated in the election of a school committee. It was only in the 50s that the ANC moved away from judging participation in state structures on tactical grounds.

What aspects of popular consciousness enabled the boards and committees to attain a degree of support? Interviews with teachers suggest the way in which the board and committee system gave ordinary community members a degree of control led to support for the system. Here are the views of two teachers:

> [Board and Committee members] could say what they liked to teachers, they could threaten teachers with dismissal.

> They were looked upon as very important bodies, which could sway the sword any way they liked against a teacher. A teacher had very little to say to any parent who came with a complaint. They would say 'I will go and tell the school board.'

Another part of the attraction of participation in the board and committee system was undoubtedly the possibilities for bribery, corruption and patronage it offered. To quote another two teachers:

> It invited much corruption. Because for promotion we knew the person [sic] to rely on was the school board, so great bribes were being provided.

> The teacher had to crawl for the school board . . . You had to buy them liquor to keep your post.

The education authorities were thus able to exploit both social cleavages and patronage possibilities.

The reality of the rapid growth of the boards and committees should warn us against a simple conception of the rise of Bantu Education. It was not simply that 'the people' rejected the system, while only a handful of 'traitors' participated in it. There was broad-based opposition to the system. However, there were also significant constituencies which, for varying motives, were willing to enter the system.

The boards intensified teachers' hostility toward the educational system, rather than incorporating them. They created new grievances in the community. The boards were placed in a position where they were responsible for carrying out Verwoerd's parsimonious state educational spending policies. They were 'allowed' to discontinue school feeding schemes if they wished. The money thus saved could then be spent on 'amenities'. These amenities were taken to include the hiring of teachers. The money raised by the committees was used for the construction of new schools. There was considerable resentment in areas levied heavily by a school committee, but which did not benefit proportionately from new school buildings.

The boards also became the instruments of the state's purge of politically dissident teachers from the profession during the late 50s. School boards made spurious charges against teachers as a way of simultaneously discrediting and getting rid of them. A teacher at Langa Methodist School was dismissed in 1956 for alleged sexual misconduct with a pupil. The student's father wrote to the school board saying there was no truth in the charge. The teacher was then summoned to a meeting with the secretary of the school board, who demanded he sign a statement admitting his guilt. A scuffle broke out. The teacher was charged with assaulting the school board chairperson. When the case was heard, the Magistrate threw it out and advised the teacher to appeal against his dismissal.

Similarly, NEUM activist V.K. Ntshona was sacked by the Moroka-Jabavu School Board for supposed neglect of duties. When he applied to another school, he obtained a temporary appointment. He was then turned down by the school board on grounds of his political activity, after they had been visited by the SB. A subsequent attempt to obtain a post for Ntshona was frustrated. The NAD informed the school board it would not provide a subsidy for any post held by Ntshona. The board duly excluded him from consideration.

Some board members positively revelled in the power they enjoyed. Rev. Lediga, the chairperson of the Langa School Board, is quoted in *The Torch* after addressing a meeting in 1958. He said that '. . . from now on he would see to it that the Board put its foot down and dealt more severely with the teachers.' He went on to inform the gathering '. . . there has never been such a learned government as we have in the present.'

The animosity between teachers and school boards was fuelled by the way in which teachers, a formerly prestigious social group, were placed under the control of bodies of people less educated than themselves. Here are some typical comments:

> . . . The teachers did not like the school boards . . . I have studied so hard to be in my profession then an ordinary person comes to interview me.

> Those were old people with old ideas. Some of them were chosen because of status. In our school boards you find that there's a member who hasn't gone to school but he is Mr So-and-so . . .

There was an anti-democratic and a democratic component in the objections raised by teachers to the new structures. The 1957 conference of the conservative CATU passed a resolution that members of school committees ought to have completed primary education, and members of school boards some post-primary education.

The Self-Destruction of CATA

The sole remaining bastion of African teacher militancy during the late 50s, CATA, undertook continuing activity against government policy. This was despite its being subjected to strong repression by the state. CATA continued its work in the rural Eastern Cape and Transkei. It was active to some extent in the Western Cape as well. CATA particularly focused its energies on the boycott of school committees and boards, defending sacked teachers, and combating the influence of the conservative CATU. The final collapse of CATA was, however, largely self-inflicted. The NEUM's sectarian hostility to the ANC ensured CATA members did not participate in or support the ANC's school boycotts in the Eastern Cape. The logic of a divisive sectarian outlook eventually led, in 1958, to a split in the NEUM itself. This caused CATA's demise.

By the end of the 50s, the state appeared to have completely subdued African teachers. Yet the Bantu Education Department (BED) could not capitalise on this victory. It was unable to draw teachers fully into the system. The ham-handed authoritarianism of the school boards and the crass racism of most education officials proved insuperable obstacles to winning teacher allegiance to the new system.

For CATA members, the implementation of Bantu Education represented both an assault on their organisation and an opportunity to expand their political influence. Their campaign for a boycott of school boards and committees developed a considerable popular resonance. The repression to which CATA was subjected was substantial. Many teachers experienced redundancy during the early stages of the implementation of Bantu Education because of the strict application of staffing quotas. By 1958 this had resulted in 157 dismissals in the Cape alone. Most of the sackings were clearly for political reasons. Between the beginning of 1955 and mid-1956, 29 CATA members were dismissed from their posts. These included the president N. Honono, secretary Z. Mzimba, magazine editor L. Sihali, and treasurer J.L. Mkentane. The Transkei and other sections of the Eastern Cape were most affected. The axe fell, during 1955 and 1956, on teachers in the districts of Queenstown, Elliot, Glen Grey, Tsomo, Umtata, Butterworth, Willowvale, Nqamakwe, Ngqeleni, Qumbu and elsewhere. The purge also spread to the urban areas. CATA members were sacked in Langa and Port Elizabeth by their school boards.

CATA was forced to stop production of *Teachers' Vision* through new regulations preventing teachers from publishing their political views. This was a major blow. The magazine had appeared regularly since the early 40s and had played a major role in spreading CATA's ideas. The January to March 1955 edition was the last to be published (an attempt to circumvent regulations and revive the journal as *New Teachers' Vision* lasted only a few editions). Detectives attended CATA meetings, raided the association's officials and tailed teacher activists when they travelled. Native Commissioners imposed stringent controls on CATA meetings. They would only grant permission for them to take place if full details, including the names of those attending, were supplied. The NAD prevented the holding of the 1956 CATA conference in Port Elizabeth. It denied CATA hall facilities, refused members the necessary pass documentation and eventually imposed a ban on public meetings in the area.

On occasion, CATA members were prosecuted for breaking regulations governing meetings. Inspectors took draconian actions to instil discipline among teachers. At Nqabara in Willowvale district, the inspector transferred all teachers who had not been appointed by the new school board within a fortnight. To justify his action, he cited the influence of CATA in two local schools and the hostility of the teachers to the school board.

However, the hardships experienced by CATA members did not prevent their launching into a new round of agitation on educational issues. The state, to publicise the 'benefits' of Bantu Education, Bantu Authorities and soil rehabilitation, took to organising frequent public meetings in the rural areas. Chiefs were usually given the task of convening these gatherings, in which CATA militants intervened energetically to spread their ideas and sabotage the NAD's initiatives. In January 1955 Chief Kaiser Matanzima called a big public meeting at Qamata. People came from all over the Transkei and Ciskei to hear a speech by the Chief Education Officer, F.J. Malan. No sooner had Malan finished his speech than CATA and AAC activists got up and began asking embarrassing questions. These included ones on 'the various taxes and fines . . . the control of Bantu Schools, the overriding powers of the Minister of Native Affairs . . .' According to *The Torch*, the meeting insisted on voting on the issues discussed. Matanzima, sensing the mood was against him, closed the meeting in a humiliating defeat.

CATA also used other methods of popularising its views. In Willowvale in late 1954, the local branch issued a series of Xhosa language leaflets. These called for a boycott of the establishment of a tribal authority and the election of a school committee. After this, the new chief was not recognised by the local people. Seven out of eight villages boycotted the Bunga elections. When an inspector arrived in the area to hold an election for the school committee, he was driven away by the populace.

CATA also attempted to defend sacked members through the courts. They raised funds for a test case for two dismissed teachers, Mangcu and the prominent CATA leader, Sihali, against their respective school boards and the Secretary for Native Affairs. At a legal level this initiative achieved a certain success. After a protracted battle through the courts, the Appeal Court found in favour of Sihali and Mangcu in September 1957. The court ruled their dismissal invalid. They had been hired under an ordinance that gave them security of tenure and which had never been repealed by any ministerial action. CATA hailed the decision as a major victory, but this was premature. Teachers hoping to be reinstated under the Sihali/Mangcu ruling were simply redismissed under other regulations that could not be challenged legally.

CATA's campaign to defend the sacked teachers evoked a degree of public sympathy. At a farewell function after the sacking of Honono and others from Nqabara Secondary School, a school student made a strongly NEUM influenced speech. Students and parents were reported to be hostile toward teachers who took over the jobs of those who had been victimised. *The Torch* reports on an incident at Lamplough

Secondary School. A teacher who had come to replace Sihali found written on his blackboard: 'Are you CATA or CATU? Are you here or are you there? – please do not erase.'

CATA continued to assert itself, with some success, against the more conservative current of Cape teachers. The mid-50s saw a considerable struggle between CATU and CATA for leadership of the Cape teachers. This was especially in areas where CATA was particularly strong, such as Tembuland and the Ciskei. CATU had the worst of this contest. Throughout the 50s, CATU's organisational efforts were remarkably unsuccessful. Perhaps this was a consequence of trying to develop a fundamentally conservative and apolitical organisation in a period of popular upsurge and radicalisation. Only in the North Western Districts, where it organised about a third of the teachers, was CATU strong. In 1954 CATU possessed only 45 paid-up members in the Western Province. By 1956, although CATU was claiming to have defeated its rival, there were complaints recorded in CATU's newsletter of 'falling membership . . . comparatively meagre finances and apparent apathy'. In 1957, the CATU regional organiser in the North East Cape 'painted a gloomy picture of his region'. In Pondoland the regional organiser spoke of 'difficulties' in trying to set up a regional organisation. Elsewhere in the Eastern Cape teachers were reported to be 'indifferent' to CATU. In Tembuland it was reportedly difficult to develop support in Umtata, Mqanduli or St Mark's. In 1958 the CATU regional organiser for Tembuland, B.M. Titus, reported that in the Transkei it was difficult 'to have any dealings with the teachers'. When Titus could convene a meeting of 10 teachers at St John's Practising School, he considered this 'a very good response'.

By the late 50s CATU was in a parlous state, with only 144 paid-up members in 1958. Such was its level of disorganisation that its President, S. Burns-Ncamashe, failed to turn up for the 1959 conference. All of this testifies both to the lack of attractive power of CATU's ideology for teachers, and to the continued strength of CATA's influence.

CATU's political direction remained fundamentally unchanged. It combined surprisingly sweeping attacks on aspects of the education system with a highly conciliatory and apolitical approach to the authorities. At their 1957 conference, criticism was directed at:

- scope of the powers of school boards and committees;
- the low level of education of many of their members;
- the low level of salaries;
- the lack of cost-of-living allowances;
- the lack of industrial schools for Africans; and

- the civil services' refusal to address African teachers as Mr, Mrs, or Miss.

In the presidential address, the Bantu Education system's emphasis on 'race or tribe' and 'language' was attacked. Despite CATU's conservatism, its members could not help reacting against the burden of the new education system. However, they did so in a way that avoided raising broader political questions. Their faith continued to be pinned on sending delegations to the government as a means of effecting change. In the political upsurge of the 50s it was only a minority of teachers who responded positively to this cautious approach.

Despite repression, CATA was able to maintain some resistance to Bantu Education in the mid-50s.

Why then did it fade away by the end of the decade? A major reason for CATA's collapse was its failure to relate constructively to the ANC's mass campaign against Bantu Education in the Eastern Cape in 1955. In contrast to CATA's campaigns against the new system, the ANC's initiative was based in the urban areas. By refusing to participate in or to support it, CATA and the NEUM missed any opportunity of linking with mass urban struggles on education issues. This was the result of the NEUM's hysterically sectarian attitude toward the ANC. A flavour of this is evident in a *Torch* article on the Defiance Campaign of 1952. It characterises the ANC as 'the reactionary, collaborationist wing of the Africans . . .' The UM offered no analysis of the ANC's social composition or its political programme in justification of such abuse. The ANC was condemned for participating in elections for Native Representatives, Advisory Boards and other state-established structures. According to the NEUM, they collaborated with the enemy. The NEUM's opposition to the ANC's campaign on education was strange as the ANC used the NEUM's hallowed tactic of the boycott. However, the NEUM's argument was that the ANC was carrying out the wrong sort of boycott. In its view, it was pointless for school students to boycott classes as this was detrimental to their own interests. It exposed them to repression while not presenting a challenge to the education system. In the NEUM's opinion, the main focus of opposition to Bantu Education should have been on boycotting the boards and committees.

The policy of the NEUM toward the school boycott was in some respects hypocritical. In 1952 it supported, along with members of ANCYL, the pupil boycott and the establishment of an alternative school at Orlando. These activities were part of the protest against the dismissal of the TATA leaders. It is difficult to avoid the impression that the NEUM's main objection to the 1955 to 1956 schools boycott was that the ANC was leading it. The consequence of the NEUM's abstention from the boycott campaign was that CATA stood aside from the most important urban struggle against Bantu Education in the Cape.

By 1958 the combined effects of state repression and its own sectarianism had significantly undermined CATA's organisational capacity. Through the 50s, certain tensions manifested themselves in the NEUM. One revolved around the composition of the NEUM's affiliate, the Society of Young Africa (SOYA), which was strong in the Eastern Cape. SOYA's leaders argued that, for tactical reasons, their organisation had to be limited in membership to Africans only. This the Cape Town based, and largely 'Coloured', leadership of the NEUM saw as a breach of the principle of 'non-European Unity'. More important, tension grew between the Cape Town leadership and the Transkei and Eastern Cape supporters of the AAC. The issue at stake was what policy should be pursued in relation to land reform. At the end of the AAC conference at Pietermaritzburg on 16 December 1958, the conflict came to a head. The conference split into two factions and the Easterners attained a majority for their position. The minority then broke away from the AAC.

At the conference of SOYA that followed immediately afterwards, a similar division took place. A majority loyal to Cape Town issued a statement accusing the AAC of revising the NEUM's programme and 'boosting up . . . nationalism, especially African Nationalism'. The movement did not divide cleanly on a regional basis, however. There was extensive conflict among affiliated organisations in the Eastern Cape. SOYA's Lady Frere branch supported Cape Town in the SOYA split. There was also strong opposition to the AAC leadership in Queenstown. CATA simply collapsed in this round of division and feuding. The inquest on CATA must return a verdict of suicide by sectarianism.

CATA did leave behind it a legacy of teacher activism that played an important part in preparing the way for the peasant upheavals of 1958 to 1961. Officialdom and its allies saw the teachers as a dangerous group in the rural Eastern Cape. *The Torch* tells of an incident at a public meeting in Engcobo in November 1960. Here, Headman Bungane Mgudlwa 'accused the "teacher bastards" of being behind the resistance to the chiefs and the "Bantu Authorities"'.

The end of CATA brought major oppositional activity among African teachers to an end for nearly two decades. This might have created circumstances favourable to the incorporation of teachers into the Bantu Education system. Not only did the NAD face a lack of structured opposition, but it could also offer significant inducements to greater teacher co-operation. The re-organisation of the education system meant inspectorial posts were opened up to blacks. The hope of personal advancement attracted some. At a 1954 meeting of the CATA branch at Mount Frere, a Mr Mahlati welcomed the Bantu Education Act. He said it gave him the chance of promotion to the inspectorate. The widespread dismissals ensuing from the establishment of the new system acted as a negative sanction, frightening teachers into quiescence in order to keep their jobs. For a teacher, loss of his or her job meant rapid proletarianisation and a new intensity of racial humiliation. These consequences are suggested by an anecdote of Huddleston's. David, a teacher, resigned in protest against the Bantu Education Act. Huddleston found him a job in the packing department of a big store. When, sometime later, Huddleston asked him how he was faring, he replied:

> It's all right, Father, except for that European lady. Sometimes, when I have to shift boxes or bales and put them on the counter, I have to move an account sheet or a weigh bill from one place to another. Then she shouts at me 'Don't touch that paper. Paperwork is white work, it's not for natives.'

The combination of promises and threats from the authorities did not generate a strong movement of co-operation with Bantu Education from any section of teachers. The strength of the African nationalist movement put considerable social pressure on teachers not to act in a way that could be construed as collaborating with the authorities. We have seen this in the case of school board elections. However, the political movements of the time were not insensitive to the problems facing teachers. They could keep them in alliance through flexibility as well as coercion. One interviewee claims that after attending a political meeting in Benoni Location, he was approached by Oliver Tambo, who lived nearby. Tambo, he says, counselled him not to attend such meetings in future in view of the risk of dismissal. The prestige and the social pressure of the nationalist movements was sufficient to keep the teachers away from conservative movements.

Bantu Education also undermined teachers' autonomy at work and the status based on that. When the link between education and the churches was broken, teachers ceased to be employees of a respected social institution. They became employees of a resented racist state. They were exposed to the strains of double-shift teaching, worsening student-teacher ratios, arbitrary sackings and poor salaries.

Verwoerd's hegemonic vision was carried out by its agents in a way which prevented its objectives from being attained. The subjective racism and the insensitivity of education officials constantly undermined their attempts to win teachers' allegiance. Educational officials acted on their commitment to white domination, rather than on their formal commitment to promote some form of separate black self-determination. The possibilities of incorporation were undermined by the staggering crudity of the administrative and ideological practises of the central educational authorities. The change from provincial to central control of the educational apparatus meant that the liberal paternalism which had characterised much of the administration of education was replaced by brute racism and authoritarianism. Inspectors with a knowledge of local conditions and African languages were often replaced by people who lacked this knowledge. Administrators with educational experience were sometimes replaced by NAD officials who knew nothing of education and were notoriously rude to their subordinates.

Official racism in black education really came into its own when W.A. Maree became the first minister of an independent Department of Bantu Education in 1958. Maree was responsible for the issuing of a circular to inspectors forbidding them to shake hands with blacks. Maree also occupied himself with such weighty matters as personally reprimanding Inspector Martin Potgieter for drinking tea with the black teachers at Lovedale. The ministerial approach rapidly permeated to local level. At Adams College the dishwasher was upbraided for washing the cups of black and white staff in the same sink. For black teachers used to the paternalism of the missions and the relative paternalism of the pre-1955 inspectorate, such experiences were shocking. Squeezed between the bullying of school boards on the one hand, and the abuse of gut racist administrators on the other, teachers fell into a grumbling acceptance of the status quo. But that did not amount to an allegiance to it.

Student Resistance

Initially, there was no spontaneous, student-led reaction to Bantu Education. As has been seen in the discussion on the ANC's school boycotts, those were essentially parent-led movements. There was an absence of spontaneous revolts by urban youth. Student discontent in rural mission schools continued much the same as in the post-war period. Occasionally there were violent outbursts, but these were generally over localised grievances and were not part of a wider political movement. There were, of course, important institutional changes in the rural mission schools as the state moved in to take over from the missionaries. By the early 60s these changes, together with the critical national political situation, brought the mission-founded boarding schools to the boil. Coinciding with the Sharpeville crisis and the 1960 emergency, there were five major incidents resulting in 360 suspensions. The militancy of the students in these schools reached its apex in 1961.

Whereas the riots of 1960 had been around food or discipline issues (even if conveying hidden political messages), the incidents of 1961 were in many cases quite explicitly political protests against the proclamation of the Republic. Transvaal schools seem to have played a greater role than before. This greater geographical and institutional spread reflects a rising politicisation of youth. Trouble broke out in at least three Transvaal and eight Eastern Cape or Transkei schools and one Natal teachers' college. The level of conflict then dropped in 1962. The SAIRR, which kept consistent records of these events, recorded trouble at only three institutions. But in 1963 there was once again a significant student upsurge centred in the mission foundations with conflicts taking place at seven schools and colleges. These resulted in at least 471 expulsions. The circumstances of these upheavals lent credibility to the SAIRR's view that they were in part students' responses to the activities of Umkhonto we Sizwe (MK) and Poqo.

When the state began to take over the mission sector and to impose its own educational model, student action did not show a dramatic, spontaneous response to this change. The tradition of student contention continued, but the number of incidents did not significantly accelerate. Nor did that tradition spread into the expanding new schools of the Bantu Education system.

If one excludes events related to the ANC's 1955 school boycotts, all the strikes and boycotts from this period occurred in mission-founded institutions, mostly in the Eastern Cape. I have found only one spontaneous student action during 1955 – at Ndaleni in Natal. This took the form of a boycott of hymn singing and a demand for an end to compulsory church services. It culminated in students setting fire to the chapel. It can hardly be interpreted as a protest against the state takeover of mission education.

However, as the boarding schools came under the control of the NAD, conditions worsened in a way that generated new frictions. There were complaints that school authorities were now tending to call in the police over trivial student offences; that African teachers found their position increasingly conflict-ridden; and that NAD officials had far more racist attitudes than the missionaries. The incidents followed established patterns. At Blythswood in March 1957 students launched a one-day food boycott, to which the headmaster refused to respond. Subsequently, the boarding master called in the police to investigate the case of boys who had taken and eaten maize from the school fields. The culprits were lashed by the police. Thereupon, the boys staged a mass walkout.

The pattern of the food riot also recurred at Lovedale in 1959 where students in the junior hostel petitioned against the quality of their food and having to do manual work. Four were expelled and 26 pupils left in protest. When further demands from the students were ignored, a boycott of school activities and church took place. A disciplinary committee refused to bend to the students' demands. The students stuck to their position. There was a mass expulsion of students, supervised by the police. Other student actions took the form of protests against classroom and disciplinary grievances.

Complaints by women students at Shawbury about their hostel conditions led to the expulsion of the entire female student body in 1957. There were similar protests at Mfundisweni in the same year. A boycott at Boitshoko Methodist Institution in 1958 was resolved without expulsions.

In some ways it was the authorities rather than the students who increased the tendency to politicise the conflict. There were relentless searches for largely imaginary 'instigators' and subversion. At Ndaleni in 1955, the chief response of the mission authorities to the riot was to blame it on 'the reading of "subversive literature" '. At Mfundisweni, African teachers who tried to resolve the 1957 dispute were reported to the authorities for inciting the students. Similarly, following the 1957 Blythswood incidents, a NAD spokesperson told a parents' meeting students were being 'poisoned' by people in positions of responsibility. He claimed 'agitators' were influencing parents in country districts.

Now, while there was a high level of political agitation in the Eastern Cape region, the authorities misunderstood the situation by adhering to a simple 'agitator' theory. Students had real grievances. These included authority conflicts, racial oppression, educational problems and material conditions. In the institutions, these factors combined with African nationalist political sentiment. Agitators were not needed to spark so explosive a mixture. In the 1959 Lovedale incident, students' concerns were certainly informed by a political awareness. They demanded an end to ethnic segregation of living quarters, stamping this as 'tribalism'. This terminology does suggest political awareness. However, the unifying grievances which focused their discontent were around food and manual labour. These issues had not been discussed with people outside the institution. Students were thus amazed to hear from the Regional Inspector that they had been 'instigated by the same people who were behind the Victoria Hospital nurses' strike in 1958'.

The desire of the authorities to track down 'subversion' frequently inflamed conflicts around the schools. In 1959 pupils of St John's,

Umtata, made Congress salutes at Minister de Wet Nel's car. One was expelled. Six teachers at the school were also dismissed by the NAD. This heavy-handed reaction prompted a joint teacher/student/parent protest – which succeeded in blocking the department's move.

The troubles in mission institutions during 1960 had the same form and focus as before, but were more frequent. Healdtown's difficulties, for example, focused on the bread ration and the special seating given to white staff in the dining hall. A protest against the quality of breakfast led to the expulsion of a student leader. The students then embarked on a boycott and set fire to the buildings. Police intervened and eight students were arrested. At Moroka Training Institution, students attacked the house of the teacher responsible for catering. Kilnerton's upheaval, similarly, was a classic disciplinary riot. Friends and relatives of students were refused admission to an annual drama night. A class boycott, arson and an attack on the hostel matron followed. At Tigerkloof the old protests against manual work resurfaced when the carpentry block was burnt down. The entire student body was arrested and held for nine days. Among these 60s actions only one had an overtly education-political focus. Fifty students at Amanzimtoti walked out over the quality of the tuition.

The next year showed decisive changes in the pattern of protest. The actions of 1961 were of three types – and two of these were new. For the first time school riots and boycotts centred on opposition to the coming of the Republic. Second, there were actions responding to unprovoked clamp-downs by the authorities. Last, there was some continuation of the tradition of food and discipline boycotts. The significance of the existence of a particular tradition or repertoire of protest, in particular educational institutions, is well illustrated by the events of 1961. In the mission-founded schools of the Eastern Cape there was an immense flare-up at the time of Republic. Schools in the regional urban centre, Port Elizabeth, were quiet. The Regional Director of Bantu Education, J. Dugard, comments: 'Boarding schools caused many heartaches while the far more numerous day schools went quietly on their way.'

A generalised political eruption took place in the Eastern Cape boarding schools. At St John's College, Umtata, students held a meeting defying the government's ban on gatherings. This culminated in the burning of a government vehicle, the college library and furniture. Altogether, 204 students were arrested in the Transkei alone around Republic Day incidents. One hundred and six were convicted of offences connected with illegal gatherings or public violence.

Action also spread to the Transvaal. At Emmarentia Bantu High School at Warmbaths on Republic Day, students refused to participate in the festivities and held a mass meeting instead. Police were twice called in to disperse them. After a two-day class boycott, 29 students were expelled.

It is not clear to what extent the new wave of student action was organised. Much of the little available data expresses the views of educational authorities who inclined to an excessively conspiratorial view of student action. A conference of senior BED officials in the Eastern Cape concluded that behind the disturbances lay 'a powerful and ruthless organisation brought to bear on the immature but politically conscious minds of young scholars'. This was supposedly part of 'a considered and prepared attack on the Government and White supremacy'. The BED believed there was a plan to oust 'Europeans' from the institutions in order to place blacks in charge. They claimed there was a plot to create 'strong Bantu political centres' which would become training grounds for 'agitators and leaders of Bantu nationalism'. This fantasy reflecting the paranoia of the white inspectorate is illustrated by inspectors' views of the issues. Regional Director J. Dugard, a humane and enlightened official, was clearly unaware that the ANC and the NEUM were separate organisations. Although he was convinced there was a 'cell' in each institution which 'dictated' to the student body, he admitted it had mysteriously proved impossible to find out who *any* of these 'instigators' were. At the officials' conference, inspectors virtually admitted their relations with both students and black teachers had totally broken down. The prefect system had been 'neutralised'. Prefects had either participated in the disturbances or become 'negative'. Those prefects regarded as 'sell-outs' were subject to physical violence. Discipline was eroding as the sensitive situation compelled the authorities to ignore breaches they would otherwise have punished. Black hostel staff and teachers who supported the authorities were being ostracised. The majority of black teachers could not be relied on in a crisis. Some were suspected of encouraging and supporting student action.

There was space for more overt forms of political action to come to the fore. The students who told the authorities at this time that 'education is not everything' expressed a new form of political consciousness. It was based on a local defeat of the legitimacy of the education system. It was to become generalised in the 70s when there was a more thorough collapse of that legitimacy.

Heavy-handed interventions by the authorities also helped to escalate the level of conflict. At Healdtown, a few days before Republic Day, police staged a raid looking for 'weapons'. The trunks of 200 students who refused to co-operate with the police were seized. A class boycott followed and the college was placed under police guard.

Following an attempt by pupils to burn down the Principal's office, the institution was closed. Measures against those who participated in protests also provoked trouble. At Lovedale in July, 400 students boycotted classes in protest against the expulsion of 50 students for participating in the May demonstrations. All 400 were expelled. At Ndaleni, 50 students walked out in protest at being required to sign a good conduct undertaking after returning from suspension over the May demonstration. At Kilnerton in June a strike took place in sympathy with 10 expelled pupils and with Healdtown and Lovedale.

Few of the incidents reported in 1961 had the character of simple food riots. The food riot had, however, served as a bridge across which students could charge onto the political offensive.

Disturbances in schools continued in 1962 although at a reduced level. However, in the first half of 1963 there was a renewed flare-up. A statement by the Minister of Bantu Education also indicated a larger number of incidents, but did not provide adequate details of them. Speculation that the incidents of this period were linked to the activities of Umkhonto we Sizwe or Poqo should not be taken too literally in an organisational sense. But at the same time the battles in the schools in 1963 did take on a bitterness and intensity which suggests a deepened political anger. The mood of the students could be summed up by a slogan written by students at Healdtown during the 1963 disturbances: 'Why must we wear uniform? Are we convicts or soldiers? We are the future leaders of South Africa.'

The last-ditch violence of the conflicts in society as a whole was reflected in the schools. At Wilberforce (Evaton), in February 1963, two students were expelled on allegations that they had incited others not to pay fees. Following this, the BED sacked Vice-Principal Jack Lekala. The BED claimed he was inciting pupils and was behind the campaign against fees. However, after his dismissal, Lekala returned to the school and spoke to some students. A student meeting ensued and the principal was stoned when he tried to intervene. The police then arrived. After being initially driven back by stones from the students, they took control of the campus with the aid of a Saracen armoured car. After a boycott the next day, all the male students were expelled. The Director of Bantu Education intervened. When he was denied a hearing by the students, he had all the women students expelled as well. In September 1962, students protesting expulsions at Kilnerton used knives and sticks to attack students who were breaking their boycott. They also burnt a teacher's car. Students at Bulwer in 1962, and at Healdtown in 1963, stoned members of staff. There was massive property damage. At Mfundisweni in April 1963, students stoned the church, smashed the mission lighting plant, and burnt down a dairy. Ninety-two of them were convicted in the Magistrate's Court.

Unlike the riots of 1961, none of the riots of 1962 to 1963 were launched on an overtly political issue. All claimed to be about a disciplinary issue, such as expulsions, or took the form of a traditional food riot. After the violent boycott and confrontation at Healdtown in 1963, the students claimed their grievances were insufficient food and broken beds. However, the riot clearly had political undertones.

As repression increased in the early 60s, students became more cautious at putting forward overtly political claims. However, the underground activities of the time did impact on the students. Not, as contemporary officialdom believed, in a direct organisational sense, but rather in that these activities gave the students a sense of continuing struggle and of the possibility of change.

Student riots in the late 50s and early 60s manifested a deep discontent among school students at the state's educational and social policies. However, certain of its features prevented its being an effective form of opposition. First, it was deeply rooted in a mission boarding school tradition of revolt against local grievances. This provided a cultural context for revolt. It also intensified the tendency for protests to be localised and to be a confused mixture of local and wider grievances. Second, as a result, the student revolts had little impact in the urban areas. Third, no strong school student organisation emerged of the kind which could make school students a coherent social force.

In the case of student rebellion, there was a dialectic of successful repression and future conflict. By the end of 1963, the authorities had stabilised the situation inside the schools.

The tradition of student revolt did not quite die out. And although it remained rooted in the rural boarding schools, in the 70s it would re-emerge, with much more devastating effect, in the new urban schools developed by Bantu Education.

Bibliography

Oral History
Interviews with Teachers. Nos 1, 4–5, 7–8, 13, 16, 18.

Archives
Cory Library manuscripts. Series MS 16 598/6.
SAIRR Press Cuttings 124.
University of South Africa Archives. Pretoria. Series AAS 212, 213.
University of the Witwatersrand Archives. Johannesburg. Series AD 1812.

Newspapers and Periodicals
New Teachers' Vision. Vol. 1 No. 3, October to December 1955; No. 5, January to June 1956.
Race Relations News. April 1964, SAIRR.
SAIRR Race Relations Survey. 1954–1956; 1959–1960; 1961–1964. Johannesburg, SAIRR.
The Teachers' Vision. Vol. 12 Nos 1 and 2, October to December 1954; Vol. 13 No. 3, January to March 1955.
The Torch. 8 July 1952, 13 January 1953, 13 January 1954, 24 January 1955, 1 February 1955, 15 February 1955, 21 February 1955, 13 March 1955, 12 April 1955, 10 May 1955, 17 May 1955, 24 May 1955, 14 June 1955, 6 September 1955, 20 September 1955, 25 October 1955, 20 March 1956, 17 April 1956, 12 June 1956, 3 July 1956, 21 August 1956, 16 October 1956, 20 October 1956, 7 May 1957, 14 May 1957, 28 May 1957, 25 June 1957, 30 July 1957, 4 February 1958, 11 February 1958, 1 April 1958, 17 April 1958, 27 May 1958, 11 November 1958, 10 February 1959, 17 February 1959, 24 March 1959, 20 October 1959, 7 December 1960, 19 July 1961, 26 July 1961, 13 March 1963, 10 May 1963.
Work in Progress. No. 31, May 1984. Hassim, K. 'Interview: Hassim on APDUSA'.

Publications
Brookes, Edgar. *A South African Pilgrimage.* Johannesburg, Ravan Press, 1987.
CATA. 'The Defeat of the NAD and School Boards'. Cape Town, CATA, undated. (A copy can be found in the University of South Africa Archives. Pretoria. Series AAS 212/13.)
Dugard, J. *Fragments of my Fleece.* Pietermaritzburg, Kendall and Strachan, 1985.
Horrell, M. *A Decade of Bantu Education.* Johannesburg, SAIRR, 1964.
Huddleston, T. *Naught for Your Comfort.* London, Collins, 1981.
Lodge, T. *Black Politics in South Africa Since 1945.* Johannesburg, Ravan Press, 1983.
South African Law Reports. Cape Town and Durban, Juta and Butterworth, 1957.
Wilson, M. and Mafeje, A. *Langa: A Study of Social Groups in an African Township.* Cape Town, Oxford University Press, 1973.

CHAPTER SIX

The Zenith of Bantu Education

The Early 60s to 70s

The defeat of opposition to apartheid education policy was part of a tightening of governmental control over the entire society. The early 60s saw the wholesale repression of popular oppositional movements. In the booming economic conditions of the 60s, the state pursued its Bantu Education policy with intensified vigour and dogmatism.

During this period the BED used education policy as a means to further 'Grand Apartheid's' aim. This was to uproot the black urban working class, and build the homelands as, supposedly, the only arena for the realisation of black political and educational aspirations. The consequences for education were disastrous.

Development of Bantu Education accompanied rapid expansion of the capitalist economy. This might seem to confirm that Bantu Education supplied an appropriate labour force to employers. The lack of public friction between government and representatives of capitalist interests might lead to the assumption they were in a symbiotic relationship. The apparent passivity of black communities, teachers, and students might encourage one to suppose that the schooling system was successfully distributing dominant ideology, and strengthening dominant class hegemony.

However, state education policy was generating a set of social tensions. The apartheid bureaucracy pursued its own ideological agenda and organisational interests. Its actions in no way served the long-term interests of capital. The triumph of racial ideology led to educational measures which were to pose a string of problems for urban business interests.

Education was harnessed to the application of apartheid policy. Development of secondary, technical, and higher education for Africans in the urban areas was strangled. Young people were driven to seek their educational future in the bantustans. The educational development that did take place was centred in the rural areas, to strengthen the homeland states and their leaders.

By denying urban African people effective access to post-primary education, bureaucrats and NP politicians were effectively ignoring the growing needs of industry for skilled and clerical employees.

The policy was also generating future political problems for the government itself. The financial and administrative structure of Bantu Education proved increasingly unable to sustain even that level of educational development that the BED wanted to pursue.

By the end of the 60s, the funding of black education was in a state of collapse. There was a groundswell of urban discontent, even if this was barely visible. Nor were teachers as effectively drawn into the Bantu Education system as at first might have been the case. Docility of the existing teachers' organisations prevented them from aggressively pursuing their members' interests. Few major improvements in teachers' conditions of service and pay were achieved. This led to disillusionment. Teachers were further alienated from the BED by its racist practices and heavy-handed administrative style. The boards were subordinate to unpopular policies of the BED and their actions were arbitrary. They were corrupt and their utilisation by chiefs in the bantustans as instruments of personal power generated considerable hostility from communities and from teachers.

While the level of student revolt was low, the tradition of riot in rural boarding schools continued. Parents, students and teachers may have unhappily accepted the education system for lack of any alternative. Mostly they did not identify with it.

Bantu Education and Territorial Apartheid

With the more vigorous implementation of apartheid policies, there was a serious disruption of the relationship that had existed between government and industry in the 50s.

By 1962, the state had accomplished the outlawing of the African nationalist movement. This removed the major political obstacle to establishing the bantustans as a 'solution' to the question of political rights for black South Africans. The crushing of workers' organisations and a vast inflow of foreign investment provided the basis for the unequalled boom in the South African economy during the 60s. This boom gave the state a rare freedom from economic constraints in carrying out its aims. Within the NP, the Verwoerdian ideologues were dominant. Rising forces of Afrikaner capital were too reliant on the political patronage of the NP to step out of line.

All Africans were regarded as 'temporary sojourners' in urban areas. They would become homeland citizens, exercising political rights solely in the bantustans. In order for this to come about the government moved towards granting the homelands self-government.

Simultaneously, energetic moves were made to reverse the flow of population to the cities. From the late 50s, the government tightened influx control. It made the pass laws more rigid and toughened policy within the labour bureau system. The early years of B.J. Vorster's government deepened this new thrust. The construction of urban housing was virtually frozen, to stem the growth of big urban townships. The Physical Planning Act (No. 88 of 1967) allowed the state to limit the proportion of black employees in new urban factories. This was part of an attempt to encourage decentralisation of industry, so that the black labour force might increasingly be based in the homelands. The educational component of this policy was that the state insisted all development of secondary, technical and tertiary education for blacks should be concentrated in the homelands. State officials saw the urban school system as a mechanism of influx control.

A policy of blocking secondary school expansion in black urban areas was adopted. It was particularly energetically pursued by Dr H.J. van Zyl, the Secretary for Bantu Education in the late 60s and early 70s. In 1966 the *Bantu Education Journal* said urban Africans should go to the bantustans for secondary technical and university education. Urban people, the article pronounced, 'will have a few high schools but never enough, because, according to Government policy, most of these schools should be in the homelands. They will never get a trade school in the white cities again.'

In a series of speeches in 1969 and 1970, Dr van Zyl reaffirmed the policy of providing no further secondary schools in urban areas. He concentrated on the provision of homeland secondary schools with hostel provision for urban pupils. While admitting existing hostel facilities were inadequate, he claimed these were being expanded. He said there were adequate rural schools to absorb urban youth eligible to enter secondary school. He accepted urban lower and higher primary pupils should remain with their parents and claimed (inaccurately) that sufficient urban schools were provided for them.

New policies removed the possibility of black communities taking the initiative in this matter. White municipalities were made responsible for school building, within tight budget restrictions and state-decreed limits on the level of facilities that could be provided.

In the early 60s, white municipalities were responsible for the provision of African lower primary schools in their areas. The building of higher primary and secondary schools was dependent on black communities raising half the cost of each new school. The rest of the money was matched by the state on a rand-for-rand basis. Raising this money was often difficult. Clearly the policy placed the burden of financing education on the urban working class. Nevertheless, it did provide a degree of community initiative in school building. This was not in line with the state's desire to control school expansion. In 1968, the government ended the system of rand-for-rand contributions. The following year, white local authorities were ordered to take over all school building in townships. The money was to be provided by a 20-cent levy on each township household. Integral to the new system was an official formula that laid down the level of facilities which municipalities ought to provide. This constituted:

- 12 lower primary classrooms for each 800 families;
- 16 higher primary classrooms for each 1 600 families; and
- 10 junior secondary classrooms for each 3 200 families.

Some municipalities, including Johannesburg, were given permission to finance building from funds other than the levy. They were, nevertheless, expected to adhere to this formula. The new system, with its grotesquely inadequate level of secondary school provision, was obviously designed to channel pupils to the bantustans.

The effects of this policy are exemplified by the case of Johannesburg's Soweto townships, the largest black urban concentration. Van Zyl made no bones about proclaiming in public, in 1970, that only one secondary school per 3 000 families was appropriate. He forbade the building of additional classrooms in Soweto high schools he considered 'too big'. He also bluntly told a meeting of Soweto school boards he would not allow Soweto schools to enrol too many pupils. He said secondary schools would be provided in the homelands.

The Department of Community Development (DCD), which also played a role in controlling school building, was equally unforthcoming. A 1971 request by the Johannesburg City Council for funds to build 674 classrooms in Soweto was refused. The DCD gave permission to build 36. After a considerable struggle, the city council gained permission to build a further 167 classrooms in early 1972. However, it could not get the funds for this out of the DCD. A little later the same year, the DCD turned down city council plans for six new schools on the grounds that they exceeded the maximum unit cost.

These policies acted as a pressure on township parents to send their children to rural schools. One teacher comments:

> . . . if a parent wanted his son to be trained he . . . had just to send his children out into the boarding school outside . . .

Another says: '. . . urban communities sent their children to the rural areas . . . where these facilities were provided.'

The education system was also linked, in much more direct ways, into the influx control system. Students from families without urban residence rights were prevented from attending schools in the urban areas. Where they had made their way into these schools, students of rural origin were, as far as possible, removed. Mr van Dyk, Van Zyl's predecessor, argued publicly that the shortage of urban school places was because of the lack of effective influx controls on migrant workers' children. This view appears to have reflected the BED's analysis.

In 1964 pupils from rural areas around the city were forbidden to attend secondary or higher primary school in the urban area. In 1968 a BED official announced students registering at schools in 'white' areas would have to produce residence permits.

Port Elizabeth was a particular centre of attempts to control rural influx through the schools. In 1970, the municipal superintendents ordered checks in the city's schools on whether pupils were registered in the urban area. They returned those who were not born in Port Elizabeth to the rural areas. To its annoyance the municipality found black headmasters were, despite warnings on the matter, continuing to enrol out-of-town pupils. Van Zyl also introduced a policy in Soweto under which pupils, even if properly and legally enrolled, could be ordered to leave school. This rule applied if there were more than 50 pupils in a secondary class or 55 in a primary class.

The BED's policy was to develop technical instruction primarily within the bantustans. In Port Elizabeth, the city council called for a trade school for Africans to be opened in the city in 1964. The BED refused the request on the grounds that technical education must take place in the rural areas. It announced a trade school would be opened in King Williamstown, Ciskei.

In 1966, the Johannesburg Chamber of Commerce acquired adequate funds and land to open a commercial college accommodating 1 000 African students. It was refused permission to carry out the project by the government. At the same time the state closed down eight Johannesburg commercial colleges, suggesting they open in the bantustans.

In the few instances where there was development of urban technical training facilities in the period, the government aimed to limit it to no more than Junior Certificate level. This was the case when the Jabulani Technical School in Soweto was established in the late 60s. As teachers were subject to influx control regulations, having trained in rural institutions, they could not take up posts in urban institutions. This was because they did not have residence rights and, besides, there was a government-created urban housing shortage. The state's restrictive educational spending policies meant there was in any case a gross shortage of teaching posts. The BED refused to use some of the best qualified African teachers because they had been trained outside the Bantu Education system. In 1966 a graduate of Roma University,

Lesotho, with a BA and Dip Ed was dismissed. He was told his training had been received outside South Africa.

The BED tried to ensure control of the expansion of the urban school system. It tried to prevent or restrict any use of funds from private business by schools. Any donations to schools of more than R50 had to be administered by the BED. In 1970 the Vanderbijlpark African School Board was 'warned' for obtaining a donation of R3 000 toward building classrooms and a library. A donation from the Anglo-American Corporation to the Soweto Secondary School, Naledi, was frozen by the BED in the same year because the gift had not gone through official channels. Mr G. Rousseau, Van Zyl's deputy, stated in 1971 the BED would not allow school boards to raise money for buildings from private firms.

The Triumph of Teacher Conservatism

The state did seem to achieve a degree of success in winning teachers' acquiescence in the existing education system. In the 50s TUATA and CATU had made little impact and mustered insubstantial support. Their apolitical, passive approach, their dedication to cultivating a professional image, seem to have had limited appeal for teachers during that turbulent decade. Popular pressure on teachers to identify with the aspiration for drastic social change was strong. One of the major successes of Bantu Education during the 60s was that this situation was transformed. Most teachers were drawn into the structures of the cautious TUATA, CATU and their equivalents in Natal and the Orange Free State. These bodies, federated together as the African Teachers' Association of South Africa (ATASA), became the dominant organisation of the teaching profession for the next two decades.

The key component in this change was the outlawing of the African nationalist political movement and the trade unions. With the destruction by the state of these movements and the exiling or jailing of their leadership, the hope of short-term social change receded. Fear of political activity became strong. A teacher from the AEM's cultural clubs, when asked to what extent she was able to inject her political ideas into her teaching in the 60s, replied: '. . . I wouldn't say that I was able, because honestly, fear for victimisation by the law . . .'

The total crushing of popular organisation created a sense of hopelessness among teachers, even at the level of influencing students with their ideas. One teacher recalls:

> . . . I wonder what indent I can make, because the situation is that you are like a sugar grain in the sea.

In these circumstances, teachers were now willing to join organisations that held out the promise of attaining piecemeal improvements in their conditions of service. The pursuit of larger social or political goals seemed unrealistic. The teacher quoted above says of the 60s:

> That was the transitional period of Bantu Education, the time when everybody was trying to look how we could improve our lot in the educational sphere. That was the time when we were pressurising some of our conditions to improve.

There were still very small possibilities for upward mobility out of the teaching profession open to African teachers. The 25 000 members of the profession in 1961 still formed substantially the largest occupational category of African salaried employees. The improvement of teachers' employment situation thus offered the only apparently viable means to a better life.

Given the changed political circumstances, certain aspects of teachers' ideology and social position facilitated their desire to find a *modus vivendi* with Bantu Education. One such aspect was a belief they could make a worthwhile social contribution by teaching, despite the political environment. For teachers who felt uncomfortable about teaching in Bantu Education schools, it came as a great comfort to find that most aspects of the syllabi remained unchanged. Here are the views of two different teachers:

> If I had discovered that what I had got from school is quite different from [what] is taught under the Department of Bantu Education, I don't think I would have remained in teaching. I consoled myself by saying even if people say the standard of education is inferior, what I am teaching is the same as what we were taught at school. I realise it was only a change of name as far as I am concerned.

> The education provided by the mission schools was actually the same . . . with that provided by the ordinary state schools today, because the syllabuses have not changed.

Another factor that aided a falling back to complacency, was the degree of respect teachers were still often accorded by local communities. This could make the teacher a relatively privileged person. According to two people who were interviewed: 'Well, the community still regarded teachers as leaders.' Again:

> If you visited a house as a teacher the people felt nervous about it. You must give them two days' notice you are coming to see them. [They] arrange the house inside and outside.

In the urban areas, the effects of state education policy had begun to undermine teachers' status, but it remained strong in the countryside:

> . . . in the rural areas the teacher was all things to all men. They were held in higher esteem than in the urban areas.

> I taught in a rural area . . . where a teacher was held in high respect by the whole community. On a Sunday, if there was a wedding, the teacher was always invited after church services . . . and accorded high respect, a special seat at the table . . . Now, unlike what you get in the urban areas.

This deference could dispose the teacher toward a certain degree of conservatism.

How did TUATA and CATU leaders utilise this favourable situation to strengthen their support base?

First, they benefited from their semi-official position. They were recognised by the BED, which had no objections to the existence of a strongly apolitical and 'professionalist' teaching body. In the Transvaal, TUATA members put pressure on their colleagues to join the association through the holding of collections for its activities. Because of TUATA's state-recognised position, teachers came to see these collections as having a compulsory character.

Second, the ATASA organisations used cultural events, especially choral competitions, as a vehicle for building support and structuring the activities of their members. Music competitions had a long history in teachers' organisations. They had flourished in the 40s as part of a wider range of cultural activities that embodied a spirit of African self-assertion. By the 60s they had taken on a much more neutral and ritualistic character. Choral competitions, arranged on a regional and national basis, became almost the central activity of teacher organisations. According to teachers interviewed:

> [ATASA] wasn't truly a teacher organisation. It was entertainment partly by music competition . . .

> TUATA has always been concerned mainly with music competitions.

Because these contests were extremely popular, they constituted a strong pressure on teachers to join ATASA organisations. Only those schools with ATASA-affiliated teachers could participate.

Third, the ascendant teachers' organisations of the 60s, although led by overwhelmingly male leadership groups, shrewdly oriented themselves toward organising women members. This was a significant departure from the practice of the 50s teachers' groups, whether of the left or the right, which had generally marginalised women members. A CATA member wrote in 1954:

> . . . We women take little or no interest in these teachers' meetings. Even when we do attend we do not participate fully in the discussions. What powers are lying dormant in us!

During the 50s, CATA's chauvinism had extended. It opposed increases in the numbers of women employed as teachers on the grounds that they would displace male teachers from their posts and that women were incapable of handling disciplinary and physically demanding work. The association described the BED's policy of equal pay for men and women primary teachers as 'fantastic'. In contrast, the organisations dominant in the 60s, despite their generally conservative views, did make some effort to relate to the concerns of their women members. In the early 60s, TUATA organised a petition against the BED's policy of discouraging the employment of married women as teachers. According to a leading teacher activist, this somewhat less chauvinistic approach increased women's participation in teachers' organisations. But there was often manipulative control of women members by teacher leaders.

The change in approach led to spectacular growth of the ATASA affiliates. Under the leadership of I.E. Zwane, who was in office as president from 1961 to 1974, TUATA underwent a rapid expansion. The association mounted a diverse programme of social and cultural activities. During the 60s, districts organised sports, ballroom dancing, plays, tours and music competitions involving teachers and pupils in choral singing. These cultural foci created a basis for rapid growth. In 1963 membership stood at 5 806. By 1972 this had risen to 11 000, by 1974 to more than 15 000.

CATU achieved an even more dramatic self-transformation. With the imposition of the State of Emergency in April 1960, many members feared they would be arrested. Presumably they believed all African organisations, regardless of political stance, would be subject to the clampdown. The result was poor attendance at meetings, a shortage of funds and a very weak 1960 conference. The demoralisation and disruption of community life that followed the crushing of the nationalist movement had its effects on CATU. Through the early 60s it struggled to survive. Its 1962 to 1963 report stated bluntly: 'The Cape Teachers' Union has no funds and must very soon close "shop".' However, the new political conditions of the 60s rapidly created an audience for CATU's pragmatic message. A key part in its revival was played by the Port Elizabeth Teachers' Union (PETU). This CATU affiliate was established by members of its Peddie branch in Port Elizabeth on 10 September 1964, with R.L. Peteni as President. In 1966 Peteni became CATU's regional organiser in the Eastern Cape. Under his leadership a crowded programme of social events – receptions, rugby and netball matches, and choir competitions – was launched. In 1968 PETU diversified further, into a beauty competition, music festival, maths classes and amateur dramatics. In this era, there was a rapid growth of membership in the Port Elizabeth area. This was significant, as Port Elizabeth had been a stronghold of the ANC in the 50s and a centre of political action. That CATU, with its political quietism and bland programme of social activities, could build itself there, reflected the depth of the defeat of the nationalist movement in the area. Teachers in Port Elizabeth, who had previously been under the pressure of popular militancy, were now free to pursue their 'professional' interests. The Port Elizabeth developments were mirrored elsewhere in the Cape. By mid-1966 the turn-about was apparent. CATU's conference at New Brighton in June was described as 'an unqualified success'. The union was reported to have about 1 000 paid-up members. By 1969 this total had climbed to 1 895, and by 1974 to 3 410 – almost half of the African teachers in the Cape.

The substantial organisations that thus emerged among teachers generated an ideology that provided far more scope for the BED than was the case in the 50s. The rolling back of teacher radicalism was a major gain for the BED. ATASA ideology satisfied teachers' discontents with state education policy. They engaged in rhetorical criticism of the absence of compulsory education, of the material impoverishment of schools, and of certain unpopular departmental policies. ATASA ideology, however, asserted that teachers should abjure any form of political activity and that political and educational concerns were absolutely separate. It praised the virtues of the Christianised African middle class, in a way that evoked the most conservative side of mission ideology. In this way ATASA developed an ideology compatible in practice with the BED.

TUATA did advocate free compulsory education. Frequent well-publicised calls for this were made, culminating in a conference held at Atteridgeville in March 1968. This gathering passed a resolution asking the BED to introduce free compulsory education for all African children between six and 16 years. TUATA conferences during the 60s also called for the end of the BED's practice of using vernacular languages throughout primary school. TUATA wanted vernacular languages to be used only up to the end of Standard 2 and a reduction of the language requirements for pupils to pass Standard 6. Such stances appeared to have given teachers a sense they were avoiding incorporation into those aspects of the educational system they rejected. Two ATASA members interviewed felt that by taking such positions their organisations had maintained their distance from the state:

> ATASA being a body that represents the various teachers' organisations . . . has never accepted Bantu Education . . . Because the various teachers organisations have never accepted Bantu Education on their own. They have rejected it from its inception.

ATASA felt Bantu Education was an education for convenience, and until it was an education for citizenship it would merely be tolerated, but not accepted.

Yet, at the same time, the ideology of the ATASA organisations explicitly rejected any form of political opposition to the state. CATU leaders continued to vilify the memory of CATA. They went out of their way to assure the authorities they would never follow its politicised path. C.N. Lekalake told the 1967 CATU conference in his presidential address:

> . . . to the members of the inspectorial staff of the various regions and to those higher officers of the Department of Bantu Education we say thank you, and promise solemnly as we did in 1953 that IT SHALL NOT HAPPEN AGAIN. Never again will the work of many years be reduced to shambles as it was in the late '40s and early '50s.

The most coherent rationalisation of ATASA's position was provided by R.L. Peteni, when he took over the presidency of CATU at its 1968 conference at Taung. In his address to the conference, he held up the African middle class as the creator of stability in an urban environment dominated by the disruption caused by the movement from the land:

> The severing of ties between . . . young Africans and their tribal homes upset their traditional orderliness and their traditional respect for law and custom . . . The ranks of anti-social townsmen grew at an alarming rate . . .

> The pattern changed slowly for the better as the urban community became more permanent and more settled. More schools were built and genuine church people grew. Some families built themselves good, solid homes, and many members of these families became sophisticated in a good sense, and assimilated many of the good things of Western culture.

He criticised the government's policies of the development of bantustans and population removals for 'upsetting the balance and stability'. However, Peteni's conclusion was a resounding reaffirmation of the concept of non-involvement in politics and dedication to 'professional' life as the best path for the teacher. His approach deemed that the effects of state policy ought not to be the concern of the teacher. Instead, it emphasised the task of intellectual and moral formation of the youth:

> . . . the movement from one part of the country to another, from one form of administration to another – these are not the real ills that beset us.

> They are not the problems that we as a teachers' organisation should concern ourselves with. There is not much we can do about these matters

in any case. Our main concern must be the individuals, the young people who have to be prepared to changing circumstances.

Conservative teachers' organisations flourished during this era. Their apolitical and pragmatic outlook appeared to many teachers to be the most viable one. ATASA leaders proved adept at developing organisational activities and an ideology that could provide teachers with a social cohesion and sense of self-worth.

A Period of Acquiescence: School Boards and Students
The further entrenching of the school board system and the decline of student contention during the mid-60s were other areas in which the state seemed to be gaining ground.

The defeat of the mass African nationalist movement in the early 60s created a wholly different political context for the school boards. From then until the early 70s, they were no longer under overt political attack. This brought about a situation in which they were potentially able to exert an influence over far wider sections of society. The new conditions did much to strengthen the boards. One senior departmental official found that in this period, holding a seat on a school board became far more acceptable in black communities. By 1969, there were 509 school boards and 4 108 school committees, involving more than 50 000 people. Some teachers established cordial relations with their local boards and committees:

> During my time they were acceptable . . . And I did not have any experi-
> ence where the school committee or the school board interfered with
> teachers.

A similar analysis would appear to apply to the evolution of student action during the next decade. With the crushing of the underground political movements, the level of student agitation subsided drastically. Incidents between 1965 and the mid-70s generally lacked the overtly political character of some of the student rebellions of the early 60s.

On the surface, Bantu Education appeared to be working well for its creators. It was used to strengthen the bantustan system and displace the black urban working class. Teacher and student revolt had been replaced by seeming co-operation.

The Limitations of the State's Policy
Each area in which officialdom made gains contained hidden conflicts of interests. These were to prevent the Verwoerdian aims of Bantu Education from being attained. Bantu Education was miring the state in vast economic and administrative difficulties. As an attempt to

impose a new hegemony it was largely a failure. The state could not win allegiance.

Bantu Education policy rendered itself increasingly unviable in three major ways.

First, the strangling of post-primary black education in urban areas meant the complementary relationship between the state and industrial capital was severely disrupted. By the 60s, industry had new labour requirements, for more educated labour, which the schooling system was not meeting. The policies pursued by the BED in the 60s were ones with which industrial capital could live in the short term. But they posed fundamental long-term conflicts of interest. This needs to be looked at in the context of the type of industrial growth that occurred during the 60s.

As the boom proceeded there was a strong tendency toward a monopoly structure in industry. This intensified the trend that had begun in the 40s. The major labour requirement within industry tended to be for semi-skilled machine operators. This need could be supplied largely by the labour of the existing urban black working class, not yet removed wholesale from the cities. A primary education was sufficient to prepare such workers for the labour market. By the mid-60s about 80 per cent of the 7–14 age group of African children was in school. By the end of the decade the total number of students had risen to more than two-and-a-half million. So during this period, state labour and education policies were reconcilable with industrialists' needs. The continued emphasis on four-year education thus evoked little criticism from industry. At the same time, the direction of state policy, in its long-term implications, threatened industrialists. It meant eventually the permanent urban working class would be uprooted. In the educational field some important secondary problems were emerging. Monopoly industry increasingly required technicians and clerical staff, who could no longer be found on the white labour market. The government's attempts to confine secondary and technical education to the bantustans and the slow growth of the proportion of African students in secondary education (from 2,94 per cent of the total number of students in 1961 to 4,5 per cent in 1971), meant the educational apparatus was not geared to this growing industrial need. By 1971 there were only 20 schools for Africans in urban areas that went up to Matric level. There were only 74 that went up to Junior Certificate level. This represented only one high school for every 80 000 urban African families. The examination performance of secondary schools also spoke of the weakness of this sector of education. In Soweto in 1967 only 225 pupils sat Matric and only 16 passed. Nationally, in 1967 only 485 out of 2 000 Matric candidates passed. In the Transvaal Senior

Certificate exams of 1969, out of 9 000 who sat, 3 000 failed and 2 500 received a third-class pass. There was a generally steady increase in the rate of matric passes, but the overall numbers remained pathetic. They rose from 182 in 1960 to 1 824 in 1970. So disrupted and inadequate was primary schooling that the median age for entry into secondary school was 16 in the mid-60s. When the economic boom ran into difficulties in the late 60s, the problems thus created for industry were to become more salient. Industry was propelled into action on the front of educational politics.

Second, the viability of the policies of the 60s became increasingly threatened within the state education's administrative and fiscal structures. The bodies established in the 50s could no longer provide the material wherewithal to execute policy makers' decisions. Even those educational services that the BED wished to provide during the 60s, were undermined by a long-term administrative malaise within the BED itself. By the late 60s the NP government was still adhering to the original 'R13 million plus four-fifths of black tax' formula for spending on black education. Only R1,5 million was added for the African universities. As inflation rose, the real value of the R13 million constantly declined. By 1968, the BED was running a deficit of R2 million on its account. A deficit of R6 million was predicted for the next year. In response, the government put a subvention of an extra R9 million into the Bantu Education account. Because this was not provided for in the legislation on Bantu Education, it remained formally a loan. Then, in 1969, changes in the black taxation system reduced the income available from that source. By the end of the decade, the BED found itself in an intractable financial crisis. It was trying to run an expanding system on extremely constricted resources.

Third, the policy pursued in the 60s was self-destructive. The impoverished facilities provided in the urban areas generated a growing resentment from teachers and communities of racial inequality in education. Teachers interviewed in the course of this research often noted the lack of resources affecting their schools in this period:

> The classrooms were mostly made out of corrugated iron, so in winter it was extremely cold and in summer it would be extremely hot . . . I happened to be the librarian and it was [so] small I had to inch my way inside. There was no laboratory, there was no staffroom . . .

> . . . there was little equipment available, libraries were sparsely . . . populated in books . . . we were demanding and asking for donations all the time . . .

> . . . Nothing was supplied by the department. We had to build our own sports fields, set our own posts.

The implicit comparisons being made in these comments are with the well-appointed libraries, sports fields and laboratories of white state schools. Bolder teachers articulated their sense of inequality to their students:

> ... we say we feel it unfair ... library and the like are provided in the European schools and we are denied them.

Similar resentments were aroused by the attempt to drive urban youth into rural schools. Contrary to the promises of Dr van Zyl, rural secondary schools did not provide a solution for urban students whose chances of furthering their education in the urban areas had been blocked by government policy. Only a limited number of urban parents could bear the extra cost of sending their children to bantustan schools. Many urban school students' education came to an early and involuntary end. A teacher points out:

> Our community being a poor community, most of them could not afford taking (their children) to those homeland boarding schools. That in itself brought about ... a high drop-out rate.

Even those urban parents who had the money to send their children to rural boarding schools were by no means certain they would find a school to take them. Despite the assertions of BED officials, there is evidence that even in the rural areas demand for secondary schooling outstripped the available facilities. A visit by a reporter from *The Star* to 17 high schools in the North Sotho homeland in 1970 showed all but four were essentially day schools serving the local community. Most were already full. Students without local relatives could not get accommodation and were turned away. A school principal commented that there were 'far too few schools in the homelands'.

Furthermore, where urban students did obtain admission to rural schools, they could find themselves strongly resented as outsiders by their teachers and contemporaries. 'Children from Johannesburg were not favoured,' a teacher comments.

The shortage of urban secondary school places was a source of deep resentment by students and teachers. By 1971 there were only eight secondary schools in Soweto as against 54 higher primaries. This bottleneck had catastrophic results. In 1969, Orlando High School had 60 pupils per class in Form 1. In early 1970, Morris Isaacson High School had an average of 70 pupils in a class. When the 1970 school year commenced, Morris Isaacson had to turn away 500 applicants. Inevitably, these massive class sizes led to increasingly ineffective tuition and to a growing demoralisation among teachers as to what they could accomplish:

... up to 80 in a class in high school, and they expect a teacher to teach ... If you have 100 it is impossible to work out the weakness of every child.

At Orlando High ... I remember I had a matric class of 72 pupils. Now, teaching can't be effective in such cases. Form One, I had a geography class of 104 children, one class ...

This shortage of urban school places gave rise to signs of growing desperation, on the part of youths, to obtain access to educational facilities. In early December 1970, primary school pupils in Soweto were reported to be queuing for admission to high school the following year. So desperate were some students to be admitted to school that in early 1970, 100 of them picketed Orlando High School for two months. Headmaster T.W. Kambule found places for them by arranging to use a church hall.

There are theoretical grounds for arguing that the state's attempts to reduce the availability of urban secondary education had the unintended consequence of raising the intensity of urban youth's demand for it. The government's attempts to 'put the squeeze' on urban secondary and technical education did little to increase the attractiveness of homeland education for urban working-class children. A person who received his or her education or training in the homeland might end with a qualification. However, as homeland residents were excluded from the urban labour market, such students were likely to be without employment opportunities. The qualified urban student, on the other hand, was well placed to get into the labour market of the cities. So any level of urban education was by definition more valuable in the labour market than an equivalent level of rural education. By increasing the scarcity of urban education, the state succeeded in raising the demand for it. The BED alienated even potentially supportive groupings by ignoring the views of even those 'representative' bodies of black opinion established by the state. The Soweto Urban Bantu Council repeatedly requested the establishment of a teacher training college in Soweto, to no avail. The government adhered to its policy of establishing all training facilities in the bantustans.

The growing discontent of black urban élites with the state's education policies was soon manifested in organised form. In 1968, the Association for the Educational and Cultural Advancement of the African People (ASSECA) was formed. The organisation was established as an educational pressure group of teachers, professionals and business people. Its initial base was in the main urban centres of the Southern Transvaal. Its formation was a reaction to the poor matric results of 1967. ASSECA called for free compulsory education for black students. The organisation established a free tutoring scheme in

Orlando for pupils who had failed matric. It also sought to make donations to high schools. M.T. Moerane, ASSECA's president and a former teacher activist, (and editor of *The World*, the Rand newspaper), launched a somewhat ambitious scheme to raise a 10-cent donation from every African man and woman in South Africa in 1970. ASSECA did manage to obtain considerable funding from the Polaroid Corporation from 1971. By 1973 this co-operation had collapsed, amid barely veiled accusations of embezzlement from Polaroid. During the early 70s ASSECA's activities extended to the Western and Eastern Cape.

Overall, ASSECA was a fairly ineffectual organisation based on the township elite. It was conciliatory in its approach to the BED. It represented an organised expression of the widespread urban discontent over BED-style education. This was the case even among the more instinctively conservative elements in township communities. Thus, the policies pursued in the 60s provided a basis for an increasing popular hostility to the state's education programmes. It was in this decade, as one teacher interviewed argued, that 'the man in the street began to suspect the intention of Bantu Education.'

The drive to use Bantu Education as an instrument of influx control cut across the possibilities of the state's building alliance with sectors of urban black communities.

Teachers: An Underlying Resentment

The servility of the ATASA organisations toward the BED was far from the full picture of teacher response to the educational authorities in the 70s. To a considerable extent, teachers' organisations failed to hold the loyalty of their members, or to reflect their true sentiments. The ideology and administrative practices of BED officialdom prevented the BED from fully capitalising on the opportunity for co-option that teacher conservatism presented. The pragmatic acquiescence of African teachers in the education system hid a deep resentment of apartheid schooling.

The very caution of the ATASA teachers' organisations, which had enabled them to grow in the changed political climate of the 60s, inhibited them. They took no form of action that could bring real material gains to their members. In the long run, the lack of gains to show in return for the moderation of the ATASA organisations undermined their members' confidence in these associations.

First, they proved to be unable to defend their members against dismissal or victimisation. For instance, in 1965 the school board of Witbank arbitrarily dismissed five teachers. TUATA took no effective action to defend them. One of the sacked teachers, J.M. Kananda of

Lynnville Township, wrote to J. Kumalo of TUATA in December 1965:

> What has become of your efforts as far as we sacked Witbank teachers are concerned? . . . Tell me, Jimmy, what's TUATA busy at? Competitions, competitions and competitions? What about the Safe Guard [sic] of so many sacked teachers we read about in the papers?

In 1967, T.W. Kambule, Orlando High's Principal and Chairperson of the local TUATA branch, made the following shrewd critique of the association's inability to protect its members:

> The prerequisite of the association is that it should safeguard the interests of the teacher against the employer. If the association can do this, much can be gained. At the moment it does not give the teacher the assurance that under its wing he can carry out his duties without fear. All it does is organise music competitions effectively. I want to see it give the teacher the courage to pursue the truth.
>
> If the association were strong, no teacher would be afraid of being victimised.

Second, the services arranged by the ATASA leaders for their members were of dubious value. Atlantic and Continental Assurance (ACA) were appointed TUATA's official insurers. ACA's business ethics appear to have been somewhat deficient. They treated TUATA members contemptuously. One TUATA member was told by ACA that he had to continue paying his premiums for three years in order to claim surrender value. He was then informed, on completion of these payments, that he would have to continue paying for a period of three months. In another case, an ACA representative, a Mr de Beer, 'sold' a policy to a teacher in KwaThema by posing as a BED 'investigator'. He told her he was sent by the BED to instruct all widows to sign the policy forms.

Last, the organisations do not seem to have been able to attain many really significant improvements in teachers' pay or conditions. The ATASA organisations would not go beyond a gentle lobbying of the BED as a means of raising wage issues. Even by the mid-70s, TUATA was unwilling to support either an open call for the closing of the wage gap between black and white teachers, or the idea of a minimum wage for teachers. ATASA organisation members interviewed on the role of both the national body and its provincial affiliates in this period were negative about their organisation's achievements:

> On my side I disagree that [the ATASA affiliates] were important, because they couldn't organise loans or houses.
>
> I've never been excited about teachers' organisations because I don't

think they serve any purpose at all. They are supposed to try to improve the lot of the black teacher but I'm not aware of any meaningful change they have brought about, and so I think what they really do is to concentrate on cultural matters like music.

[ATASA] were always criticising [Bantu Education] but as a force to take action, they were poor.

Yet the hostility of many teachers to the BED was not only due to their organisations' inability to extract a better employment package from it. The state's failure to obtain real teacher support was also underpinned by its inability to draw teachers into a new perception of their role, in line with the aims of apartheid institutions. It is true the BED and its publications did make much of the concept of professionalism, which had a resonance with sections of teachers. However, the BED's ideologists put forward themes that were crudely racist and loaded with menace against any form of dissent. These approaches could scarcely gain the allegiance of many black teachers. The BED's mouthpiece, the *Bantu Education Journal*, provides notable examples of this. On one occasion it informed its teacher-readers that to them South African whites were the most important whites in the world: 'They are honest and sincere in their actions to all, people whose word is their bond and who will not be frightened by violence.' Even more bizarre was this 1965 editorial in the journal:

It is about time that we take a look at our South African Bantu population to see in what respects they have exceptional qualities . . . choral singing is one of our strong points . . . Another talent which is manifested in our children is their neat handwriting . . . *subversive activities* and *sabotage* are not our strong points. There are some of our fellow men who, following the instigation of strangers attempted this but they were bound to fail. They failed because these things have never had a share in our traditional way of life and because they are not intrinsic abilities of the Bantu.

These messages of white superiority were incapable of forming an ideological rallying point for the educated black strata of society. They could only be counter-productive for the state. The racism of BED officialdom was, in fact, subverting their own attempts to create a coherent ideology.

The BED's racism was coupled with an authoritarian administrative style which further reduced the possibilities of integrating teachers into the education system. Some teachers had positive experiences of personally helpful and well-disposed inspectors. They seem to have been individual exceptions. The approach generally failed to accord recognition to teachers and stifled their professional autonomy. Teachers' experience of the BED's administrators was often bitter:

> The Department of Bantu Education obviously dictated . . . all decisions
> were from them. There was no consultation. If there was consultation, it
> was what we call rubber stamp consultation.

Ideologically, the disaffection of teachers expressed itself in a pro-
found dissatisfaction with elements of the syllabus. They put across
their objections to the syllabus to their students. As suggested above,
changes in the school syllabus after the introduction of Bantu Education were often not experienced as particularly dramatic by teachers.
But the history syllabus, heavily loaded with themes derived from the
work of Afrikaner NP historians, did contain material which teachers
often found deeply offensive. One particular idea in history text-books
– that the 'theft' of Boer cattle by Africans during the early colonial
period was the cause of frontier wars – seems to have become a symbol
and condensation of all that teachers resented in the education order. It
seems to have evoked a feeling of deep injustice. It stigmatised Africans as criminals, whereas from an African nationalist perspective,
they were the victims of settler depredations. Indeed, the removal of
African land and cattle was seen as the primal act of colonial dispos-
session. When teaching such material teachers would often use it as an
occasion to give vent to their resentment of the existing political
dispensation. That such a process occurred is further evidence of the
inadequacy of the 'brain-washing' view of Bantu Education. Far from
simply reproducing dominant ideology, its classrooms were often an
arena of ideological contestation. Teachers recall:

> . . . with History, I changed certain things I had read in the books – Kaffir
> wars, the stealing of cattle – I tried to correct it.

> I was very unhappy with the kind of History I was teaching: where you
> had to tell your students that their forefathers were thieves, they stole
> cattle from the whites . . .

While teachers were often in a state of considerable fear, some
found stratagems which were hard for the authorities to pin down:
'Those who are clever hear it eventually, those who don't hear you,
leave them alone.'

The apparent practical accord between the BED and ATASA thus
hid a great reservoir of teachers' anger and frustration. Teachers'
organisations were viewed with scepticism by many teachers. They
resented ATASA's inability to defend them, to provide good services
or to win increased benefits. The BED's racist ideology and brutal
administrative methods were loathed. The high point of Bantu Education saw substantial teacher resentment of the whole education system,
and their place in it, lurking just beneath the surface.

The Tyranny of the School Boards

Verwoerd's conception was that school boards would play a crucial role in drawing black communities into a new hegemonic political order centred on tribal loyalties and the bantustans. But as time passed, it became apparent the state was only securing the adherence of limited minorities. At the same time, it was creating deep discontent between teachers and other sectors of black communities. The administrative abuses, corruption and association with unpopular state policies of the school boards constantly threatened their credibility. In the rural areas their utilisation by chiefs and traditionalist elements as instruments of power made them unpopular.

Teachers were placed in a structurally powerless position by the school board system. This explains, to a major degree, their lack of incorporation in the new education order. Through the 60s and 70s there were complaints from teachers and parents about intimidation by the boards; about manipulation of boards by the inspectors; about what one teacher called the 'incompetent and unscrupulous management of our schools'; and about extortion of bribes by board members in matters of teachers' employment, transfer or promotion.

An editorial in *The World* in 1966 reflected the attitudes of black salaried employees when it denounced the situation where teachers 'are more and more being exploited by small men who are in power over them in some school boards'.

Teachers interviewed in the course of this research echoed these complaints. They had often experienced contemptuous treatment by the boards and committees:

> Those people had a tendency of not consulting the teachers, of just giving instructions of how the school was to be run, and how things are to be done. You do it this way, failing which you are fired.

> They were rather viewed with a 'bad eye' in the community, in the sense that they were always threatening a number of people with expulsion.

The complaints of bribery and corruption also seem justified. In the Rand townships, the school boards took bribes and engaged in sexual exploitation. A teacher says of the period:

> Some were even threatened with dismissal if they didn't pay the secretary of the school board in cash or kind. For instance, in one area of Wattville, it was a known fact that if you didn't bring a bottle of brandy, you won't get a post, and for ladies, it was something else they had to bring.

While the numbers of those serving on the school boards may have increased, their structure and policies of the boards continued to generate friction between them and community members. The lack of accountability of the boards to parents allowed them to trample over grassroots opinion. A memorandum by Transvaal teachers in 1966 complained that school boards were ignoring or overturning recommendations made by school committees. The board and committee system continued to be used by the state to extract financial contributions to education from parents. By 1971, these contributions had risen to the level of R1,7 million – of which only R350 000 was spent on repairs and new buildings. The remainder was spent on teachers' salaries. Urban parents, in particular, bore a heavy burden because of officialdom's determination, during this period, to restrict funds spent on urban black schooling. In 1964 in Moroka, 100 out of 600 teachers were being paid by the board. This practice also further alienated teachers from the boards as board salaries could be 45 to 55 per cent lower than regular departmental salaries. The authorities thus generated a relatively limited amount of extra finance for education services. At the same time they created a powerful source of parent and teacher disaffection.

The BED's treatment of urban school boards themselves also served to undermine their credibility and their loyalty. Members of boards and committees who were politically suspect were arbitrarily removed from their positions. In at least one case where the BED disapproved of the actions of members of a school board, the board was dissolved. The BED also stifled the initiative of the boards by refusing them permission to raise funds from outside donors.

The contradictions of the boards were further intensified through their being loaded with responsibility for the state's policy, introduced in the late 60s, of separating out urban schools on an ethnic basis. The policy did to some extent have its intended effect of increasing ethnic consciousness among black communities.

> . . . it really happened that there was war: Zulus and Sothos.

> Instead of bringing the children together to know and understand each other at an early stage, children were led to view each other differently . . . to the extent that there were physical clashes, even on sports fields, when a Zulu school was playing against a Tswana school, for instance . . .

However, the effect of this ethnic separation was by no means only that desired by the state. In part this was because of the way the change of policy was imposed from without on urban communities which were already fairly well integrated. A teacher comments:

> The administrative chaos which resulted from the new ethnic policy adversely affected the quality of urban schooling. This further undermined its popularity with parents and students.

The communities, I think, saw through it, and it tended to cement relationships between the different ethnic groups.

When the ethnic policy was set up in Meadowlands in 1968, artificial overcrowding was created in the Tswana schools. In other cases disastrous mismanagement of the ethnic reorganisation brought about such consequences as the allocation of junior primary students to a secondary school.

The BED acted with its customary lack of finesse in the matter. It engaged in the wholesale expulsion of Zulu-speaking students from a Soweto school where they constituted the majority in 1973. By 1975 there were no junior secondaries for Tsonga and North Sotho speakers in Diepkloof. All of this scarcely brought much lustre to the boards.

During the 60s and 70s, school boards in the bantustans increasingly became a means by which the chiefs and homeland politicians exercised their sway over rural society. The boards provided these groups both with ways of disciplining parents and teachers and with profitable sources of misappropriated funds. These tendencies were accelerated from 1967 when the state moved to transfer administrative control over education in the bantustans to their 'territorial authorities'. The rural school boards exercised their authority over the teachers ferociously. At one school in the Tswana Territorial Authority, the vice-chairperson of the school board told the school committee: 'Teachers are but dogs. We can dismiss them at any moment.'

The arbitrary way in which rural school boards exercised their authority alienated many teachers and parents. The dominant groups in the bantustans tended to loot the institutions which were placed in their trust for wealth and power, rather than using them as instruments of a hegemonic strategy. It is not surprising that in a village in Sekhukuneland the school board were viewed as 'agents to the chief'.

Illustrative of these processes is the story of Philip M. Malebye, the Principal of Itotleng-Baralong Secondary School, Lichtenburg area, during the late 60s. Malebye came into conflict with the local authorities over the various forms of corruption to which they subjected the school. The local chief imposed a R6 tax on those pupils who came from outside the Ratlou Baralong tribal area. The tax was paid into tribal funds. The school committee raised a R3 a head levy from students for the building of latrines but then did not carry out this work. In November 1968, it bought 100 bags of cement for the flooring of four new classrooms. The cement was mysteriously used up without the planned work being done – it was presumably appropriated by members of the committee.

Malebye's resentment of such corruption apparently engendered tensions between him and the school board and school committee. The conflict was finally precipitated when a pupil approached Malebye in 1968 with evidence she had been sexually harassed or abused by the primary school principal. Malebye passed this evidence on to the school board for their action. However, the primary school principal was an ally of the chief. Instead of attempting to investigate the issue, the chief and school board tried to get rid of Malebye. An allegation of embezzlement was then brought against Malebye. But an investigation by the responsible administrative official found no money was missing.

Malebye was then charged in the Delareyville Magistrate's Court with the theft of a R15 cheque from the local storekeeper. However, during the trial, in February 1969, the storekeeper admitted he had conspired with the chief to frame Malebye for the offence. After a brief respite, the board and committee simply moved to dismiss Malebye. His post was advertised in *The World* and he was given notice to quit by 1 April 1969. To add insult to injury, the chief's henchmen also stole some of Malebye's property. Although Malebye had plans for legal action, it seems little came of this.

Malebye's tale illustrates well the manner in which those who exercised power in bantustan structures enhanced their power through their control of the school boards. It also shows how this control was not exercised in such a way as to bring these bodies greater popular support.

Some of the most intense conflicts involving teachers in rural areas took place in the central and Northern Transvaal during the early 70s. Two dimensions of bantustan politics need to be understood here.

First, in Lebowa the period was dominated by a conflict between the chiefs and a grouping who stood for a reduction in the chiefs' power. Up to 1972, the Lebowa Territorial Authority had been led by Chief Motodi Matlala, a stern traditionalist and extreme conservative. However in 1972, with the transition of Lebowa to 'self-governing' status, Matlala was replaced by Cedric Phathudi. He became Chief Minister as the leader of an anti-traditionalist faction. In 1975, after Phathudi had failed, because of South African government opposition, to force the chiefs into a separate upper house in the Lebowa legislature, he brought about a compromise with Matlala. They joined together to fend off attacks from a group around the former Interior Minister, Collins Ramusi, who wanted a more determined attack on the chiefs.

Second, there was considerable political turmoil within Lebowa, Bophuthatswana and surrounding 'white' areas over the creation of KwaNdebele. The NP government had originally not intended to establish a separate Ndebele homeland but rather to allow the existence of Ndebele territorial authorities within Lebowa and Bophutha-

tswana. However, a combination of the particularism of the existing
bantustan leaders who wanted to force out 'foreign' elements; some
forces among the Ndebele chiefs; the labour needs of the Southern
Transvaal industrial region; and the ideological dynamics of the state's
commitment to a distinct ethnic basis for bantustans brought about,
during the 70s, an attempt to construct a single ethnic unit for the
Ndebele. The result was the formation of the least viable of all the
homelands – KwaNdebele. This process involved considerable friction between Ndebele communities and the Lebowa and Bophuthatswana authorities.

The 70s thus saw much friction in the region. This had a severe
impact on teachers in particular. There were incidents in which teachers were forcibly circumcised by traditionalist elements. These actions
underscored the conflict in rural society between rural elites. Teachers,
the bearers of a heavily westernised identity, defined themselves against
the forms of tradition invoked by the more conservative elites. A
teacher who had been subjected to such a forced circumcision replied
in this fashion to his cross-examination during the trial of the culprits
in the Potgietersrus Regional Court.

* Was the circumcision done according to Bantu custom?
* I don't know.
* Do you have no knowledge of the customs of the tribe involved
  here?
* The heathens, yes, they use this custom.

Here the distance between 'the heathens' – a term of abuse drawn
straight from a missionary vocabulary – and the teacher is clearly
demarcated.

In another such case, Amos Motsepe, Principal of Metsangwana
Primary School and TUATA Elands River Branch Chairperson, was
the victim. On 31 May 1970, Motsepe was dragged out of his motor-
car. He was beaten and taken to a circumcision school run by Headman Lesolo Maloka, under the control of Chief Matlala. The next day
he was forcibly circumcised. Motsepe was later moved to another
camp, and held until the end of July, when he was released. In 1974,
with the financial assistance of TUATA, Motsepe brought a legal case
against Chief Matlala, Headman Maloka and their henchmen. Motsepe
duly won the case and considerable damages against Chief Matlala.
However, when he tried to collect these damages he found it virtually
impossible. Motsepe's attempts to recover what had been awarded to
him were an abject lesson in the difficulties faced by anyone trying to
challenge chiefs' power in the bantustans.

An investigator sent to the chief's area by Motsepe's attorneys found that the chief and his brother Chief Mokogome Matlala had a considerable income. They imposed their own poll tax in the area and an annual levy on patients at the local mission hospital. They received salaries as officials of the Lebowa government, split the proceeds of tribal funds between them, and pocketed half of any fines imposed in their 'lekgotla'. In addition the chiefs received a portion of the produce of all land farmed. But it was very difficult for Motsepe to lay his hands on any of these assets. Matlala dispersed his cattle among the herds of the local people, thus making it impossible for them to be identified and seized. It became clear that further investigations would place the attorneys' agent in danger. When the attorneys tried to serve a writ on the chief, they could not find a Deputy Sheriff who was willing to enter the area for this purpose. In 1980, the attorneys were still struggling to have the judgement enforced, even though Matlala had now suffered a decline in his fortunes and was in jail on a charge of stock theft.

In other cases, the results of forced circumcision were more tragic for those involved. In 1971, a group including school teachers was forcibly taken to a circumcision school in the Zebedelia area and subjected to circumcision. One teacher, Gideon Mokoena, suffered a sepsis and died as a result. When those charged with the crime appeared in the Potgietersrus Regional Court, they were let off with a fine.

Another aspect of the conflicts within the bantustans was the way in which the Bophuthatswana authorities tried to use schooling to force non-Tswana minorities out of their 'state'. There was a determined attempt in the mid-70s to force the ama Ndebele-a-Moletlane under Chieftainess Ester Kekana, to leave for KwaNdebele. The Bophuthatswana authorities tried to force the schools to teach in SeTswana, but this was met with resistance from the 'tribal' authority. Eventually Chieftainess Kekana was deposed.

In summary, there was extensive conflict within bantustan elites. In this conflict the school boards often became instruments of those who were strongly placed within the bantustan social order – especially the chiefs. The most conservative of these elements often saw teachers as bearers of ideas contrary to their interests. Because of the avenues of corruption school boards opened up, they were often operated by chiefs in a way which adversely affected teachers and parents. The boards brought some benefits to dominant bantustan elites. However, they did not really serve to build large, strong constituencies supporting the apartheid order.

The Continuation of Student Protest in the Heyday of Apartheid

The apparent quiescence of students in the mid-60s did not continue for long. In the rural, mission-founded boarding schools the long tradition of riotous behaviour, especially over food, continued. From 1965, the familiar pattern of protest began to flare up again. It generally took two forms – the one, a food or discipline riot – the other, anonymous acts of arson. Overt political issues were never raised. The occasional hint of underlying political discontent did sometimes emerge. The level of action fluctuated but the pattern never quite disappeared. Interestingly, despite continuing urbanisation, it was in the rural boarding school that the tradition of student upheaval remained. Few incidents occurred in the expanding urban primary-school sector. Students in the boarding institutions responded to the change in the national political situation which had occurred by the mid-50s. In the repressive situation of the mid- and late 60s they could not make political calls for mobilisation which were as overt as those of a few years before. Nor did they have the scope to be as aggressive. Their attention turned to the internal conflicts of the school. Once again, food and discipline became the metaphors of power.

At Botshabelo Training Institution, Middelburg, there was a strike in April 1965. The boarding master had dismissed student complaints about the food and medical facilities. A protest against the hostel master at Vryheid Government Bantu School in November 1967 led to 19 expulsions. There were expulsions at Nongoma Vocational Training School in February 1968, following a food riot. In September 1968, 200 boys were detained at Clarkesbury following a riot over food in which buildings had been stoned and two cars damaged.

Various disciplinary issues also became a basis for protests. In 1965, Mariannhill pupils broke windows in protest against expulsions. The same year a search of a classroom at Moroka Mission by prefects looking for weapons led to attacks on buildings. The following year at Lovedale, 300 pupils were expelled. They had refused to attend the classes of two teachers they said were unqualified.

Despite the generally lower level of conflict, some incidents had violent outcomes. At Moroka Mission, following the 1965 incident, arsonists set the mission on fire, causing R30 000 damage. Shortly thereafter, Roodekuil Community School at Brits was burnt to the ground. There were still signs of deeper political meanings in school disturbances. During the 1965 food riot at Botshabelo, the students were heard to be singing ANC songs. While the level of student unrest did not rise sharply on a national scale before the mid-70s, there was one localised revival of activity in the Transkei/Eastern Cape, around

1970 to 1971. This regional upsurge was fairly intense, with high levels of violent rioting taking place. Interestingly, of the 13 institutions in the Transkei and Eastern Cape at which there is evidence of student action, five were missionary-founded boarding institutions. These were St John's, Clarkesbury, Mvenyane, Buntingvale and Healdtown.

The motivations for this wave of student action are not particularly clear. At Healdtown a teacher commented that when students who had attacked the headmaster's house were interviewed,

> their complaints were all very petty indeed . . . the trouble does not lie with any individual, but with the boys who will not accept the rules and discipline . . .

In a sense this grasps the nub of the issue. The breakdown in the internal social relations of rural boarding schools had never been overcome. Neither Bantu Education nor the neo-Bantu Education of the Transkei and Ciskei 'states' could restore the credibility of the educational process sufficiently to reintegrate the students into it. They thus turned to violence around issues which could focus their broader resentments at the authority relations of the school and at society. It is tempting to suggest that the moves of the Transkei and Ciskei toward self-government were a focus of the discontent of the students. There is, however, no hard evidence of this. But it is clear the political tensions involved in this process sometimes served to provide the students with more room in which to act. In the case of the 1971 Healdtown incident, a row had broken out between the warden of Healdtown, who had closed the hostel and suspended classes, and the Ciskeian Territorial Authorities Education Department. The department reprimanded the warden for taking this action. It felt he should have tried to bring the school back to normal. The Ciskei's Acting Director of Education wrote:

> The Church is running the hostel for the territorial authority which represents the Xhosa people of the Ciskei, the parents of the children. The executive councillor must be able to say that every possible effort was made to keep the hostel operating, and that the Department was satisfied of the need to close.

The point is that the Ciskei bantustan leadership wanted to build its political base and that the suspension of the children of the local elite who attended Healdtown was an obstacle to this. This is not to suggest the particular configuration of events at Healdtown was widespread. It does suggest that the strains of transition to pseudo-independence may have contributed to the Ciskei and Transkei authorities' difficulty in handling students at this time.

Conflict continued at a reduced level in 1972. There were 296 arrests of students at five schools, in connection with which there were 37 convictions. In 1973, there were arrests at six schools resulting in 472 convictions. These incidents took place in Lebowa, the Transkei, Zululand and Ciskei. The classic pattern of the food riot often continued. At Bulwer in August 1973, the students were affected by food poisoning on a large scale. A doctor was called for consultations. But after he had left, the students were still ill and no action was taken. A meeting to discuss this was held with a teacher, Mr Hlengwa. He refused to show students the minutes he had taken. On Sunday, 12 August, the male students announced there would be a boycott. Once it started on Monday, the police were called, but the boycott went ahead. On the Monday evening the students met with the circuit inspector, whom they presented with a list of no fewer than 92 grievances. The boycott continued throughout the day. In the evening students met with the Principal, Mr Mthiyane. Four main demands were made:

- that a doctor should be called;
- that the students should have access to the minutes of the meeting;
- that staff should stop opening students' letters;
- and that there should be no hitting – 'klapping' – of students by teachers.

The head agreed only to the last of these demands. On the Wednesday the students went back to school. Shortly thereafter a teacher struck a female pupil. This incensed the students. During the night they attacked school buildings. The police arrived and fired on the students. Two female students were wounded. The remaining students fled into the countryside. On the Friday school was suspended. After a few weeks students were allowed to return but, when they found some were being expelled for trivial offences, others left voluntarily. This was a classic food riot situation. While there were real material issues – the students being poisoned by their food and the lack of medical attention – there were also underlying feelings that this situation was part of the injustice intrinsic to students' relations with authority. 'To our surprise,' one of the students wrote, 'the police were called within five minutes after school time was past, but the doctor was not called immediately after we had eaten poison.' It was this sense of injustice in the student experience of dealing with authority that fuelled their anger around more concrete issues.

Student resentment of the racist and authoritarian structure of school and society clearly had not been uprooted effectively in the areas where, in the 40s and 50s, it had posed problems for the authorities.

The existence of a tradition of student revolt and a repertoire of actions expressing this revolt in the rural boarding schools provided an accepted means of expression for student discontent which they could use in a way appropriate to the changed political situation. The authority relations in rural schools had apparently not been successfully reconstructed either by BED officials or by homeland authorities.

The NP bureaucrats would have had some justification for regarding the era from 1962 to 1972 as a triumph for their policies. The administrative structures of black education had been fully mobilised in the service of apartheid policy. Teachers had apparently submitted completely in the political sphere. School boards were functioning, student activity was dormant. But this success was to give rise to new crises. Schooling no longer met the labour needs of industry. The BED's financial structure was not viable. The starving of urban education produced widespread popular resentment. Moreover teachers, students, and parents were largely hostile to the education system. In the apparent calm of the 60s, conflicts multiplied. The next decade would give them expression.

Bibliography

Oral History
Interviews with Teachers. Nos 1, 3–8, 10–11, 15–20.

Archives
Cory Library manuscripts. Series MS 16 598/5.
University of South Africa Archives. Pretoria. Series AAS 120, 121, 212.
University of the Witwatersrand Archives. Johannesburg. Series AD 1181.

Newspapers and Periodicals
Bantu Education Journal. April 1965, February 1970, March 1970, April 1970.
Cape Argus. 6 March 1969.
Cape Times. 18 June 1964.
Daily Dispatch. 12 June 1971.
Die Vaderland. 19 January 1968, 13 January 1969.
Eastern Province Herald. 7 June 1969, 1 May 1971.
Evening Post. 13 January 1964, 30 January 1964, 1 May 1964, 21 May 1966, 11 February 1969, 30 May 1969, 14 February 1970, 23 February 1970.
Journal of Southern African Studies. Vol. 10 No. 2, April 1984. (Charney, C. 'Class Conflict and the National Party Split').
Natal Mercury. 2 September 1975.

Natal Witness. 17 February 1964, 16 August 1965, 4 February 1966, 25 May 1970.

Race Relations News. Johannesburg, SAIRR, 1969.

Rand Daily Mail. 4 February 1964, 5 July 1964, 15 April 1965, 26 October 1965, 18 January 1966, 14 September 1966, 3 November 1966, 16 December 1966, 5 September 1967, 9 September 1967, 16 September 1967, 13 December 1967, 17 January 1968, 24 January 1968, 25 January 1968, 26 January 1968, 27 March 1968, 30 March 1968, 2 May 1968, 29 May 1968, 19 July 1968, 15 January 1970, 28 January 1970, 31 January 1970, 10 March 1970, 2 May 1970, 10 June 1970, 3 October 1970, 8 November 1970, 17 November 1970, 19 November 1970, 18 March 1971, 19 March 1971, 14 December 1971, 21 December 1971, 15 January 1972, 18 January 1972, 15 March 1973, 4 December 1973, 5 March 1975, 28 April 1975.

SAIRR Race Relations Survey. 1968–1969, 1972–1973, 1975–1976. Johannesburg, SAIRR.

South African Labour Bulletin. Vol. 10 No. 3, December 1984 (Hyslop, J. and Tomlinson, R. 'Industrial Decentralisation and the "New Dispensation"').

Sunday Times. 18 September 1966, 18 February 1973.

The Teachers' Vision. Vol. 21 No. 3, September 1951; No. 4, April to June 1954.

The Friend. 16 February 1966, 24 October 1968.

The Star. 6 May 1964, 16 October 1965, 18 October 1965, 28 June 1966, 1 February 1967, 12 June 1968, 29 January 1969, 12 February 1969, 21 February 1969, 14 March 1969, 16 May 1969, 28 January 1970, 16 February 1970, 18 February 1970, 19 February 1970, 23 February 1970, 12 October 1970, 17 November 1970, 26 January 1971, 26 March 1971, 3 June 1971, 26 January 1972, 1 February 1974, 30 December 1974, 4 March 1975, 16 May 1975, 9 June 1975, 28 July 1975.

The Torch. 25 November 1952, 1 April 1958.

TUATA. May 1965, May 1966, December 1966.

Theses and Papers

Hindson, D. 'The Pass System and Differentiated Labour Power'. Law Society Seminar Paper, University of the Witwatersrand, 1985.

Khuzwayo, W. Letter, Dlangezwa. 3 October 1973. In possession of Luli Callinicos.

Posel, D. 'Interests, Conflict and Power: The Relationship Between the State and Business in South Africa during the 1950s', Association for Sociology in Southern Africa Conference Paper, Cape Town, 1985.

The 1961 Education Panel. 'Education and the South African Economy' (Second report). Johannesburg, Witwatersrand University Press, 1966.

Matlala, Chief M. Speech, from Verbatim Report of the 1974 Session 4–15 March: Second Lebowa Legislative Assembly. Lebowa Government, 1974.

Publications

Davenport, T.R.H. *South Africa: A Modern History.* Johannesburg, MacMillan, 1981.

Dugard, J. *Fragments of my Fleece*. Pietermaritzburg, Kendall and Strachan, 1985.

Innes, D. 'Monopoly Capitalism in South Africa'. *South African Review 1*. Johannesburg, Ravan Press, 1983.

Kane-Berman, J. *South Africa: The Method in the Madness*. London, Pluto, 1979.

Peteni, R.L. *Towards Tomorrow: The Story of the African Teachers' Association of South Africa*. Morges, (Switzerland), World Confederation of the Teaching Profession, 1978.

Skocpol, T. *State and Social Revolutions: A Comparative Analysis of France, Russia and China*. Cambridge, Cambridge University Press, 1985.

Surplus People Project. *Forced Removals in the Transvaal: The SPP Reports. Vol 5: The Transvaal*. Cape Town, SPP, 1983.

CHAPTER SEVEN

Change

Educational Policy in 1972

The period from 1972 onwards saw a major shift in government policy toward black education. This was the outcome of conflicts caused by the underlying contradictions of the Bantu Education system.

The relationship between Bantu Education and capitalism was contingent and changing, rather than fixed. Accomplishment of rigid apartheid policy in the educational sphere took place in the 60s at the same time as a boom in the capitalist economy. However, it does not follow that the former process helped the latter. The state's education policies from the early 60s to 1972 undermined the possibilities of economic development. They failed to meet the needs of the most advanced sections of industry for skilled labour. In 1972, education policy fell more into line with capital's labour requirements. Nor did the shift of 1972 unproblematically bring the education system into line with the needs of the dominant classes. It prepared the way for the revolt of 1976.

The state educational system is a contested field of social relations, in which conflicting social forces are embodied. There was no *absolute* necessity that state education policy would change in the early 70s in a way beneficial to the leading sectors of capital. This consequence was the result of a political struggle waged by capital to assert its interests inside the state. Without this struggle the reorganisation could have taken other forms. The state only responded to capital's interests to the extent that capital was able to organise cultural, ideological and political interventions. A powerful campaign by business interests and a changed composition of the NP's social basis made a victory for capital possible. However, the outcome was not guaranteed.

The lack of viability of the BED's internal financial structure was a major impetus toward restructuring education policy. This problem had a dynamic of its own, which cannot be reduced to a reflection of external social forces. If the state had been adequately able to finance the BED's activities within the existing financial-administrative structure, it is doubtful the pressure toward change would have been so acute.

The specific interests and nature of the bureaucracy go some way to explain the earlier insistence of the bureaucracy on pursuing policies that varied with capital's needs. Following the NP's 1948 victory, the civil service had been reforged to pursue the interests of the NP's alliance of Afrikaner workers, petit-bourgeoisie and agriculturalists. It was therefore unresponsive to the needs of big business. Bureaucracy flourished, on the basis of and in pursuit of, apartheid policy. Monopoly capital had virtually no access to the levers of power in the state. There is thus no reason to expect bureaucrats would have been particularly amenable to capitalist interests.

Bantu Education policy cannot be seen as simply reproducing unskilled labour. State policy was directed toward reproducing different forms of labour at different times. In the early 70s, there was a major attempt to reorientate the system toward the reproduction of skilled labour. The shortages of educated employees facing industry and commerce had become acute for industrialists. They began putting public pressure on the state to change its restrictive policies toward urban secondary and technical education.

This process was helped by the way in which, during the 60s, liberal groups developed a critique of state education policy as an obstacle to economic development. They argued that educational reform could help contain political conflict. These themes of liberal thought were deployed by commerce and industry in their attack on state policy. After some resistance, the state did change its orientation.

Two factors were particularly important in the state's eventual shift in policy.

First, the rising influence of Afrikaner industrialists in the NP created a greater degree of flexibility in the carrying out of apartheid policy. The NP still aimed at full apartheid in the long term. However, the economic difficulties that these policies presented soon became apparent. Shortages of skilled labour and the slowing of industrial growth threatened. The NP was prepared to make short-term, pragmatic policy adaptations in the interests of industry and commerce.

Second, the internal organisation of the BED had reached a point of critical difficulty. The state's commitment to Verwoerd's 'R13 million plus four-fifths of black taxation' formula for spending on schools had hamstrung the BED. Policies pursued before 1972 could not be funded on such a budget. The state was having to make loans to the BED to prevent it going bankrupt. Clearly a re-organisation was needed. The result of these pressures was that from 1972, the state did allow the expansion of urban secondary and technical education. It began to fund the BED directly from revenue, thus raising the amount available for black education considerably. The state also began to push private sector initiative in education, while capital became active in the funding of educational projects. However, far from helping to stabilise the educational arena, the rapid urban school expansion made the Bantu Education system increasingly unstable.

Political Struggles around Education Policy: 1968 to 1971

Between 1968 and 1971 a policy conflict between important sections of capital and the state, and within the NP political leadership, became inevitable. This conflict was resolved through an overhaul of education policy. The state brought education into a far closer alignment with the needs of urban industrial capital. It expanded urban secondary and technical education provision, thus producing a far greater range of types of labour.

The course of the conflict can briefly be outlined as follows. During the boom of the 60s, industry showed little interest in criticising government education policy. The economic conditions of the time were buoyant. Shortages of skilled and clerical labour could be borne. Educational matters were only addressed by two significant groupings within white politics. The first were liberals – the Progressive Party (PP), the SAIRR and others. They placed a great deal of emphasis on education for blacks as part of a long-term political aim of gradual change and improvement in economic opportunity. The others were the UP-controlled white municipalities, notably Johannesburg. The UP was generally moribund on the education issue. However, the municipalities it controlled were up against the practical problem of directing the reproduction process of the working class within their areas. They found the resources the state allowed them for school provision were inadequate for this role. They therefore fought a long battle with government for greater resources in African education.

When the main wave of the boom of the 60s came to an end in 1968, industry rapidly came to feel the consequences of the prevailing educational order. The recession allowed further concentration of capital to take place. Now, with monopoly conditions totally dominant in industry, the need for the technical and clerical staff became more acute. Given the change in the economic climate, efficiency became a pressing concern for capital. By 1971, organised business began to take up the educational themes that had been advanced by ideologists and politicians associated with the liberal and municipal educational lobbies. Industry and commerce began to make a major pitch for new policies to develop urban black education. This was particularly so at the secondary and technical levels.

This shift in stance coincided with certain developments inside the NP. As Afrikaner capitalist interests had become stronger during the 60s, the wing of the NP sympathetic to a pragmatic adaptation of policy to industrialists' needs became stronger. There was opposition from this wing to some of the NP government's more spectacular attempts to undermine the existence of the urban working class. This development gave rise to the 'verligte-verkrampte' division in NP ranks. Business interests, the urban middle class and Cape agriculture were broadly on one side; conservative intellectuals, the lower middle and working classes, and northern agriculture on the other. The Vorster leadership largely succeeded in straddling these diverse interests. However, by about 1972, Vorster's policy tilted in favour of the 'verligtes'. Although its political ideology remained based on the ideas of classical apartheid, there was a limited shift. There was greater accommodation of the long-term reality of an urban working class and the expression of this in policy development. In education this resulted in a considerable expansion of funding, especially for urban education. This meant better technical and secondary provision in the urban areas. Close co-operation on these issues developed between capital and the state. The education system remained that of classic Bantu Education. However, there was, within that framework, a greater degree of articulation with the reproductive process necessary to a successful capitalist economy.

Liberal Pressure and Education

During the period from the mid-1960s to 1971 most public pressure for change in state education policy came from liberals. These included the PP, the SAIRR, journalists on the *Rand Daily Mail, The Star* and others newspapers. Education was seen as a gradualist strategy for change. Liberals felt trapped between submission to a juggernaut state on the one hand, and the equally unpalatable option of a revolutionary attack on it on the other.

The mid- and late 60s saw rising levels of liberal activism on educational issues. The English press played a prominent role in criticising government education policy. *The Star* and the *Rand Daily Mail* criticised the low level of spending on black education. They also criticised the lack of secondary education and skill training. There was also some vocal criticism from such bodies as the Witwatersrand Council of Education, and a constant flow of critical statements and analysis from the SAIRR. One of the most important initiatives was the 1961 Education Panel (EP). This body was dominated by the English-language universities and by Anglophone educationists, with a few representatives of major capitalist concerns. The EP's second report, published by the Witwatersrand University Press in 1966, focused on the economic implications of the government's educational policies. The report's message was twofold. Unless there was a liberalisation of racial restrictions and more skills training for blacks, the shortage of skilled labour would increase and economic growth would be threatened. The panel called for big increases in expenditure on black education and teacher training. It also advocated an end to school fees. The panel's liberalism, however, had its limits. It believed 'teachers should be of the same cultural group as their pupils.' The exception? It was considered advisable to use 'Coloured' teachers in African schools, in order to raise the standard of English and Afrikaans! The EP advocated the country maintain a two-tier education system: one level was based on the 'best modern standards'. The other aimed at 'educating the balance of the population as best it can'. This was viewed as inevitable in a developing country. However, the EP argued the division should no longer be on strictly racial lines. There should be an 'advanced section' of black education, which was equal in quality to white education.

Particularly in the years around 1969 to 1971, there was a great deal of liberal activism at a local level in education. For instance, in the Eastern Cape, the SAIRR and the 'African Books Committee' engaged in energetic fund raising to buy books for black school students. A group of white school students in 1970 organised a public meeting of 800 people in Rondebosch Town Hall. This called for the issue of free books to African pupils, greater spending on education and established an 'African Scholars' Education Fund'. A body known as National Youth Action circulated a petition for the issue of free books to African pupils among young whites. It succeeded in obtaining 5 000 signatures in Natal alone. However, most sections of business and their UP political representatives, showed little interest in campaigning on these issues. Benjamin Pogrund, a *Rand Daily Mail* journalist in this era, has written of it:

> . . . the business community was in general monumentally unconcerned with the debased nature and standard of 'Bantu Education': as an illustration, trying to get money out of business people to contribute to the Rand Bursary Fund (which was backed by the *Rand Daily Mail*) to provide small scholarships to keep youngsters at school was a grinding, humiliating and largely unsuccessful battle.

John Jordi, the editor of *The Star*, commented in 1971 on the initial 'disappointing' response of business to his paper's attempt to raise money for black education: 'There are none so blind as those who cannot recognise their own self-interest.'

The UP displayed little enthusiasm for taking up the issue of black schooling. When it did, its proposals were less than sweeping. In 1970 Member of Parliament (MP) Catherine Taylor advocated compulsory education up to Standard 2. Another MP, Walter Kingwill, called for the training of blacks as motor mechanics. He argued whites could be moved up to supervisory positions. The PP was considerably more vigorous on education issues. However, with only one MP and a narrow support-base at this time, they were able to have little impact.

The Johannesburg Levy Conflict

The most important conflict over education policy in the period of the late 60s and very early 70s took place between the Johannesburg Municipality and the state. At issue was the development of schooling in Soweto. While the state sought to restrict educational growth in the city, the city council opposed this policy. There were two reasons for this conflict.

First, the city council, an entity dominated by the UP, reflected interests more in line with those of manufacturing capital.

Second, the municipality was, as a bureaucratic entity, responsible for the administration of Soweto (this being before the introduction of administration boards). It had an interest in maintaining a level of social services that could maintain the process of reproduction of the working class.

It may seem strange that the city council received little direct backing from business interests in this conflict. The council's campaign was apparently in the interests of Johannesburg-based manufacturers. The explanation is to be found in the nature of the chief issue at stake. The city council wanted to raise funds for school expansion through a large increase in the levy imposed for this purpose on township residents. The government refused to allow this increase. Now for business, such a levy was a double-edged sword. On the one hand, it would provide industrialists with labour of a higher calibre. On the other, it would raise the level of the minimum wage necessary for social reproduction of the working class, and therefore raise the wage bill. Hence the lack of enthusiasm from industry for the city council's stand.

There was a search to find funds for the financing of educational expansion in Soweto. The advisory board (from 1968 the Urban Bantu Council (UBC)), the state-established representative body for urban blacks, reached an agreement with the Johannesburg Municipality. The education levy imposed on township residents would be raised by 20 cents, from 18 to 38 cents. The proposal was by no means popular with all Soweto residents. Mr S.W. Pikoli of the Joint Soweto Residents' Committee led a campaign of denunciation against it. But there appears to be no evidence of mass opposition to the levy.

Before 1969, only the older areas of Soweto had paid the levy. The government now decided to allow municipalities to impose a 20-cent levy through the UBCs for education, which meant the new sum would be paid by all Soweto residents. The city council believed the current shortage of schools – which they put at 10 secondaries, 24 higher primaries and up to 63 lower primaries – could not be met from the levy. They would require an increase to the 38-cent sum. However, a request to the minister for this increase was refused. At the end of 1970, a major row broke out between the city council and the UBC. The city council announced that because it was R55 000 in debt on the maintenance of the Soweto schools, the money from the levy would have to be used for that purpose. With understandable exasperation, a UBC member asked:

> How are we going to tell the people who elected us that the money they are paying for extra classrooms is being used for something else?

However, members of the UBC who went with a school board delegation to Secretary Van Zyl of the BED must have found him even more unsympathetic. He merely argued that those who could not find places in Soweto schools must seek them in the homelands. In December 1970, the Johannesburg City Council met with Deputy Minister of Bantu Administration and Development Piet Koornhof, who repeated Van Zyl's argument in more diplomatic terms. Koornhof argued the government could only countenance the 38-cent levy if the extra 18 cents raised was spent on homeland education. The situation was worsened by new government restrictions on the building of higher primary schools by local authorities. As a partial sop to the municipality, this was relaxed early in 1971. Local authorities with surplus funds from lower primary construction were allowed to use them for higher primaries. By early 1971, a city council survey estimated the school shortage at 450 classrooms. Further approaches were made to the Minister of Bantu Administration and Development on the levy issue. As the year dragged on, despite some hopefulness on the part of the municipality as to a change of policy, no positive reply was received.

Business Moves on Education Policy: 1971

During 1971 big business and its allies moved decisively to a more activist stance on education, a result of the coming together of several different factors. The recession of 1968 to 1969 had forced business into a reappraisal of future strategy. It became clear the issue of the lack of black employees with suitable education and training had now come to the crunch. The concentration of capital in the monopoly sector, with its growing demand for administrative and technical staff, was stronger than ever. At the same time, liberal agitation on the issue of education had popularised the question of schooling. Ideas and criticisms on educational policy were made available to business. Furthermore, the more politically perceptive sections of business were becoming aware of the strains on the fabric of working-class life which current state policy imposed. They began to sympathise with the liberal view of education as a panacea for social and political ills.

It is important, though, that one should not take the rhetoric of 'skill shortage' which capital advanced, at face value. The shortage of skilled and clerical workers was real enough. In 1963 it had been estimated by the EP that employers needed 49 000 white apprentices at a time when there were only 23 000. Demand for black clerical labour was exploding. In the construction industry black clerical labour increased about tenfold between 1964 and 1976. But as Eddie Webster has shown in *Cast in a Racial Mould,* the basic thrust of social transformation in industry in the 60s and 70s was toward a semi-skilled proletariat.

Industry saw the skill shortage as both crisis and opportunity. It wanted not so much to replace white artisans with black artisans as to replace expensive skilled white workers as far as possible with cheaper, semi-skilled forms of black labour.

The 1966 report of the EP had identified employers' concerns when it complained that apprentice-trained artisans comprised a 'conservative and unadaptable' workforce. It also expressed the fear that the lack of training of many of the blacks who *de facto* carried out artisan work would also render them less adaptable. The model the report put forward was a workforce with a 'formal and theoretical' training, without the rigidity of those coming from an artisan tradition. The opening of more skilled work to blacks was seen as offering the possibility of saving on the wage bill. Percy Thomas, the Secretary of the Natal Chamber of Industries, argued in 1971 that artisan wages were inflated. He said newly introduced black skilled workers could not expect to receive the wages of their white counterparts.

During 1971 there was a rapid shift in the position of business toward a more engaged attitude on the question of education training. Public criticism of current education policy was voiced by Dr Frans Cronje of Netherlands Bank. B.R. Cooke, the President of the Natal Chamber of Commerce, asserted that better education and vocational and technical training for blacks would have economic benefits for capital. It would create a higher standard of living which would enlarge the domestic market. This, he argued, would bring down unit costs to an extent, which would improve South Africa's position in external markets. The Free State Chambers of Commerce Conference called for a free supply of books to students at African schools. At the annual conference of Chambers of Commerce, the Johannesburg Chamber proposed a motion calling for action to improve educational facilities for Africans. The chamber urged the establishment of vocational training centres in or near the main economic centres.

Another new phenomenon was that of substantial business donations toward educational causes, which emerged as a trend in 1971:

- Polaroid (partly because of anti-apartheid activism in its US plants) donated funds to the black education group, ASSECA;
- Reckitt and Coleman declared it would invest R100 000 in bursaries and school extra-curricular activities;
- Anglo-American donated R160 000 to the Johannesburg City Council for a junior secondary school in Soweto;
- Barlow Rand set up the CS Barlow Foundation. Its first project entailed spending R700 000 on establishing a trade school in Lebowa.

Such donations were possible because they were made to the city council or individuals, thus bypassing the BED's prohibition on gifts to schools.

At the same time, the wing of the UP most closely linked to monopoly capital, the so-called 'Young Turks' group of Harry Schwarz, began to address the issue more vigorously. It called for equal educational facilities for all ethnic groups. Schwarz urged large firms to offer low-interest loans for school buildings and demanded greater government spending, a crash programme of school building, and an intensive teacher training programme. Schwarz also convened a committee of chairpeople and managing directors of leading companies to raise money for the building of schools in Soweto.

Another initiative that gave great impetus to business involvement in education was the launching by *The Star* of its Teach Every African Child (TEACH) fund. Schwarz also appears to have been linked to this. The fund aimed to raise money to supplement the Johannesburg City Council's school-building efforts. It can partly be seen as a response to the crisis arising from the debacle over the levy increase. The campaign nicely combined altruism with more down-to-earth aims. *The Star* of 8 October 1971 said the campaign's motives were:

> Simple justice to a section of Johannesburg people whose educational institutions were starved of funds,

and

> ... the enlightened self-interest of employers whose firms will gain immensely in efficiency if their African staff are trained to be literate and responsible.

Dr R. Jordan, the President of the Chamber of Commerce, amplified the latter point in calling for support for TEACH. He said that 'basic primary and secondary education is a pre-requisite for more advanced technical and vocational training.'

Initial business response to the fund was sluggish. Len Miller, OK Bazaars' Chairperson, donated R1 500 for a classroom in January 1972, and called on his colleagues to do the same. After that, there was a rapid increase in the level of donations.

Policy Shift in the NP: 1969 to 1972

The pressure from the business community during 1971 was just one component of an array of forces pushing the Vorster administration towards accepting the continued existence of the urban black working class. An important force in bringing about such a shift was the increased strength of Afrikaner urban capitalist interests within the NP. These interests, although tied into the NP by state economic patronage and political tradition, were nevertheless increasingly experiencing the same difficulties resulting from the government's labour policies, as their Anglophone counterparts. As early as 1968, leading Afrikaner industrialists such as A.J. Wessels of Veka and Dr P. Rousseau of Sasol were publicly calling for more technical training for blacks. Simultaneously, the break-away of Dr Albert Hertzog's Herstigte Nasionale Party (HNP) from the NP in 1969, removed an important faction of the party which believed Vorster's policies involved educating Africans 'too fast' and spending too much money on black education. This enabled Vorster to move in the direction of more pragmatic policies, as 'verligtes' became ascendant in the NP and the Broederbond.

During 1970 there were strong signs of tensions over urban labour policy within the NP. In his 1970 budget speech, Dr N. Diederichs said he favoured more non-white labour being available for industries in 'white' areas. More conservative ministers vociferously denied Diedrichs had been referring to African (as opposed to 'Indian' or 'Coloured') labour. However, to contemporary observers the real import of the speech was clear. There was a shift in the rhetoric of some top NP members on labour issues toward the 'skill shortage' idea. In 1970, T.J. Gerdner, Administrator of Natal, stated in a public speech that black education and training could 'help to ease the manpower shortage'. The government's confidence in carrying through a dogmatic Verwoerdian vision of apartheid was clearly eroding.

In 1969 a bill to prevent any further acquisition of Section 10 black urban residence rights was dropped. In 1970, measures introduced to impose draconian forms of job reservation were first undermined by the conceding of extensive exemptions, and then never followed through.

The government backed down on the Physical Planning Act's restrictions on the employment of black labour in urban industry in 1971. Now the establishment of new industries in all areas except the Southern Transvaal was deregulated. Even there industries which were 'locality bound' or 'white-labour intensive' were exempted from labour controls. By late 1971, the basis had been laid for important changes in state labour and education policies.

A New State Policy Toward the Education of the Urban Working Class: 1972 to 1976

Around the beginning of 1972, government policy toward black education changed. This was part of a wider policy turn. It represented a renewed attempt to adapt to the requirements of capital for skilled and permanent urban labour. There was no break with the overall ideological rationale of Grand Apartheid. There was, however, a willingness on the part of government to accept, within that framework, the continued existence of the black urban working class. There was recognition of the need to do more to meet the reproductive needs of that class. In education this meant a greater commitment to government spending, a rationalisation of the school system and a new acceptance of urban secondary and technical education.

The decisive shift came early in 1972. The government finally accepted that spending on urban black schools would be financed from state consolidated revenue funds. It was no longer linked to black taxation. An important factor in this decision appears to have been the obvious impracticality of continuing with the existing funding formula for black education. The government had in the immediately preceding years already bent the Verwoerdian rules for spending on black education considerably.

From the late 60s, Bantu Education had been subsidised from the loan account. In 1970, in order to prevent Bantu Education's becoming hopelessly in debt to the loan account, the government contributed R17 million from the revenue account. With the 1972 decision to remove statutory controls on educational spending, the total budget of Bantu Education rose sharply. It went up from R55 million in 1970/71 to R72,1 million in 1972/73, and R97,45 million in 1973/74. The per capita expenditure ratio between white and black students began to narrow. It contracted from 18 to 1 in 1971 to 1972 to about 15 to 1 in 1975 to 1976.

The change in spending policy provided the financial basis for a considerable expansion of secondary and technical education for the urban African working class. Dr van Zyl articulated the new policy as enthusiastically as he had the old. In a 1972 statement, he stressed the need for a 'diversified system of secondary education (academic, general, technical and commercial)'. This, he said, would meet the need for 'trained middle and top manpower' in the white areas as well as the bantustans. This was a major initiative toward providing urban training facilities for black workers. The *Rand Daily Mail* of 6 February 1974 reports on the government's involvement in a scheme to establish 16 training centres in the major urban areas (half of them run by the state and half by industry). The *Eastern Province Herald* mentions favourable consideration was being given to the setting up of trade schools in the urban areas.

A shift in educational ideology now prevailed in government circles. Leading NP ideologues and technocrats like Dr S.P. du Toit Viljoen of the Bantu Investment Corporation used the rhetoric of skill shortage to support the development of the skill centre programme. TEACH was publicly praised by Deputy Minister Punt Janson, Dawie de Villiers, MP, and even by Dr van Zyl himself.

In the Johannesburg-Soweto area, the policy change had a dramatic impact. At last the 38-cent levy was granted, coming into effect in August 1972. *The Star* of 15 March 1972 reported that the government had given the Johannesburg City Council the go-ahead for a programme to build 500 classrooms at a cost of about R1 million. A follow-up story in the *Rand Daily Mail* of 11 April 1972 reported that the city council received the first R250 000 of this as a government loan to be paid off at six per cent a year.

During the subsequent year, the pace of school building increased rapidly. The housing section of the city's Non-European Affairs Department had to double the number of its employees. By mid-1974 there were 40 new schools in Soweto. Half of these had been financed by TEACH. This suggests the Johannesburg Municipality had to rely much more heavily on the private sector than originally envisaged. The new policies on urban training were reflected in the opening of two new industrial training centres in Soweto in 1975. In 1974 urban teacher training was reintroduced in Johannesburg when 70 student teachers enrolled at Jabulani Technical College.

The Growth of Private-Sector Educational Intervention

State educational policy changes unleashed a virtual stampede of industrial participation in educational projects. It made more sense to industry to put money into education now that the state was prepared to produce the clerical and technical workers needed by enterprises. The period 1972 to 1973 saw increasingly substantial employer involvement in attempts to upgrade the education system. Examples include the following:

- General Motors began to provide free school books for children of employees;
- South African Breweries announced it would donate R100 000 to black education over a three-year period;
- the sugar industry put R25 000 into its bursary fund;
- Associated British Foods and Twins Pharmaceutical Holdings each donated R25 000 to TEACH;
- Mobil Oil gave the KwaZulu authorities R50 000 for technical training;
- the Stellenbosch Farmers' Winery sank R25 000 into the establishment of an education fund;
- an electrical company provided R25 000 for a school in Daveyton;
- the Elandsfontein Industrialists' Association donated R50 000 to education in Tembisa.

The industrial unrest of 1973 raised the intensity of employer concern about the inadequacy of the education system. Concern increasingly centred on two issues.

These were the political implications of a failing urban educational system and the need for technical and clerical workers. Spokespeople for commerce and industry presented lack of educational opportunity as a grievance which had given rise to the strike wave. They argued that moves to improve the education system would quieten the political situation. In this way, the liberal conception of educational change as an alternative to political change began to infuse business thinking. For capital, education was an alternative to worker power and independent trade unionism. Not unnaturally Durban, the centre of the strike wave, produced some of the most vigorous activism from business leaders along these lines. The statements of the Durban Chamber of Commerce reflected the feelings of a business community which had been deeply shaken. In May 1973, Walter Lulofs, the outgoing President of the Chamber, was reported in the *Natal Mercury* as telling the Chamber's annual conference that a 'radical rethink' of the country's educational policy was necessary. He asserted neglect of

African education was a cause of worker discontent. Unless action was taken, Lulofs argued, a 'national emergency' would result. Rev. A. Hedgeson, of the Bureau of Literacy and Literature, noted in 1974 that labour unrest had created pressure on employers to address the problems of 'improving relationships' and the training of blacks.

Concern with the technical and clerical training issue was reflected in far more concrete thinking by spokespeople for industry on what problems they faced in this regard. Lulofs pointed out that inadequate basic education would undermine the success of technical training schemes. This theme was enthusiastically taken up by *The Star*. The newspaper solicited donations from industry and commerce to its TEACH scheme. It argued it was in the interest of employers to ensure that 'in 10 years they will be able to call on a more educated – and therefore a more "trainable" workforce.'

One of the clearest projects to link school education with technical training was that of Consolidated Gold Fields, which gave R186 000 to TEACH for junior secondary schools. These were planned to be sited next to the industrial training centres, so that pupils could be taken to the centres for technical courses. In the field of clerical labour, there was growing concern as well about the need for facilities to translate the general skills learnt at school into specific office skills. A sub-committee meeting of the Johannesburg Chamber of Commerce in February 1975 discussed a plan to establish a commercial college in Soweto. Members were concerned about the need to train black 'cashiers, clerks, secretaries', 'the young person with a Junior Certificate interested in clerical work' and 'bank clerks in Soweto'.

To a considerable extent industry and commerce's inability to assert their interests within the state during the 60s had left them with a backlog of difficulties in the field of labour reproduction. This was not easy to solve, even in the context of a more receptive policy on the part of government. The NP leadership now shared industry's skill-shortage fears. It endeavoured to provide a more extensive basis for the reproduction of the urban working class. However, it did not see the issue of urban education's explosive possibilities in the way that Lulofs dimly but accurately did.

Initially, aspects of the new policies were well received by black urban communities. State acceptance of secondary school expansion in the townships removed the pressure on urban parents to send their older children to school in the rural areas. As one interviewee put it:

> The community felt this was a good idea in the sense that they did not necessarily now have to send . . . their children . . . to boarding schools outside, and pay a lot of money. The children could live at home, and go to school daily.

The expansion of urban specialised facilities, especially technical training and teacher training, evoked some positive responses as well. A teacher claims:

> Particularly technical training was accepted open handedly by the black because it was something they had not had before. The expansion of education in general was welcomed by most blacks as a step in the right direction.

Yet the restructuring did little to defuse, and much to increase, the tensions in the educational system. An enormous amount of distrust of state education policy had been built up by urban peoples' experiences of the previous decade. According to one teacher: 'there were still suspicions . . . the coming of these [changes], did not really mean a clear benefit.'

What is more, the re-organisation of schooling taking place would put great pressure on the school system and build up new social tensions.

Bibliography

Oral History
Interviews with Teachers. Nos 8, 10, 17–18.

Official publications
Hansard. Vols 2, 4 1977.
South African Statistics. Pretoria, Central Statistical Services, 1982.

Newspapers and Periodicals
Cape Argus. 9 September 1970, 19 June 1972.
Cape Times. 14 August 1970.
Daily Dispatch. 3 May 1969, 18 March 1971.
Eastern Province Herald. 20 January 1972, 20 July 1972, 1 December 1972, 17 August 1974, 30 September 1974.
Evening Post. 12 July 1969.
Journal of Southern African Studies. Vol. 10 No. 2, April 1984. (Charney, C. 'Class Conflict and the National Party Split').
Natal Mercury. 13 February 1971, 25 February 1971, 24 September 1971, 16 October 1971, 9 May 1973, 18 June 1973.
Race Relations News. Johannesburg, SAIRR, 1964.
Rand Daily Mail. 28 January 1966, 22 September 1967, 30 May 1968, 17 January 1969, 30 January 1969, 9 March 1970, 2 June 1970, 31 October 1970, 5 November 1970, 8 December 1970, 22 January 1971, 27 January 1971, 24 February 1971, 25 February 1971, 18 March 1971, 30

June 1971, 31 August 1971, 19 October 1971, 2 February 1972, 11 April 1972, 22 April 1972, 6 July 1972, 17 March 1973, 6 November 1973, 7 November 1973, 6 February 1974.

SAIRR Race Relations Survey. Johannesburg, SAIRR, 1973.

South African Labour Bulletin. Vol. 10 No. 3, December 1984. (Hyslop, J. and Tomlinson, R. 'Industrial Decentralisation and the "New Dispensation"').

Sunday Times. 6 September 1970.

The Friend. 12 March 1971.

The Star. 3 June 1964, 3 December 1964, 25 March 1966, 9 November 1966, 18 January 1968, 29 January 1968, 18 April 1968, 2 November 1968, 10 February 1969, 19 June 1970, 4 August 1970, 13 May 1969, 28 February 1970, 2 November 1970, 17 November 1970, 18 May 1971, 30 June 1971, 7 October 1971, 8 October 1971, 13 October 1971, 9 December 1971, 15 June 1973, 1 November 1973, 13 August 1974, 15 August 1974.

Transvaler. 14 August 1975.

Vaderland. 14 August 1975.

Weekly Mail. 20 December 1985.

Theses and Papers

Johannesburg Chamber of Commerce. 'Ad-Hoc Committee of the Non-European Affairs Committee'. Minutes, 12 February 1975. (In the author's possession.)

The 1961 Education Panel. 'Education and the South African Economy' (Second report). Johannesburg, Witwatersrand University Press, 1966.

Publications

Chisholm, L. 'Redefining Skills: Black Education in South Africa in the 1980s' in Kallaway, P. (ed). *Apartheid and Education: The Education of Black South Africans.* Johannesburg, Ravan Press, 1984.

Davenport, T.R.H. *South Africa: A Modern History.* Johannesburg, MacMillan, 1981.

Horrell, M. *A Decade of Bantu Education.* Johannesburg, SAIRR, 1964.

Horrell, M. *Bantu Education to 1968.* Johannesburg, SAIRR, 1968.

Kane-Berman, J. *South Africa: The Method in the Madness.* London, Pluto, 1979.

Webster, E. *Cast in a Racial Mould: Labour Process and Trade Unionism in the Foundries.* Johannesburg, Ravan Press, 1985.

CHAPTER EIGHT

Student Revolt: 1972 to 1976

This chapter sets out to explain the origins of the school student uprising of 1976.

The changes in education policy described in the previous chapter created conditions that sharpened school students' sense of common identity and grievance. The period leading to the 1976 revolt saw significant changes in urban black youth sub-culture. These changes helped produce a new political culture among young people. This provided the basis for a potentially transformative challenge to Bantu Education.

The state, by rapidly expanding the urban secondary school population from 1972, inadvertently caused the growth of a highly politically combustible social force. This was intensified by a badly managed re-organisation of schools' year-structure from the beginning of 1976. These changes created intensified discontent between urban pupils and teachers.

This structurally overstretched school system began to encounter a rising ideological challenge from the youth.

One important political influence was Black Consciousness (BC), which emerged out of black university campuses in the late 60s. BC spread into the schools through young teachers, providing school students with new political ideas. Students were receptive to these influences for several reasons. There was discontent over school over-crowding. The changing political situation made the state look more threatened than it had in the 60s. There was growing economic uncertainty as the boom of the 60s tailed off. The rising influence of BC reduced the political influence of conservative black elites in the educational sphere.

The events that triggered the uprising of 1976 were another effect of the restructuring in education. Conservatives within the BED reacted against the pragmatic policies of the 70s. Their attempt to enforce the teaching of Afrikaans was a reaction against what this wing of the bureaucracy saw as a dilution of apartheid policy. The BED refused to take any notice of the opposition that the language policy aroused from its own creatures, the school boards.

In 1976, the determination of a reactionary inspectorate to enforce this policy collided with the radical aspirations of a new generation of school students.

The Impact of Educational Restructuring

The most important result of the education policy turnabout of 1972 was the rapid expansion of the number of students in secondary schools. Previous policies had led to almost total neglect of this sector. By 1965, there were a mere 67 000 African secondary school pupils. Largely bantustan-based growth had allowed this figure to rise to 122 000 by 1970. With the new policy, secondary school enrolment soared to 389 000 by 1976. By squeezing larger numbers of older pupils into an under-resourced school system, the state generated an environment in which rebellion might grow.

Moreover, the higher level of state expenditure also allowed the continued expansion of primary education. In 1955 only 10 per cent of the African population had been school students. By 1975, 21 per cent of all African people were school students.

The injection of larger numbers of students into an educational system of limited resources led to declining educational standards. Two teachers explain their demoralisation and disaffection:

> . . . from the beginning of the '70s . . . when our classrooms in the secondary schools were becoming overcrowded . . . I noticed that there had been a remarkable change. Now, in the methods of teaching applied by the teachers in the schools . . . no longer do you find teachers marking the individual student's books or scripts. Students are told to exchange books and mark their own books . . . if you are not satisfied with that type of thing, and you still feel that you want to pile yourself with books to mark . . . you become very unpopular in the schools.

> . . . it was now obvious classes were too big . . . The teacher himself was now sick of the set up.

The strains of overcrowding and lack of resources also encouraged the use by teachers of harsh methods of corporal punishment. The resulting student resentment led to what one student described as a 'deadlock' between pupils and staff.

Part of the re-organisation of Bantu Education after 1972 was a fateful decision to change the year-structure of black schooling. The structure had traditionally comprised an eight-year primary course and a five-year secondary school course. The 1972 decision was that there was now to be a six-year primary course and a six-year secondary course. Implementation was planned for the beginning of 1976. This affected both those who had passed Standard 5 in 1975 and those who had passed Standard 6 in 1975; both groups would go into secondary school. The 1976 first-year secondary class would be at least twice the size of the class in the previous year. Applied on a small scale, and on an experimental basis, the new structure had been tried out in Soweto schools. Headmasters had found it an educational success.

However, the implementation of the policy on a mass scale would be a different story. The expansion of school building in Soweto from 1972 had taken some pressure off the schooling system. More buildings allowed the top secondary schools to specialise in teaching only the upper levels of students (Forms 4 and 5).

When the ill-planned measure of 'doubling up' was carried out at the beginning of 1976, the result was chaotic overcrowding and overstrained facilities. A teacher recalls:

> It brought about absolute confusion . . . although [the government] planned it, but they had not prepared for it . . . they didn't have ready grants for teachers to be able to cope with those numbers . . . they did not have accommodation . . .

Teachers found the change a strain because the younger classes of children promoted from primary school were not equipped to cope with secondary school work. One teacher comments: 'It had a bad effect because the kids were not ready to go to secondary school.'

There were unbearable strains on an impoverished and debilitated educational service. The bad conditions produced further disaffection among teachers and kindled a greater level of resentment among school students. Paradoxically, it was the youth's common experience of a poor quality mass schooling system that created a common sense of identity and grievance. As one teacher memorably put it: 'Bantu Education made us black.' Yet it is unlikely that this student resentment would have been sufficient to generate the basis for the 1976 uprising. More important, these developments interacted with the growth of a new political culture among urban youth.

The New Political Culture of Urban Youth

The expansion of secondary education brought a new generation into the schools. It was not just a new chronological generation, but what C. Bundy, drawing on K. Mannheim, calls a sociological generation. This is a group with its own generational consciousness. As H. Lunn has shown, the period saw the growth of a distinctively urban youth culture. Youths became relatively educated and totally urbanised. They were sympathetic to statements of black political identity. They began to differentiate out from the previously dominant, 'gangster' sub-culture of the 'mapantsula'. From the early 70s, historical process was rapidly reshaping the consciousness of this generation.

The changing internal and external situation of the regime had the effects of creating the conditions for a new outlook. The 1973 strike wave presented the state with the first oppositional mass mobilisation for more than a decade. Labour's discontent made an impact on students. A teacher comments that students:

> . . . listened to their parents talking and listened to how their parents are treated by their employers, and became aware that their parents are underpaid and therefore are unable to afford the bare necessities that the children require. I think that's one of the most important things that influence the children politically.

The period also saw the fall of Portuguese colonialism in Angola and Mozambique. South African military intervention in Angola had failed. There was guerrilla warfare in Zimbabwe and Namibia. These events placed the South African state, which had seemed so invulnerable in the 60s, under pressure. It was isolated and could be challenged.

The political thinking of urban school students about their own ability to affect the course of events began to change. One student wrote in a study conducted by L. Maree at a Soweto High School in April 1975: 'Riots are now going to occur. We are going to event things for ourselves [sic].'

The rapid expansion of the job market that had taken place in the 60s slowed very considerably in the 70s. Rapid educational expansion is likely to generate unrest if, as was the case in the 70s, employment opportunities do not increase at a similar rate. Yet while the overall number of jobs was growing slowly, many more blacks than in the past were being taken on in clerical, technical, skilled and supervisory jobs. This created a volatile compound of ambition, frustration and economic fear among students. Particularly intense was the anguish of those students who had entered secondary school, but were not able to pursue their education far enough to secure the jobs they desired. These students found themselves, as a teacher puts it, 'too educated to sweep floors, but too uneducated to join management'.

The common experiences of youth provided the basis for a new outlook. These included, centrally, the experience of a segregated and inferior school system, which was increasingly resented. Economic developments created new aspirations and new fears.

These experiences created a generational consciousness. This was transformed into a political culture largely by the influence of a new ideology.

The political calm of the 60s ended with the emergence in 1969 of the university-based South African Students' Organisation (SASO). It spearheaded a new political current – Black Consciousness. BC stressed the need for blacks to reject liberal white tutelage. It called for the assertion of a black cultural identity, psychological liberation from notions of inferiority, and the unity of all blacks including 'Coloureds' and 'Indians'.

BC was weak in the organisational sphere. From 1972, its school student arm, the South African Students' Movement (SASM) was active in the schools, but it never developed really strong structures. However, the ideological content of BC had a pervasive influence on urban youth. BC views were prevalent at the time among younger teachers, especially those who had passed through the separate black universities established during the 60s. These teachers passed on their political ideas to their pupils. A teacher who graduated from the University of Zululand in the early 70s and taught on the Rand in the period from 1972 recalls how he tried to raise the political consciousness of his pupils:

> A student that got through varsity during the SASO era was so conscientised that you just get into class and really be prepared to conscientise. When the very same students reached Standards 9 or 10, they were already conscientised . . .

Another teacher who was in the profession in the early 70s recalls: 'the staff were divided into young and old – they called us [the young teachers] SASO.' Older teachers agreed in interviews that the newer generation of teachers had a powerful impact on their students:

> Children came to understand through these young men, that the battle for political rights had started long ago. Young teachers started to talk freely about the black leaders . . . it was the young teachers, and I must say, particularly from Fort Hare that brought about the revival of the political history of our people.
>
> . . . at that time the Black Consciousness movement was already strong and the teachers were from the universities, and in a way they did influence the children by making them aware of . . . the fact they were being given an inferior type of education, so certainly they played an important role in making the children conscious.

BC activists also influenced school students through publications. Members of the BC organisations wrote the texts of the magazines disseminated by SASM.

Increasingly, the influence of conservative black political groups such as ASSECA and TUATA was reduced. On the other hand, township elites became more critical in their stance toward the BED. In early 1971, ASSECA met with representatives of SASO and five other bodies to discuss the setting up of a BC organisation. The leaders of the BC current were at this time still groping towards a definition of their role. Their emphasis tended to be on the need for blacks to transform their attitudes towards themselves, and on community action, rather than on overtly political activity. It was this lack of political emphasis and stress on 'practical' projects that enabled ASSECA to co-operate with them. At a follow-up conference in August 1971, a committee was established, chaired by M.T. Moerane, to draw up a constitution for the projected organisation. However, at a third conference in December, it became clear the strata of youth and intelligentsia grouped around SASO wanted a political movement. The ASSECA delegation resisted this. Nevertheless, the majority of the other delegates backed SASO. When the Black Consciousness Movement (BCM) was founded in July 1972, it was on SASO's terms.

A similar estrangement developed between BC activists and the ATASA teachers' organisations. Conservative teacher groups increasingly lost the initiative to the young radicals. In the Transvaal, TUATA proved unable to respond to the challenge of BC. During 1972, SASO subjected the teaching profession to a stern critique for its lack of political militancy. TUATA responded defensively, declaring in a magazine editorial:

> We are not going to prejudice our case and course in order to please SASO's generals by being militant . . . We shall always criticise the Department of Bantu Education, and the Government of the day, as we always do, in a manner suitable to us, and in our own responsible way . . . SASO's attitude is bound to lead to head-on collisions . . . Why can't SASO live and let live?

TUATA was infuriated by the radicals' criticisms of the way in which it worked with the BED. It saw these attacks as undermining its status and that of the educational system. Among teachers, the influence of a younger and more radical generation began to undermine the prestige of the ATASA organisations. One of its former members comments:

> Many teachers lost confidence in the provincial organisations like TUATA as a result of the ideas of the young teachers who came into the field.

This process in turn led to conflicts between teachers and principals about how to handle the new political awareness in the schools. As one teacher puts it:

> Principals feared the spirit of Black Consciousness . . . whereas it was something exciting to the students . . . you found there was polarity

>between the teachers and the principal, because the principal feared if this would come out there would be trouble . . .

A shift in urban political attitudes was taking place, especially in urban black politics. This lessened the impact of the conservative currents which had flourished in the different circumstances of the 60s.

Conversely, those elements of the urban elite who wanted to be more politically assertive were strengthened. The school board system provides a case in point. In the early 70s, school boards and committees in urban areas became foci of protest against aspects of state educational policy.

With the rise of new oppositional politics, there was an increasing confidence on the part of urban black elites in their ability to assert themselves. In some urban areas, especially on the Rand, there was growing protest from school boards and committees about various state policies from around 1971. This is not to suggest that the boards and committees were simply transformed into some form of popular leadership. However, in certain areas they began to articulate themes contrary to those of state policy.

The first such issue around which conflict arose was the state's attempt in the early 70s to separate urban schools along ethnic or 'tribal' lines. The government wanted to establish similarly distinct school boards for different ethnic groups. In late 1971, at a meeting with BED officials, members of Soweto school boards expressed their opposition to the state's plans to re-organise the boards. They said this move would create administrative problems and generate conflict between different groups. The following year, in March, a meeting of Soweto school committee members and parents objected to the scheme to establish 'tribal' schools. Parents threatened to withdraw their children from the schools if the plan was imposed. In Alexandra township in 1973, school committees and parents met and protested about the ethnic separation of the schools. The Alexandra School Board then withdrew its instructions to principals to pursue this policy.

There were also some incidents in which school boards came to the defence of politically victimised teachers. There were two such incidents in 1972. In one, the BED ordered that Abraham Tiro, the Turfloop (University of the North) student leader (later to be assassinated in Botswana), and Edward Kubayi, who had also been expelled from Turfloop, be removed from the teaching posts they had taken in Soweto. However, the responsible school boards both refused to carry out the BED's decision. Thus by 1974 urban school boards, at any rate on the Rand, had developed a degree of autonomy from the BED.

The changed social and political environment began to create a student movement of a type never seen before. During 1974 student activity displayed its traditional pattern. Transkei schools continued to predominate as the main centres of action. There were also isolated incidents in the Orange Free State and Natal and in the older rural boarding schools. But the following year showed a striking change in the geographical and spatial location of unrest. Student action spread to the urban areas of the Eastern Cape and to urban areas outside the Cape. A number of incidents also took place in Pretoria and Mafikeng. The secondary and higher primary schools of the townships were awakening politically, for the first time developing their own autonomous tradition and repertoire of action. This represented both a break and a continuity with the history of the mission schools. A break because it was marked by a new strength, political vision and coherence of organisation. A continuity because the tradition of challenging authority relations in education through the tactics of boycott and riot were carried over into the new period.

The new-style struggles in urban day-schools were far more organised and more explicit in their aims than the actions that had been mounted in the boarding schools. One school where these new currents emerged was Thembalabantu High School at Zwelitsha. In October 1974, three students there were expelled for contributing to SASM's magazine. In May 1975, pupils presented a list of grievances to the head, who responded by expelling one of their number. The students then called a strike and held a meeting to discuss the issue. The police arrived and 140 students were arrested. A similar new combativeness was demonstrated by students at Morris Isaacson School in Soweto in September 1975. When the Security Police returned to school a student they had been interrogating, they found their way blocked by protesting students.

Another incident took place at Nathaniel Nyaluza High School, Grahamstown, during 1975. Here students clearly articulated and ferociously fought for their demands. In May they staged boycotts and demonstrations. They put forward serious complaints. The teachers, they said, were poorly qualified, had drinking problems, sexually harassed female pupils and punished students for exposing their misdeeds. There were also complaints about the conduct of the inspector, disciplinary procedures, shortages of books and the poor quality of the buildings. For the first time the serious and central problems which students experienced within Bantu Education were being articulated by them, and in action. Even more striking was the determined form of action the students took. They occupied the school buildings for two weeks. They held mass meetings to discuss progress. The teachers, who were objects of much of the students' wrath, fled the school, fearing they would be attacked. Eventually 19 of them were sacked for refusing to return to their posts. A new and tempestuous generation had arrived.

The Issue of Afrikaans

This new militancy was to be transformed into mass revolt by a particular issue – that of enforced use of Afrikaans in the school system. The BED had strongly carried out this policy from 1974. It would seem at first glance that the language policy of the mid-70s merely arose out of some reckless ideological drive to propagate Afrikaans. However, it was a by-product of the internal struggle in the NP. It was generated by a shift in the orientation of the NP leadership in the early 70s.

The language policy represented part of a reaction by the NP's right wing, and its supporters within the state administration, against that shift. The more extreme wing of the NP feared that the coming together of the NP leadership with Anglophone business interests represented a sellout of Afrikaner interests. The promotion of the use of Afrikaans was a symbol of national self-assertion. It was an attempt to test government commitment to Afrikaner identity. The policy cut across the need of students to prepare to sell their labour-power on the labour market of urban centres dominated by English-speaking concerns.

For most of the period from 1958 to 1976, the BED was quite ready to subordinate the NP ideological drive toward the promotion of Afrikaans to the needs of the labour market. The BED accepted the reality that few black teachers were fluent in Afrikaans. From the start, it formally subscribed to the policy that in secondary schools, half of the exam subjects should be taught in English and half in Afrikaans – the so-called 'fifty-fifty rule'. However, this policy was not practicable, given the small numbers of African teachers who spoke Afrikaans. The BED introduced a system under which schools were given permission to depart from the rules concerning equal use of language. During the 50s, a majority of secondary schools were granted such permission. The BED was willing to consider other factors than lack of teachers with the right linguistic abilities (such as shortage of textbooks) as a basis for exemption. In 1959 there was an attempt to tighten up on exemptions. The lack of teaching staff with the right language aptitude was declared the only basis for exemption. This rule seems to have been flexibly enforced. The language of local employers became the main determinant of which official language was used in the classroom. J. Dugard, as a senior department official, found in the 60s that African teachers in the Orange Free State and parts of the Northern Transvaal had a good grasp of Afrikaans. Those in the Cape, Natal and on the Rand did not.

In 1973, the BED moved to consolidate this tailoring of language policy to the needs of the labour market. Departmental Circular No. 2 of that year laid down that exam subjects could now be taught either purely in English or purely in Afrikaans. This policy was acceptable to both parents and students as it enabled students to study in the language that would be of most use to them in obtaining work. It reflected the new element of pragmatism and accommodation with industry in BED policy.

However, this relatively widely acceptable language policy was soon to be dramatically reversed. In the early 70s there was a political re-orientation by the NP leadership. While remaining close to the traditional political ideology of apartheid, the NP attempted a greater degree of detente with the needs of capital. This led to intensive infighting between the 'verligte' faction supporting the new orientation, and the 'verkrampte' group who represented traditional interests. In 1972, Gerrit Viljoen, a leading 'verligte', displaced the 'verkrampte' Andries Treurnicht from the leadership of the Broederbond. Subsequently, in 1974, Viljoen beat off a challenge by Treurnicht to regain the leadership. It seemed that the verligtes were clearly ascendant within the NP. However, Treurnicht rapidly emerged as the leader of a strong conservative group in the party. Prime Minister Vorster, in order to contain the dissension in the ranks, began to tilt in his public pronouncements towards the 'verkramptes', directly attacking the 'verligtes' in a 1974 speech.

In this context, right-wing NP members within the educational apparatus came to see the role of Afrikaans as an issue of symbolic political importance. The lack of assertiveness in BED policy on the use of Afrikaans was seen as part of a pattern of weak commitment to traditional NP values. This feeling emerged most clearly at the 1975 conference of the 'Federasie van Afrikaanse Kultuurverenigings' (Federation of Afrikaans Cultural Societies). The conference passed a motion calling on the government to promote Afrikaans in all possible ways to achieve its 'rightful position' in schools for blacks and Asians. Proposing the motion, Professor J.H. Senekal said there was concern about the position of Afrikaans as a language of use among black people, especially in the black urban schools. For the continued existence of Afrikaans it was important that it should become 'a language of use of the black man'. Former Minister W.A. Maree supported the motion.

The 'verkramptes' within the BED had already launched an offensive on the issue. A meeting of Transvaal inspectors in January 1974 resolved that arithmetic and social studies ought to be taught in Afrikaans. Departmental Circular No. 6 of 1974 re-asserted the need to apply the fifty-fifty rule. The Afrikaans version of the circular added the qualification 'where possible', but the English version did not. The circular stressed the need for application to be made to the secretary of the BED for any deviation from the fifty-fifty rule. It thus represented a clear policy reversal. From late 1974, there was a stricter application of the fifty-fifty rule, and a greater rate of refusal of applications for exemption. This was especially the case in the Southern Transvaal. Regional Circular No. 2 of 1974 imposed the earlier decision of the inspectors to force the teaching of maths and social studies in Afrikaans. The circular failed to draw attention to the possibility of obtaining exemption.

The policy of enforcing instruction in Afrikaans was almost universally unpopular in urban areas. It forced teachers to teach in a language in which few of them were proficient. Few pupils understood it. Here are a sample of teachers' views:

> Almost all the African teachers were never taught through the Afrikaans medium . . . and therefore could not teach . . . children.

> . . . only some of us understood Afrikaans and it was difficult for us to express ourselves, then what about to teach? . . . A lot of kids didn't even know what to do or how to write anything in Afrikaans.

ATASA was sufficiently antagonised by the policy to send a delegation to Pretoria to complain about it.

The insistence on the new policy by elements of the white inspectorate generated immense friction between the BED on the one hand, and teachers and students on the other. One headmaster speaks of:

> . . . the intransigence of the inspectors who were predominantly Afrikaners and who were not interested in the black child at all, but they were interested in the black child being Afrikanerized.

He had found the inspectorate totally unsympathetic to the fact that many teachers who had claimed to have been able to speak in Afrikaans, in order to get a post, were unable to do so. Another principal, finding that his students were making no headway in mathematics when using Afrikaans, instructed his teachers to change to English. He lobbied the BED through the school board for approval of this change. The response of the inspectors was to have him summoned to the BED to account for his deviation from departmental policy.

The new policy thus not only failed to strengthen the ideological influence of Afrikaner nationalism on blacks, but also created a new grievance in the educational sphere. This was strongly felt by teachers and students alike.

Writings on the student uprising of 1976 have generally ignored the role of the school boards in opposing the imposition of Afrikaans as a teaching medium from 1974. Yet popular opposition to the policy first manifested itself in the resistance of certain school boards. However, throughout the period from 1974 to 1976, the BED showed no inclination to listen to these views. It responded to the boards' opinions with threats or disciplinary action. The authorities wanted the boards to incorporate blacks into a sense of participation in the education system, but they were not prepared to give them decision-making powers. The BED wanted community participation in education, but only as long as the community's views coincided with its own. This approach guaranteed the failure of boards as a hegemonic structure.

Discontent about the Afrikaans policy resulted in a meeting of 91 delegates from school boards of the PWV and Western Transvaal areas, held in Atteridgeville on 21 December 1974. The tone of the meeting was relatively mild. Nevertheless, it strongly opposed the use of Afrikaans as a medium of instruction. A memorandum was drawn up demanding an end to the policy. A deputation was chosen to meet the BED on the matter. The views of the meeting were couched in terms of support for the homeland leaders' views that secondary education should be conducted in English. The meeting also supported the idea of seeking a Supreme Court injunction if the BED proved to be intractable. Some, however, did express more combative views. Mr M. Peta, a member of Atteridgeville School Board, called for a school boycott if the policy were not reversed. The very limited demand of the school boards was met with implacable opposition from the BED.

A further meeting of school boards was held in January at which 'great dissatisfaction' was expressed at the BED's refusal to compromise with the boards. However, the BED was determined to repress any opposition to its policies. A planned joint meeting of school boards at Sebokeng was later banned by the circuit inspector of Vereeniging. In Atteridgeville, the chair of the school board was sacked for his opposition to the Afrikaans policy. This provoked a school boycott. Circulars Nos 6 and 7 of 1975 were issued by the BED to firm up its position. They reaffirmed the fifty-fifty English-Afrikaans rule and forbade school boards to decide on the medium of instruction in their schools. W.C. Ackermann, the Regional Director of Bantu Education for the Southern Transvaal, told one school board, which had instructed its teachers to use English, that its grants for teachers' salaries would be cut off if it did not co-operate.

These strong-arm policies did not crack the school boards' opposition to the Afrikaans medium of instruction policy. Several school boards in Soweto persisted in instructing their teachers to use English as the sole medium. Boards in the Port Elizabeth area also took up the issue. School boards from townships there presented a joint memorandum to the inspector in the area, calling for abandonment of the fifty-fifty policy, in February 1975.

With the beginning of the 1976 school year, the conflict in Soweto deepened. On 20 January, the Meadowlands Tswana School Board met the local circuit inspector to discuss the issue. The inspector took an approach characteristic of the BED. He argued that as all direct tax paid by blacks went to homeland education, urban black education was being paid for by whites. The BED therefore had a duty to 'satisfy' white tax payers. Not surprisingly, the board members were unimpressed by this analysis. They voted unanimously for English as the medium of instruction in schools under their control. Following this, two members of the school board were dismissed by the BED. The other seven members resigned in protest.

The story of the period leading up to June 1976 is, in part, one of the refusal of the BED to listen to its own school boards.

Despite the widespread evidence of the unpopularity of the policy on Afrikaans, the NP government did not act in a way likely to reduce tension on the issue. Rather, underestimating the potential of popular opposition, it went in the opposite direction, playing to its rightist constituency. To a considerable extent Vorster's policy was one of giving the NP's right wing their head in the cultural and social sphere, while carrying out a slightly more pragmatic orientation in the economic field. As part of his attempt to placate the 'verkramptes', Vorster reassigned the notably reformist Deputy Minister of Bantu Administration and Development, Punt Janson, in 1976. He replaced him as Deputy Minister of Bantu Education with the 'verkrampte' leader, Andries Treurnicht. This clearly strengthened the hand of the extreme right within the educational bureaucracy.

Treurnicht's unshakable commitment to the hard line language policy played an important role in triggering the uprising. He relentlessly pursued the fifty-fifty policy in secondary education, despite the opposition of parents and teachers and rising student discontent. On 11 June 1976, he announced that applications to depart from the fifty-fifty rule by five Soweto schools had been rejected. He took this position even though these schools were on strike. During the parliamentary discussion he protested ignorance of a violent incident at Naledi, on which the Cillie Commission commented that it was 'hardly possible that the [Deputy] Minister would not have received the correct and full details'.

The intransigence of the BED over the Afrikaans issue provided a single political focus for the pent-up anger and frustration of school students. The new political urban youth culture began to express itself on a wider scale, and more forcefully. School students of Soweto began to revolt against the BED's policy from the beginning of 1976. The BED had opened up a situation where the students could no longer hope that mediation through township elites would resolve their problems.

The first indication of trouble in Soweto schools over the Afrikaans issue took place on 24 February. Students at Mofolo Secondary School argued with their headmaster, and he called in the police. During March the Black Peoples' Convention (BPC), SASO and SASM were active in Soweto schools on the issue. In the next month, strikes took place in schools around the sacking of three school principals by the Tswana School Board in a row related to the Afrikaans issue. Orlando West Junior School emerged as a storm centre of the crisis. On 30 April, students there went on strike against the Afrikaans medium of instruction policy. On 17 May they held another boycott over the dismissal of a member of the school board, bombarding the principal's office with stones. They drew up and presented a memorandum of their grievances to the head. By 16 May, a boycott over Afrikaans had started in Phefeni Secondary School. It then spread to Belle Higher Primary School, and on to Thulasizwe, Emthonjeni, Khulo Ngolawazi Higher Primary Schools. The involvement of higher primaries is significant because their highest form was affected by the BED's Afrikaans decree. The actions were of a militant character. They included a demonstration at Thulasizwe and at Belle, the locking out of staff and of boycott-breaking students by the militants. On 24 May, pupils rejected a call to go back to school by the Orlando-Diepkloof School Boards. The strike spread to Pimville Higher Primary. SASM moved to consolidate the situation. It held a conference at Roodepoort at the end of May that discussed the campaign against the enforced use of Afrikaans.

The explosive anger of Soweto youth is suggested by two incidents which occurred at this time. On 12 May, a woman teacher was walking to school when she was stopped by two youths who intended to rob her. She yelled for aid and more than 100 students from Orlando North Secondary School rushed to help her. They pursued the robbers, caught them and beat them to death. In another incident during May, a teacher at Pimville was stabbed by a student. When police tried to arrest the student, they were stoned by his colleagues. These events suggest a rising willingness on the part of students to define what was just for themselves, and a willingness to use force to back those conceptions.

The intensity of the Afrikaans conflict continued to mount. In early June there was fighting at Senoane Junior School and elsewhere between boycotters and students trying to return to school. On 8 June the Security Police arrived at Naledi High School and attempted to arrest the secretary of the SASM branch. Students attacked and stoned the police officers and burnt their car. The policemen had to be rescued from the principal's office by reinforcements. The next day police who returned to the school were driven off by stone-throwing pupils. The situation worsened as exams began. Students at several schools refused to write. By this time collective action was being called for. SASM convened the meetings of June, which founded the Soweto Student Representative Council (SSRC). This body then organised a mass student protest against the use of Afrikaans for 16 June.

When on that day, police and students met, the subsequent shootings by the police and the ensuing nationwide revolt by students turned South African history in a new direction.

Bibliography

Oral History
Interviews with Teachers. Nos 1, 3, 5, 7–8, 11, 13, 16–18.

Official publications
South African Statistics, 1978 and 1986. Central Statistical Services, Pretoria.
Report of the Commission of Inquiry into the Riots at Soweto and Elsewhere from the 16 June 1976 to 28 February 1977 (Chairman: Cillie, J.). Pretoria, Government Printer, 1980.
Department of Education and Training. Annual Report for 1981 and 1986. Pretoria, Government Printer, 1982 and 1987.

Newspapers and Periodicals
Daily Dispatch. 25 October 1974, 27 February 1975, 17 May 1975.
Eastern Province Herald. 24 May 1975, 27 May 1975, 10 October 1974, 19 February 1975.
Journal of Southern African Studies. Vols 10 No. 2, April 1984. (Charney, C. 'Class Conflict and the National Party Split'); 13 No. 3, April 1987. (Bundy, C. 'Street Sociology and Pavement Politics: Aspects of Youth and Student Resistance in Cape Town, 1985').
Natal Witness. 30 October 1972.
Pretoria News. 29 January 1975.

Rand Daily Mail. 11 February 1970, 30 May 1972, 20 October 1972, 31 October 1972, 15 March 1973, 10 April 1973, 6 July 1974, 23 December 1974, 13 January 1975, 29 January 1975, 15 May 1975, 27 May 1975, 13 June 1975, 23 September 1975.

SAIRR Race Relations Survey. Johannesburg, SAIRR, 1974 and 1976.

Sunday Times. 7 July 1974.

The Friend. 14 February 1975.

The Star. 2 November 1971, 11 October 1972, 23 December 1974.

Transvaler. 10 July 1975.

TUATA. August 1972, May 1973, February 1975.

Weekend Post. 22 February 1975, 24 May 1975, 21 June 1975.

Theses and Papers

Chaskalson, M. 'Apartheid with a Human Face: Punt Janson and the Origins of Reform in Township Administration, 1972–6'. African Studies Institute Paper, University of the Witwatersrand, Johannesburg, 1988.

Crankshaw, O. 'The Racial and Occupational Division of Labour in South Africa, 1969–1985'. Second Biennial Labour Studies Workshop, 31 October to 1 November 1987, University of the Witwatersrand, Johannesburg.

Lunn, H. 'Antecedents of the Music and Popular Culture of the African Post-1976 Generation'. MA Dissertation, University of the Witwatersrand, 1986.

Publications

Dugard, J. *Fragments of My Fleece.* Pietermaritzburg, Kendall and Strachan, 1985.

Gastrow, S. *Who's Who in South African Politics.* Johannesburg, Ravan Press, 1985.

Gerhart, G. *Black Power in South Africa: The Evolution of an Ideology.* Berkeley and Los Angeles, University of California Press, 1979.

Hirson, B. *Year of Fire, Year of Ash. The Soweto Revolt: Roots of a Revolution.* London, Zed Press, 1979.

Kane-Berman, J. *South Africa: The Method in the Madness.* London, Pluto, 1979.

Lodge, T. *Black Politics in South Africa Since 1945.* Johannesburg, Ravan Press, 1983.

Maree, L. 'The Hearts and Minds of the People' in Kallaway, P. (ed). *Apartheid and Education: The Education of Black South Africans.* Johannesburg, Ravan Press, 1984.

Montsitsi, S. 'Lessons from 1976' in NUSAS *Beyond the Challenge of Change.* NUSAS, 1983.

SAIRR. *South Africa in Travail: The Disturbances of 1976–7: Evidence Presented to the Cillie Commission by the Institute of Race Relations.* Johannesburg, SAIRR, 1978.

CHAPTER NINE

Beyond the Revolt:
1972 to 1987

It was ultimately urban youth who blocked forever the state's plans to build apartheid on Verwoerd's blueprint.

The 1976 to 1977 Soweto uprising, starting as it did with school-children, so harnessed mass support that it injected a new stamina into all facets of the liberation movement.

Renewed student action, in 1980 to 1981 and later in 1984 to 1987, detonated the biggest explosion of worker and community struggle the regime had ever encountered.

On every front, including education, the state's reform policy was obstructed and threatened with permanent defeat. Youth and students formed the front line of the resistance, engaging in street battles, organising mass action and mounting pickets.

The student movement can only be understood in the changing historical context. It is not enough to explain student uprisings as a form of resistance to an unchanging Bantu Education system.

By the late 60s, the Vorster government's policies were hindering industrial capital's attempts to recruit adequate numbers of black semi-skilled operatives, skilled workers and clerical employees. The regime's attempt to stifle urban black secondary education, and its prohibition of urban black technical training, created major problems for management.

Big business started to contest these policies in the early 70s. Increased pressure on the state eased up some policies. These included statutory discrimination in skilled employment and restrictions on the number of blacks in urban industry.

In 1972, in line with this 'verligte' approach, the state changed its budgetary policy in relation to urban schooling. This has been covered in great detail in earlier chapters. More money was made available for schools and private capital was encouraged to sponsor urban educational projects. Some technical training of black youth in urban areas was finally allowed. These developments were to have important social consequences.

The number of secondary school students tripled between 1970 and 1975. Yet there was no equal expansion of job opportunities. While more blacks were being employed in clerical and technical jobs, the numbers of unemployed high school drop-outs multiplied. As if those factors were not enough to create volatility, the state restructured the black school system from a 13-year to a 12-year curriculum. At the beginning of 1976, the last two years of primary school were pushed into the first year of secondary school.

The growing pressure on space at the schools, co-existed with another development. This was the growth of political consciousness within urban working-class youth culture.

The year 1969 had seen the emergence of the university-based SASO, the first of the BC organisations. The school arm of this was called SASM. Unity of black people, including 'Coloureds', and Indians became the BCM's rallying call.

The ideological content of the BCM was vital in providing a new political awareness among students. The sense that it was possible to overthrow the regime was further inspired by regional events. These included the collapse of colonialism in Mozambique and Angola and the military struggle in Zimbabwe and Namibia. At home, worker militancy and the mass strikes of 1973 provided further impetus.

Signs of the new militancy among students were first evident in late 1974 and into 1975. In 1975, the Eastern Cape branch of SASM was involved in strikes over educational grievances.

The spark which set off the explosion was the insistence on the use of Afrikaans as a medium of education, detailed in the previous chapter.

In Soweto, the first school went on strike in April 1976. The strike spread to another eight schools. On 13 June, SASM convened a delegate meeting at Naledi High School that established the SSRC. The SSRC called for a demonstration for 16 June.

The violent response with which the police met the students has been well documented. The uprising spread throughout the Southern Transvaal and later, the Cape. It is now known that thousands lost their lives to police action from June 1976. The closure of state schools by the education minister and the dropping of the Afrikaans decision failed to check the spread of the upheaval.

Resistance and boycotts at schools spilt over into an attack on the government instituted Urban Bantu Councils (UBCs), where students forced the resignation of councillors.

The boycotts only started to fizzle out in late 1977. Thousands of students had left the country to join MK. The BCM had been banned, and political exhaustion could not sustain mass resistance during that period.

The SSRC effectively ended state regulation and control over Soweto. It mobilised on broader working class issues and provided a model for students elsewhere in the country to follow.

While the influence of the BCM is undisputed, it is still unclear to what extent the ANC provided the underground inspiration for the Soweto uprising. What is known is that it was in the aftermath of the uprising that the ANC really began to link with the new political generation. Some 6 000 to 10 000 students who had left for guerrilla training or simply as refugees moved into ANC organisational structures.

The state was reeling in the period following the 1976–1977 uprising. This had as much to do with the upsurge of popular resistance as with the internal power squabbles within the NP ruling elite. Conservative proponents of traditional apartheid led by Connie Mulder were pitted against the technocratic alliance of Afrikaner business and military chiefs around P.W. Botha.

Some stop-gap measures were taken, including in the educational arena. Afrikaans as a compulsory language of instruction was dropped. Compulsory education was proposed in some areas and teacher upgrading programmes were developed. The BED became the Department of Education and Training (DET).

Student organisation meanwhile strengthened and identified its position. The Congress of South African Students (COSAS), formed in 1979, based its stance on the Freedom Charter. Another student organisation, the Azanian Students Movement (AZASM), continued to identify with the BC tradition.

The second cycle of student struggles began in February 1980 when school boycotts broke out in the 'Coloured' schools of the Western Cape. These boycotts were sparked by the student outcry at South African Defence Force (SADF) national servicemen teaching in schools. There was also a demand for free and compulsory education and a call for re-admission of barred pupils. The boycotts spread to 'Coloured' and Indian schools elsewhere in the country, and subsequently to DET schools.

The struggles of 1980 to 1981 displayed a broader degree of political participation. In the Western Cape boycotting students participated in a red meat boycott in solidarity with striking meat workers. In the Eastern Cape students also began to demand the withdrawal of police from their areas, and to reject compulsory homeland citizenship. Seventy-seven African schools were closed by the DET in this period.

It was clear the state would have to do an about-turn to address itself to the task of formulating a policy of restructuring in education. Stopgap measures would not satisfy students.

The state's reform strategy, in the era of P.W. Botha, was aimed at defusing the revolutionary potential of student and worker movements. It simultaneously catered for the needs of industry, which needed to employ more blacks at semi-skilled, skilled, clerical and managerial levels.

The first stage of reform was at the economic and market levels. In accordance with recommendations of the Riekert and Wiehahn Reports, urban residence and employment rights were extended to sections of blacks. Black trade unionism was legalised. Simultaneously, the state went all out to encourage the formation of a black business class.

The second phase of reform saw a combination of attempts at political co-option of sections of the black population. People were co-opted for bodies such as the tricameral parliament and the Regional Services Councils (RSCs). However, the might of the state – the military and the police – stayed firmly within white control.

Both stages were incorporated into Broederbonder Professor J.P. de Lange's report on the reform strategy for education. De Lange's proposals, which dovetailed with Botha's 'Total Strategy', were aimed at reducing racial differentials but intensifying class ones. It thus formed a central component of state reform strategy.

De Lange wanted a more class-stratified schooling system but equal education for all ethnic groups. He proposed free and compulsory primary schooling with two streams at secondary level – a vocational stream subsidised by industry and an academic stream subsidised by parents. Tertiary education would also be integrated and have a greater technical component.

During the 1980s the DET budget increased massively: from R143 million in 1978/79 to R709 million in 1984/85. The state, in 1984, spent seven times more on white children than on black. An appalling discrepancy, although in sharp contrast to the situation in 1970 when the ratio was 18 to one.

The number of African secondary school pupils increased from under 600 000 in 1980 to more than one million in 1984. The same year saw a dramatic increase in the number of school buildings being built and conversion of a number of schools into technical schools. These developments occurred within urban areas and the bantustans. In Bophuthatswana, 15 new technical institutions were set up from 1977 to 1982.

Employers who did in-service training were granted huge tax breaks.

Private schools could get subsidies and the statutory racial restrictions on entrance to them and to universities were allowed to lapse. However, De Lange's agenda was denied legitimacy by students.

A second form of opposition came from within the NP. The NP was then divided into pro- and anti-reform camps and ultimately experienced the breakaway of the Conservative Party (CP).

When the White Paper on education was published in November 1983, it emerged that some of De Lange's proposals were refused. Christian National ideology was emphasised. A single education ministry was rejected.

The same year both COSAS and AZASM got a boost from two new legal political fronts. COSAS became the school wing of the United Democratic Front (UDF), while AZASM was drawn into the National Forum (NF).

In 1984, boycotts began anew, initially because of the 1983 matriculation examination. There are several written accounts detailing the poor and corrupt administration of this examination. Pass rates had dropped sharply between 1980 to 1983, leading to suspicions that the authorities were trying to limit the number of high school graduates.

Students at one school in Atteridgeville, Pretoria, found unmarked scripts from the previous year in their school – after the marks had been published. COSAS took up the matric question as well as several other student demands: an end to sexual harassment, scrapping of the age limits enforced in schools and an end to corporal punishment. COSAS also launched a system of Student Representative Councils.

The initial boycotts started in Atteridgeville and at Cradock in the Eastern Cape. The Cradock boycott began when a popular headmaster, Matthew Goniwe, was transferred from Cradock to a neighbouring town, Graaff-Reinet. During the boycott Goniwe was detained. Graaff-Reinet students joined the boycott.

Matthew Goniwe was one of four UDF activists who were later assassinated. A later inquest proved military intelligence involvement.

When the boycotts spread to the Southern Transvaal, the DET initially suggested a form of student representation including teachers, principals and official school committee members. This was rejected by teachers. From then on the DET started closing down boycotting schools.

The 1984 students' grievances had begun over local education issues. However, students could now take up issues nationally through COSAS, which had grown into a mass movement. In this way short-term demands could be linked to national political issues.

Student activists took the initiative, during 1983 and 1984, to found the 'youth congresses' among mainly unemployed young blacks in the townships.

Between August 1984 and December 1985 youth became the shock troops in a battle for control of the township streets. The issue at stake initially was the state's elections for the 'Coloured' and Indian houses of the tricameral parliament. Both COSAS and NF student organisations set up school boycotts as part of a wider boycott of the elections. About 800 000 students, mostly from 'Coloured' schools, participated in the boycott of the election for the 'Coloured' chamber on 22 August.

These boycotts did not last in most areas. However, in the Vaal Triangle police killings and subsequent rioting transformed school boycotts into a leading part of a national political struggle. More than 200 000 students in the Vaal Triangle joined the boycott, which gained momentum nationally in September and October. The state's response was to close down boycotting schools.

A new development was the support activities by community, trade union and political organisations for the students. Joint planning bodies, embracing COSAS, community organisations and major trade unions found a model in the township of KwaThema on 22 October in support of school students' demands. This planning group called a Southern Transvaal stay-away which supported student demands, including establishment of SRCs. They also raised wider economic demands, such as an end to rent and bus-fare increases and called for the withdrawal of the army from the townships. When the stay-away took place on 5 to 6 November 1984, about 400 000 students from more than 300 schools and anything between 300 000 and 800 000 workers participated.

Similar joint planning bodies in other areas did not always run as smoothly. In numerous cases there was antagonism between students and workers when students tried to railroad workers into giving specific forms of support.

When the student boycotts continued to spread through the entire country in the remainder of 1985, the state tried to quell the boycotts by force. In July, a state of emergency was declared in regions of the Eastern Cape, Southern Transvaal and Northern Free State. COSAS was banned and large numbers of COSAS members were arrested.

The emergency sparked off the outbreak of student protest in the Western Cape, which had been politically quiet except for the demonstrations around the 'Coloured' elections. A month after the emergency, there were boycotts at schools controlled by the ('Coloured') Department of Education and Culture and the DET. Three months of fighting between students and police, mass rallies, consumer boycotts and harsh repression followed. Students elected a strong co-ordinating body, the Western Cape Student Action Committee (WECSAC), which led their campaign.

The DET tried to close down the schools in early September, but students responded with a mass occupation of schools on 17 September. At the peak of student rebellion, the government imposed a state of emergency in the Western Cape at the end of October.

During 1985 it became clear students' demands had shifted from specific educational demands to broad political ones. Demands included withdrawal of troops from the townships and the release of detainees.

Student rallies featured songs of praise to Mandela, Tambo and the ANC's armed wing, MK. Student political culture increasingly expressed allegiance to the ANC. Clashes with police became frequent, as youths tried to barricade streets and police tried to break up student meetings.

Some student militants enforced the boycotts by mounting pickets at school gates or bus stops. The state attempted, during 1985–86, to supplement repression with boosting expenditure on black education each year, in line with the De Lange strategy.

A new structure was set up by government to co-ordinate educational restructuring – the Ministry of National Education. It took on the role of co-ordinating educational policy and developing uniform administrative policies.

However, the DET – or 'Bantu Education' as it was always known – had lost any shred of legitimacy. No amount of money tossed in by the state could buy credibility among the students, who were thoroughly aware of the limitations of the changes. White schooling was still far better funded; black teachers remained inadequately trained; the new administrative structure stopped well short of a single education system. Students saw the education system as just one aspect of their experience as oppressed people. They sought radical transformation of society.

But the students had a millenarian expectation that the transformation would come overnight. This outlook has been described as 'immediatism', and led to the popularising of slogans such as 'Liberation Now, Education Later'. Assuming that revolution was imminent, some students began to view any return to school as a betrayal. Boycotts became a principle rather than a tactic. By the end of the year, students were making calls for 1986 to be 'The Year of No Schooling'.

Students out of school could not be organised; there was also · tension between the 'immediatists' and those who wanted to return to school.

Problems also arose in areas where students tried to whip up support for community initiatives. In some instances there were rifts between students and teachers; the former often regarded the latter as 'sell-outs'. This rift was not entirely mended by the formation in 1985 of the National Education Union of South Africa (NEUSA) which organised younger, more radical teachers. The more cautious, older teacher kept up their membership of the conservative ATASA.

There was a fear by many of the older generation that student militancy would fragment, rather than cement, their community. This was particularly the case when students took it upon themselves to avenge the death of fellow students. Often the guilt of those attacked was open to question. Students' actions had the effect of terrorising the community rather than creating an alternative form of justice.

Several violent incidents illustrated the dangers present in an excessively amorphous movement of township youth. In August 1985, a march called by boycotting students in Durban's Inanda area attacked Indian-owned housing and shops. In the last third of 1985, violent clashes took place constantly between student supporters of the UDF and the NF. People seen to have the 'wrong line' were constantly accused of being 'police agents'.

By the end of 1985, urban black education had totally collapsed. Out of 25 584 DET matric class students in 'white areas', only 10 523 wrote the final examination and less than half passed. (In the bantustans, with the exception of the Transkei, students were largely unaffected by the student movement.)

The fear that rural-urban divisions would be entrenched and that incidents of violence could affect the entire movement, were averted with the rise of a new organisation in 1985 to 1986. The National Education Crisis Committee (NECC) with its strategy of 'People's Education' would save the student movement from devouring itself.

Although there were organisations like the Parent-Teacher-Student' Associations (PTSAs) in the Western Cape, the beginnings of a national response emerged in Soweto in late 1986. In October the Soweto Civic Association convened a mass meeting of parents. From this meeting came the formation of the Soweto Parents' Crisis Committee (SPCC). Its mandate was to negotiate with the DET on the issues of postponement of the end-of-year exams and the withdrawal of troops from the townships.

As parents became aware students were preparing a 'Year of No Schooling', they rallied to the SPCC. This body worked hard at roping in teachers too – not just those from NEUSA but also the ATASA teachers.

Although it improved community-student relations, the SPCC needed to make an impact nationally. This was important if it was to address the situation properly and to provide an alternative to the 'Liberation before Education' attitude. The SPCC called a National Education Crisis Conference at the end of December. (During Christmas 1985 an SPCC delegation visited Harare for discussions with the ANC.) The conference, which took place at the University of the Witwatersrand on 28 and 29 December 1985, spelt out that the ANC did not support an indefinite boycott until liberation.

'People's Education for People's Power' became the new slogan after the ANC intervention. It meant that those in the educational struggle should try to impose their priorities on the state schools rather than opt out of them.

Crisis committees, under the umbrella of the NECC, were set up throughout the country. These committees created a network of PTSAs, which formed an alternative educational authority, challenging state control of education and holding mass meetings far and wide. Students agreed to return to school on 28 January rather than the official opening date of 8 January. The state was given three months to respond to a set of educational and political demands. COSAS was to be legalised, the emergency was to be ended, detainees were to be released.

The NECC succeeded in breaking the grip of 'immediatism' and also inspired ATASA to withdraw from state education bodies and begin to support political calls to action. At the end of March 1986, the NECC consolidated its progress with a conference in Durban. The event began with a clash between Inkatha Freedom Party (IFP) vigilantes, who had gatecrashed the conference, and delegates. It ended with the decision to continue to return to school even though the state had not delivered on the three demands. However, while the NECC's return to school held nationally, it crumbled in some areas. The boycott continued in the Durban region, in the Southern Transvaal, and parts of the Northern and Eastern Transvaal.

A contributory factor in the confusion was the poor relationship between the UDF and the NF. The latter made independent calls for mass action of different dates from those put forward by the NECC. Within the bantustans, homeland education departments refused to talk to the NECC. Vigilantes in KwaNdebele and KwaZulu unleashed their wrath on students.

The double messages from the state about how it would respond to the NECC's demands reflected, once again, the debate raging within the NP on the way ahead. The securocrats insisted order had to be restored before reform could continue. Others favoured a combination of force with practical changes in policy that could generate some support for the regime.

During the early part of the year the NECC was able to negotiate with Deputy Minister Sam de Beer, a leading light in the conciliatory faction. A number of government leaders dropped hints that a degree of change in education policy was possible. However, around April, the hardliners seem to have won the battle in the cabinet. Negotiations were refused, NECC officials were arrested on a wide scale, and the government declared a national state of emergency in June.

The schools, which were on holiday at the time, had their reopening delayed until mid-July. Government announced all students would have to re-register and would be issued with identification, and that other new security measures would be introduced at schools. This led to renewed boycott activity in Southern Transvaal, where returning students burnt their new ID cards. In the Eastern Cape many students refused to register.

Once again clashes between students and police became the order of the day. More than 300 000 students who refused to register were excluded from school. The DET closed some 73 boycotting schools.

The NECC still succeeded in convincing the majority of students to organise themselves within the schools rather than move back to indefinite boycotts. Through the concept of 'People's Education' they persuaded students to see the school system as an arena of struggle. They encouraged students to write their end-of-year exams and rejected the actions of groups of youths who attacked examinees. Despite the difficult circumstances, students in some parts of the country battled to continue with the construction of PTSAs.

A vindication of the NECC's approach came at the beginning of the next school year, in January 1987. Despite various state measures that were introduced to ban people's education activities, students engaged in a disciplined return to school.

It was largely through the NECC that the rift between community and students was healed, and that students were able to get a practical political perspective.

Ten years later, South Africa finally has one education ministry trying to consolidate 13 systems of education into one national programme.

But 16 June 1996 – 20 years after the Soweto uprising – was a sad reminder of the legacy of Bantu Education.

Several newspapers marked 16 June with interviews with some of the original 'revolutionaries' who stood trial as leaders of the student uprising. Otherwise the news was not good.

For months racial tension had simmered at a school in Potgietersrus.

Right-wing white parents refused to send their children to school with black children. After a protracted legal battle, the white parents were ruled out of order, but racial violence then broke out.

The South African Broadcasting Corporation (SABC) carried a report about the Cape Flats, where a large class of children was being taught in a bottlestore, because there was no building for them.

Journalist Amma Oman of the *Sunday Independent* interviewed students from 1976. Majakatha Mokoena, now a prominent business-man, returned to his old school in Soweto. He discovered the syllabus hadn't changed in 20 years.

But one would have to look hard to find a more disillusioned voice than that of Sandile Mamela. Writing in *City Press*, he said: 'Whatever promises of a better life 16 June might have aroused in the townships, today it is mocked by a prevalence of violence, lawlessness, lack of discipline and family breakdown.'

Bibliography

Newspapers and Periodicals

Africa Perspective. Spring 1980. (Levin, R., 'Black Education, Class Struggle and the Dynamics of Change in South Africa' and Bird, A. 'Black Adult Night School Movements on the Witwatersrand 1920–1980'); No. 24, 1984. (De Clerq, F. 'Education and Training in the Homelands: A Separate Development? A Case Study of Bophuthatswana').

Cape Times. 2 November 1985.

City Press. 6 October 1985, 17 November 1985, 8 December 1985, 20 July 1986, 16 June 1996.

Die Suid Afrikaan. Spring–Summer 1987. (Zille, H. 'People's Education: A Lost Opportunity').

Eastern Province Herald. 16 March 1985.

Frontline. March 1981 (Pottinger, B., 'The Eastern Cape Boycotts: Where Crisis Has Become a Way of Life').

Indicator. January 1984 (Hartshorne, K. 'Can Separate Mean Equal? A Commentary on the White Paper on Education'); Vol. 2 No. 4, January 1985 ('A Chronology of Township Unrest'); Vol. 4 No. 2, Spring 1986 (Bot, M. 'The Future of African Education: Two Opposing Strategies' and Hartshorne, K. 'African Matric Results: The Disintegration of Urban Education').

Journal of Southern African Studies. Vol. 7 No. 1, October 1980 (Southall, R. 'African Capitalism in Contemporary South Africa'); Vol. 13 No. 3, April

1987 (Bundy, C. 'Street Sociology and Pavement Politics: Aspects of Youth/Student Resistance in Cape Town 1985').

Leadership. Vol. 5 No. 5, 1986 (Hartshorne, K. 'Back to Basics').

New Society. 10 January 1986 (Bundy, C. 'Schools and Revolution').

Rand Daily Mail. 25 April 1985.

Reality. September 1986 (Anon. 'Political Conflict and Civil Unrest in African Townships in Natal').

SAIRR Topical Briefing. (Shindler, J. 'African Matric Results 1955 to 1983'). Johannesburg, SAIRR, 1984.

SAIRR Race Relations Survey. Johannesburg, SAIRR. 1985 and 1986.

Sash. Vol. 27 No. 4 February 1985 (Brown, V. 'Our Debt to DET?'); Vol. 29 No. 2 August 1986 (Yarwitch, Joanne. 'Kwandebele – a Rural Trojan Horse').

SASPU Focus. Vol. 3 No. 2 November 1984.

Saturday Star. 15 June 1996.

South African Labour Bulletin. Vol. 10 No. 5, March to April 1985 (Cobbett, W. et. al. 'Regionalisation, Federalism and the Reconstruction of the South African State'); No. 6, May 1985 (The Labour Monitoring Group. 'Report: The November Stay-Away').

Sowetan. 3 June 1985, 23 August 1985, 29 October 1985, 1 April 1986, 8 April 1986, 5 May 1986, 7 July 1986, 14 June 1996, 17 June 1996.

Sunday Independent. 16 June 1996.

Sunday Mirror. 12 May 1985, 26 May 1985.

Sunday Star. 24 August 1986.

Sunday Times. 16 June 1996.

The Citizen. 3 May 1985, 15 June 1996, 17 June 1996, 3 December 1986.

The Star. 5 August 1985, 7 August 1985, 10 August 1985, 14 August 1985, 23 August 1985, 29 August 1985, 13 September 1985, 17 September 1985, 18 September 1985, 16 October 1985, 7 December 1985, 17 September 1985, 14 August 1985, 7 December 1985, 30 December 1985, 6 January 1986, 7 January 1986, 8 January 1986, 31 March 1986, 14 June 1996, 17 June 1996, 25 August 1986, 21 January 1987.

Transformations. No. 1, 1986 (Sisulu, Z. 'People's Education for People's Power'. Keynote address for the Second NECC Conference).

Weekly Mail. 17 January 1986, 27 March 1986, 4 April 1986, 27 March 1986, 16 May 1986.

Theses and Papers

Davies, J. 'Politics, Schooling and Resistance in South Africa'. Unpublished Paper, 1986.

Khanyile, V. 'Speech to ASP conference in Pietermaritzburg'. Unpublished Paper, 3 December 1986.

Lunn, H. 'Antecedents of the Music and Popular Culture of the African Post-1976 Generation'. MA Dissertation, University of the Witwatersrand, 1986.

NUSAS. 'Why a National Day of Protest?' NUSAS Projects Committee Leaflet, Johannesburg, 30 May 1984.

Orkin, M. 'The Black Matric Rate: Points for Discussion'. Unpublished paper, 1985.

Publications

Alexander, N. *Sow the Wind: Contemporary Speeches*. Johannesburg, Skotaville Publishers, 1985.

Bot, M. *School Boycotts 1984: The Crisis in African Education*. Durban, Indicator Project, 1985.

Chisholm, L. and Christie, P. 'Restructuring in Education'. *South African Review 1*. Johannesburg, Ravan Press, 1983.

De Clerq, F. 'Some Recent Trends in Bophuthatswana: Commuters and Restructuring in Education'. *South African Review 2*. Johannesburg, Ravan Press, 1984.

Hirson, B. *Year of Fire, Year of Ash. The Soweto Revolt: Roots of a Revolution*. London, Zed Press, 1979.

Kane-Berman, J. *South Africa: The Method in the Madness*. London, Pluto, 1979.

Lodge, T. *Black Politics in South Africa Since 1945*. Johannesburg, Ravan Press, 1983.

Molteno, F. 'Reflections on Resistance – Aspects of the 1980 Students' Boycott', in Lawrence, M. (ed). 'Kenton-at-the-Stadt Conference Proceedings.' Mafikeng, University of Bophuthatswana, 1984.

Muller, J. 'People's Education'. *South African Review 4*. Johannesburg, Ravan Press, 1987.

Randall, P. *Little England on the Veld: The English Private School in South Africa*. Johannesburg, Ravan Press, 1982.

SPCC. *Report of National Consultative Conference on Crisis in Education*. Johannesburg, SPCC, 1986.

Swilling, M. 'Stayaways, Urban Protest and the State'. *South African Review 3*. Johannesburg, Ravan Press, 1986.

CHAPTER TEN

Conclusion

The Death of Bantu Education

In concluding, it is important to return to some issues raised earlier.

I have argued that educational systems were part of the state, a contested field of social relations. Such an approach enables us to integrate the valuable insights of reproductionist and culturalist theories, without falling into their respective over-emphases of the objective and the experiential.

I also examined in great detail the social history of African education and educational conflicts from 1940 to 1976, hopefully proving the validity of a different theoretical approach. This chapter will review how my historical study has provided support for the central propositions put forward earlier in the book. It will also suggest how my account of the period since 1976 supports the type of analysis developed here.

There was no fixed and necessary relationship between Bantu Education and capitalism, but a contingent and changing one. Reproductionists have tended to see apartheid education as fulfilling the needs of capitalism. The 'liberal' critique of apartheid has implied that state policy, including educational policy, blocked capitalist development. Yet neither of these simple, one-dimensional relationships holds consistently.

In certain periods and in certain ways, Bantu Education met the needs of capital. At other junctures, and in other ways, it obstructed capitalist development. In the 50s, by drawing urban youth into the school system and providing semi-skilled labour, state policy did answer the needs of urban capitalists for social control of the urban working class and the reproduction of the industrial labour force. The financing structure of the policy enabled it to be set up without imposing a massive tax burden on employers. During the 60s, officialdom pursued apartheid policy in a much more ideologically rigid way. The deliberate refusal of government to develop black urban secondary education ran directly against industrial capitalists' interests. A resulting lack of adequately educated employees became a major problem for industry by the end of the 60s.

It was only after a major political campaign by industry in the early 70s that government moved to remedy the situation. It expanded black urban secondary education and reintroduced urban black further education from 1972. Thus, the relation between Bantu Education and capitalism was supportive in some conjunctures and conflictual in others.

The independent interests of the bureaucracy were apparent in the campaign for Afrikaans language instruction in the 70s. This cut across the earlier policy under which the predominant language of employers in a particular area dictated the medium of instruction. The Afrikaans instruction policy was a negative response by conservatives in the NP to the pragmatic, pro-capitalist shifts in apartheid policy made by the Vorster regime. While the policies pursued by the educational bureaucracy and the needs of capital overlapped on occasion, they were not necessarily linked.

The Bantu Education system did not, as reproductionists assert, only reproduce an unskilled, migrant labour force. Education policy had the effect of reproducing different forms of labour at different times and in different places. Emphasis on primary education in the 50s effectively generated a semi-skilled workforce. The move to a greater emphasis on secondary education in 1972 helped create a labour force with a much greater proportion of black technical and clerical employees. Rural education was geared to supporting the bantustan structure in a more effective way than was urban education. The relation between schooling and the labour market changed across time, and differed between urban and rural situations.

Urbanisation and secondary industrialisation were central to the origins and evolution of Bantu Education. The neglect of secondary schooling during the 60s increased internal strains in the education system and the labour market, which focused in cities. The change in policy in 1972 was a desperate attempt to overcome these tensions.

Seeing the state as a contested field of social relations, I have argued the shape of the education system was moulded in part by popular struggles. The 50s restructuring of the cities, of which Bantu Education was a part, was to a significant extent a response to the urban social movements of the period. Although popular resistance in that decade was unable to stop the implementation of Bantu Education, it did impose limits on how drastically apartheid could be set up. Paradoxically, the resistance itself constituted part of the demand for education which government tried to contain through the new education system.

The absence of popular organisation in the 60s was a major reason government could pursue so extreme a variant of apartheid education policy. I have shown how concern over popular discontent with education in the early 70s increased pressure on government for restructuring.

It has also been suggested the struggles that shaped Bantu Education were not only between dominant and subordinate classes. The conflicting interests within the dominant classes shaped the education system, as did divergences within the bureaucracy.

I have argued that the struggle over Bantu Education was one that involved a battle for hegemony. The regime did have a conception that it needed to lead the masses, rather than merely repress them. The NP administrations hoped bantustan policy would provide the basis of such a new hegemony. Bantu Education, in so far as it attempted to win popular allegiance to the bantustan system, did have a hegemonic aim. The state achieved some successes in this direction in the late 50s and the 60s. The school board and committee system did actively incorporate many people into the running of Bantu Education.

Teachers gave their support to organisations prepared to bargain within the existing educational system. The expansion of the education system, by providing more people than ever before with *some* schooling, was a material underpinning for mass participation in the education system.

Yet, we have seen Bantu Education was unable to win the active support of the mass of the population. It faced severe resistance in the 50s from the ANC's school boycott, local boycotts of the school board system, and from the campaigns of radical teacher organisations. A combination of factors ensured the defeat of these movements. These factors were repression, the attractions of an expanded schooling system, and parents' knowledge that state schools had a monopoly of certification accepted in the job market. However, officialdom undercut its own attempts to build a new educational hegemony. The racism and authoritarianism of the department's officials alienated parents, students and teachers. The education board and committee system generated great resentment. It was too little of a democratic policy-making structure to attract lasting popular support. It had enough power at a local level, though, to act in a tyrannical fashion toward teachers and thus lose their sympathy. More fundamentally, it has been shown that the material deprivation to which the NP government subjected the education system created constant new resentments. This is true particularly in the light of the obvious racial inequalities in education.

The events leading up to 1976 typify this failure to win allegiance.

The government imposed the Afrikaans instruction policy despite the protests of school boards and students. The popular response to the education system in the 60s and early 70s has been characterised as one of acquiescence: acceptance of a pragmatic kind, lacking any element of active identification.

The most coherent attempt to generate an educational counter-hegemony was the ANC's school boycott campaign. Despite its remarkable achievements, it could not compete with the state system's capacity to provide childcare and marketable qualifications. The re-emergence of student protest in the early 70s was initially small and ideologically incoherent.

I have argued for the significance of popular culture in moulding responses to the education system. We have seen that in the 50s, the predominance in urban areas of an individualistic, gangsterised street sub-culture created an inhospitable environment for the ANC's attempts to organise youth. A strong sub-culture of localised, anti-authoritarian resistance existed in the rural mission-founded boarding schools. It caused a series of riots reflecting student hostility to racial authority. Urban schools, on the other hand, proved passive. Bantu Education had helped create, by the early 70s, a new sub-culture among youth. A common education created a common experience and identity for youth. This new sub-culture was to prove more conducive to politicisation than the forms of youth sub-culture that existed in the 50s. By the mid-70s a repertoire of resistance was developing in urban schools. The differences in the 50s and 70s youth sub-cultures underpin the insistence in this book that not every form of oppositional behaviour has constructive, transformative potential.

Analysis of teachers' responses to the educational system needs to be informed by the understanding of their ambiguous structural position. It was their status that made them vulnerable to political and ideological cross-pressures.

The social crisis of the 40s hastened a teacher radicalisation. In mass popular resistance in the 50s, radical teachers' organisations came to the fore. The repressive conditions of the 60s, on the other hand, created ideal conditions for the growth of conservative teachers' organisations.

The ideology of professionalism was ambiguous in its implications for teachers. While for some it was an ideological prop for conservative views, for others it engendered a deep sense of dedication to education, which was outraged by state policy.

There was an ultimate irony in Bantu Education's effect on students. Its flagships, the homeland universities, produced, by the early

70s, a new generation of radicalised teachers who went on to 'conscientise' their pupils.

I would argue that events after 1976 further reinforce the validity of such perspectives. The relation between apartheid education policy and capitalism continued to be shifting and complex rather than straight-forward. During the 80s, the ruling party shifted from an overtly racial ideology of education to a technocratic one. The linking of education policy to capitalist economic development was expressly advocated by government leaders.

In keeping with this ideology, tertiary education and private schools were desegregated. Private sector initiative in education was encour-aged. Racial inequality in educational spending narrowed markedly. In part, this reflected the greater weight of capitalist interests in the NP, as compared with earlier periods. Yet the NP government had a com-mitment to racial structuring in education that cannot be reconciled with any view of the state educational bureaucracy as an instrument of capital. State schooling remained effectively racially separate until the democratic elections in 1994. Integrationist measures such as the creation of a single education ministry, which were strongly supported by leading capitalist groupings, continued to be rejected by the NP leadership right until the formation of the Government of National Unity in 1994. The NP's policies might have overlapped with those of capital, but were in no sense simply dictated by them.

The manner in which the education system reproduced the labour force changed dramatically. The late 70s and early 80s saw a vast expansion of black secondary education, to more than one million pupils in the mid-80s. This underpinned a continuing shift toward higher levels of skilling of the workforce. Bantu Education was, even less than in the earlier period, simply a source of unskilled labour.

Between the mid-70s and the mid-80s, total black primary and secondary school enrolments grew massively from 3,7 million to six million. The number of formal sector jobs available virtually stag-nated. Popular political pressures for educational provision played a role in this expansion. So too did calculations by government that schooling would control youth discontent.

Urban issues remained at the centre of policy conflicts and changes in education throughout the 70s and 80s. The mass school student movements of the period were centred in the towns. Government educational policy in the 80s focused on addressing the educational problems of the urban economy and the political pressures of predomi-nantly urban popular movements.

Popular movements continued to shape education policy. The upris-ing of 1976 led to the withdrawal of the Afrikaans instruction policy and some modifications of departmental policy. The De Lange Report, which proclaimed the attempt to reform education in the 80s, emerged from the period of the 1980 school boycotts. It finally brought home the lack of viability of Verwoerdian educational policy. The reduction of racial inequalities in educational spending was part of government's attempts to refashion education to contain the massive youth revolts of the 80s.

More clearly than in the 50s too, a popular challenge for hegemony in the educational sphere emerged. The NECC made, during the mid-80s, the most substantial attempt yet to forge a popular vision of education. It attempted to unite teachers, students and community. This experience has had a formative influence on post-apartheid education.

Finally youth culture, for better and for worse, has moulded popular response to educational issues. A culture of militancy developed among youth. It did, on the positive side, generate unprecedented levels of organisational and political coherence among youth. More negatively it also legitimised random violence and factional strife. It thus seems more valid than ever to make a distinction between transformative and non-transformative oppositional behaviour.

Teachers continued to be cross-pressured by changing political and ideological currents. African teachers' organisations continued to take a conservative position until the early 80s. However, with younger teachers joining more radical organisations and conflict between pupils and teachers, a realignment took place. In the mid-80s, both the more staid and more militant teachers' organisations allied themselves with the NECC. The militancy of the 50s seemed to have re-emerged. Yet teachers were often also deeply demoralised and poorly trained, and a lack of motivation and effective teaching was widespread.

As this discussion suggests, the consequences of Verwoerdian educational policy are still very much with us. South Africa's people will be tragically burdened with them in confronting the task of creating a post-apartheid educational system.

Bibliography

Official Publications
Department of Education and Training. Annual Report 1986. Pretoria, Government Printer, 1987.

Index

South African Police (SAP)   18, 74, 99,
130, 163, 171–2
  Security Police section of   157, 164
  Special Branch (SB) of   35, 36, 43, 74,
  86
South African Students' Movement
(SASM)   154, 157, 163–4, 167
South African Students' Organisation
(SASO)   154–5, 163, 167
Soweto Civic Association   173
Soweto Parents' Crisis Committee
(SPCC)   173, 174
Soweto School Boards (including
Meadowlands)   156, 162–3
Soweto Secondary School, Naledi   107
Soweto Students' Representative Coun-
cil (SSRC)   164, 167, 168
Soweto Urban Bantu Council   117, 139,
140
Star, The   116, 137–8, 142, 145,147
Stellenbosch Farmers' Winery   146
Student, The   12

Tambo, O.   29–30, 93, 172
Taylor, C.   139
Teachers' League of South Africa
(TLSA)   38, 41
Teachers' Vision, The   28, 29, 31, 32,
40, 41, 42, 46, 88
Teach Every African Child (TEACH)
142, 143, 145, 147
Thembalabantu High School   157
Thomas, P.   141
Thulasizwe Higher Primary School   163
Tigerkloof (school)   97
Tiro, A.   156
Titus, B.M.   90
Torch, The   12, 18, 38, 42, 46, 83, 84,
87, 89, 91, 92
Transkei Organised Bodies (TOB)   19,
42
Transvaal African Teachers' Association
(TATA)   26–8, 30, 33–5, 36, 37–
8, 41, 44–5, 91
Transvaal African Teachers' Union
(TATU)   34, 37, 44–5
Transvaal Education Department (TED)
34–6, 37, 45
Transvaal United African Teachers'
Association (TUATA)   45, 107,
109–11, 118–19, 126, 154–5

Treurnicht. A.   159, 162–3
Tshaka, R.   34
Tshume, W.   19
Tsotsi, W.M.   42
Twins Pharmaceutical Holdings   146

Umkhonto we Sizwe (MK)   95, 99,
168, 172
United Democratic Front (UDF)   170,
173–4
United Party (UP)   5, 6, 7, 53–5, 136,
138–9, 142
Unity Movement (UM)   *see* Non-
European Unity Movement
University of the Witwatersrand   174
University of Zululand   154
Urban Bantu Council (UBC)   140, 167

Vanderbijlpark African School Board
107
Van der Byl, P.   28
Van Eck Commission   6
Van Schalkwijk Committee   4–5
Van Zyl, H.J.   104–6, 116, 140, 145
Veka   143
Verwoerd, H.F.   2, 52, 55, 59–62, 65,
74, 86, 93, 122, 135, 166
Viljoen, G.   159
Voice, The   35
Vorster, B.J.   104, 137, 143, 159, 162,
166, 180
Vryheid Government Bantu School   128

Webster, E.   141
Welfare Department   4
Wessels, A.J.   143
Western Cape Students' Action Com-
mittee (WECSAC)   172
Western Province Bantu Teachers' League
46
Wiehahn Report   169
Wilberforce Academy   12, 99
Wilson, M.   85
Witwatersrand Council of Education
37
World, The   118, 122, 125

Xuma, A.   28

Zwane, I.E.   110